Mastering Go for DevOps

Master building, automating, and scaling cloud infrastructure with Go

Engin Polat

<packt>

Mastering Go for DevOps

Portfolio Director: Kartikey Pandey

Relationship Lead: Preet Ahuja

Project Manager: Sonam Pandey

Content Engineer: Arun Nadar

Technical Editor: Simran Ali

Copy Editor: Safis Editing

Indexer: Hemangini Bari

Proofreader: Arun Nadar

Production Designer: Ganesh Bhadwalkar

Growth Lead: Amit Ramadas

First published: December 2025

Production reference: 1011225

Published by Packt Publishing Ltd.
Grosvenor House
11 St Paul's Square
Birmingham
B3 1RB, UK.

ISBN 978-1-83702-733-0

`www.packtpub.com`

To my wife, Yeliz—my constant uptime, keeping me running even when deployments failed.

To my children, Ada and Ege— my greatest projects, forever in active development.

You are the true production environment I strive to serve every day.

— Engin Polat

Contributors

About the author

Engin Polat is a senior software engineer at Microsoft, based in Seattle, Washington. With over two decades of experience in software development, he has worked across industries—from manufacturing and media to enterprise-scale cloud solutions—building robust, scalable, and future-proof systems.

Specializing in DevOps and GitOps practices, Engin has deep expertise in C#, Go, TypeScript, Terraform, Bicep, Docker, and Kubernetes. He has contributed to high-impact projects including Microsoft's Azure Bicep language, the Power Platform Terraform provider, and popular Azure DevOps extensions used by thousands of teams worldwide.

Passionate about clean, sustainable code and modern software delivery practices, Engin enjoys sharing his knowledge through open source contributions, technical writing, and community engagements. In his free time, he experiments with new programming paradigms and continues to refine his craft as both a developer and problem solver.

For Engin, technology is not just a profession but a lifelong passion—and *Mastering Go for DevOps* reflects his commitment to helping others build tools that thrive in today's fast-paced, cloud-native world.

I would like to extend my thanks to my family for accepting that I needed to work long hours on this book during family time.

About the reviewers

Łukasz Pawłowski is a tech manager and software engineer with over a decade of experience in software development, DevOps, and process automation. He has worked with a wide range of technologies, including Go, PHP, JavaScript, Python, Terraform, AWS, GCP, and more.

Before joining Boozt, he served as CTO at VAO, where he defined and automated company-wide development processes, gaining hands-on experience. His focus included not only process automation but also DevOps culture. Working with multiple clients, he developed various solutions centered on cloud architecture. In the last years working at Boozt, he has worked more with Golang, GCP, Terraform, and GitLab CI/CD.

Łukasz leads various technical initiatives aimed at improving collaboration between software and infrastructure/operations teams, supporting developers in building efficient, secure, and scalable solutions. While his current role is more strategic and mentoring-focused, he remains actively involved in technical design and discussions, working on specific proofs of concept and helping software engineers grow and stay aligned with modern DevOps practices.

Anuj Tyagi is a senior site reliability engineer with more than twelve years of experience in cloud infrastructure and DevOps. He actively contributes to Go-based cloud-native projects and manages production Kubernetes and Terraform deployments at scale. He is a regular speaker at multiple tech conferences, delivering talks on infrastructure automation and DevOps practices.

Table of Contents

Chapter 4: Writing Go Exporters for Prometheus 67

Preface

Go has rapidly become one of the most important programming languages in the DevOps world. Designed at Google with simplicity, concurrency, and performance in mind, Go offers the perfect combination of speed, readability, and robustness, qualities that align perfectly with the needs of modern cloud-native systems and automation workflows.

In the world of DevOps, we deal with distributed systems, microservices, automation scripts, container orchestration, and CI/CD pipelines on a daily basis. Many of these systems demand highly efficient and reliable tooling; this is where Go shines. From building blazing-fast CLI utilities to developing scalable backend services, Go has become the go-to language for many DevOps practitioners and platform engineers.

In this book, we will move into DevOps-focused patterns, building tools for automation, creating APIs, and integrating with cloud services.

We will explore how to do the following:

- Build production-ready CLI tools for DevOps workflows
- Work with REST and gRPC APIs for cloud infrastructure automation
- Write concurrent and parallel applications that handle large-scale workloads
- Integrate Go with Kubernetes, Docker, Terraform, and GitHub Actions
- Develop monitoring, logging, and observability tools

Along the way, you'll see real-world examples of Go being used to solve infrastructure and operations challenges, from building custom Kubernetes operators to creating deployment automation systems.

This book is not just about learning Go; it's about mastering Go for the unique challenges and opportunities within DevOps. Whether you're coming from a systems administration background, a cloud engineering role, or software development, you'll learn how to leverage Go to create tools and systems that are fast, maintainable, and tailored for modern infrastructure.

Who this book is for

This book is for DevOps engineers, SREs, platform engineers, and developers who want to build powerful tools and services using Go in a DevOps context. A basic understanding of DevOps practices, cloud platforms, and containerized environments will help you get the most out of this book. Familiarity with at least one programming language is recommended, but you don't need to be a Go expert; we'll get you there.

What this book covers

Chapter 1, Developing Command-Line Interfaces with Go, introduces you to creating effective and user-friendly CLI applications, covering command parsing, argument handling, output formatting, and practical examples to build flexible CLIs.

Chapter 2, Packaging and Distributing Go CLIs, explains how to build executable binaries for multiple platforms and create Docker images to simplify deployment across environments.

Chapter 3, Integrating Go Applications with Prometheus, explores setting up Prometheus and Grafana, instrumenting Go code to expose metrics, and implementing alerting and monitoring strategies.

Chapter 4, Writing Go Exporters for Prometheus, dives into designing custom metrics exporters, implementing counters, gauges, and histograms, and ensuring accuracy and performance of exported data.

Chapter 5, Building and Consuming RESTful APIs with Go, covers creating API servers, handling requests and responses, managing routing and middleware, and consuming external APIs.

Chapter 6, Working with gRPC and Microservices Architecture, introduces defining service contracts with Protocol Buffers, setting up gRPC servers and clients, implementing streaming, and best practices for microservices communication.

Chapter 7, Using Go to Build Custom Terraform Providers, explains Terraform's provider model, implementing CRUD operations, and managing resource state to extend Terraform with Go.

Chapter 8, Writing Unit Tests and Integration Tests for Terraform Providers, teaches you how to write effective tests for provider CRUD operations, mock API calls, and use Terraform SDK testing tools.

Chapter 9, Documenting and Publishing Terraform Providers, guides you through generating provider documentation, writing clear resource docs, versioning, changelogs, and publishing providers to Terraform Registries.

Chapter 10, Automating Testing in Pipelines, shows how to integrate testing into CI/CD workflows with tools such as GitHub Actions, run tests automatically, generate reports, and manage failures.

Chapter 11, Integrating Go Applications with the AWS SDK, demonstrates how to use the AWS SDK to interact with services such as S3 and EC2, handling uploads, instance management, and scaling cloud resources.

Chapter 12, Integrating Go Applications with the Azure SDK, covers setting up authentication, working with Azure Storage and Virtual Machines, and managing Azure resources programmatically.

Chapter 13, Serverless Computing Using AWS Lambda, introduces creating, deploying, and managing Lambda functions, configuring triggers, and integrating with AWS services for event-driven applications.

Chapter 14, Serverless Computing Using Azure Functions, focuses on building and deploying Azure Functions, setting up triggers and bindings, and integrating with Azure services such as Storage and Event Hubs.

To get the most out of this book

To follow along with the examples in this book, you'll need a working Go development environment and some basic tools commonly used in DevOps.

Before you begin, make sure you have the following:

- **Go installed**: You can download it from `https://go.dev/dl`. The book uses Go version 1.25 or later.
- **A code editor**: Visual Studio Code with the Go extension is recommended for editing, running, and debugging Go code.
- **Git**: To clone repositories and manage source code.
- **Terraform**: Needed for the Terraform chapters if you want to run the examples yourself.

You should be comfortable using the command line, editing configuration files, and running shell commands.

All examples are written to be self-contained, so you can copy, modify, and run them directly on your own machine. The code samples are designed to work on Linux, macOS, and Windows.

Whenever you see commands that include variables or file paths, adjust them to match your own environment.

Finally, remember that this book is hands-on—the best way to learn Go for DevOps is by writing and running code yourself. Don't hesitate to experiment with the examples, extend them, or adapt them to your own projects.

Conventions used

There are a number of text conventions used throughout this book.

`CodeInText`: Indicates code words in text, database table names, folder names, filenames, file extensions, pathnames, dummy URLs, user input, and Twitter handles. For example: "Go allows us to run tests that are conditionally compiled based on `//go:build` tags using the `-tags` flag in the `go test` command."

A block of code is set as follows:

```
package main
import "fmt"

func sayHello() {
    fmt.Println("Hello from Windows")
}
```

Any command-line input or output is written as follows:

```
$ mycli cloud create --name example
$ mycli cloud delete --id 123
```

Bold: Indicates a new term, an important word, or words that you see on the screen. For instance, words in menus or dialog boxes appear in the text like this. For example: "Click **Add service account token**, provide a name, and copy the token shown."

> Warnings or important notes appear like this.

> Tips and tricks appear like this.

Get in touch

Feedback from our readers is always welcome.

General feedback: If you have questions about any aspect of this book or have any general feedback, please email us at `customercare@packt.com` and mention the book's title in the subject of your message.

Errata: Although we have taken every care to ensure the accuracy of our content, mistakes do happen. If you have found a mistake in this book, we would be grateful if you reported this to us. Please visit `http://www.packt.com/submit-errata`, click **Submit Errata**, and fill in the form.

Piracy: If you come across any illegal copies of our works in any form on the internet, we would be grateful if you would provide us with the location address or website name. Please contact us at `copyright@packt.com` with a link to the material.

If you are interested in becoming an author: If there is a topic that you have expertise in and you are interested in either writing or contributing to a book, please visit `http://authors.packt.com/`.

Free Benefits with Your Book

This book comes with free benefits to support your learning. Activate them now for instant access (see the "*How to Unlock*" section for instructions).

Here's a quick overview of what you can instantly unlock with your purchase:

PDF and ePub Copies

- Access a DRM-free PDF copy of this book to read anywhere, on any device.
- Use a DRM-free ePub version with your favorite e-reader.

Next-Gen Web-Based Reader

- **Multi-device progress sync**: Pick up where you left off, on any device.
- **Highlighting and notetaking**: Capture ideas and turn reading into lasting knowledge.
- **Bookmarking:** Save and revisit key sections whenever you need them.
- **Dark mode**: Reduce eye strain by switching to dark or sepia themes.

How to Unlock

UNLOCK NOW

Scan the QR code (or go to `packtpub.com/unlock`). Search for this book by name, confirm the edition, and then follow the steps on the page.

Note: *Keep your invoice handy. Purchases made directly from Packt don't require one.*

Share your thoughts

Once you've read *Mastering Go for DevOps,* we'd love to hear your thoughts! Scan the QR code below to go straight to the Amazon review page for this book and share your feedback.

`https://packt.link/r/1837027331`

Your review is important to us and the tech community and will help us make sure we're delivering excellent quality content.

Part 1

Go Foundations - CLI, Monitoring, and APIs

Part 1 focuses on building a strong foundation in Go for creating practical DevOps tools. We will start by learning how to build **command-line interfaces** (**CLIs**) that automate workflows and make daily operations easier. Then, we will move on to packaging and distributing the CLIs so they can be used across different platforms and environments.

After that, we will learn how to integrate Go applications with Prometheus for monitoring, followed by building custom Prometheus exporters to collect and expose metrics from systems.

Finally, we'll dive into developing web services, both RESTful APIs and gRPC microservices, to create scalable, high-performance backend systems that can power automation and cloud-native applications.

Together, these chapters give us the skills to design, build, and ship production-ready tools and APIs, the building blocks of modern DevOps engineering, with Go.

This part of the book includes the following chapters:

- *Chapter 1, Developing Command-Line Interfaces with Go*
- *Chapter 2, Packaging and Distributing Go CLIs*
- *Chapter 3, Integrating Go Applications with Prometheus*
- *Chapter 4, Writing Go Exporters for Prometheus*
- *Chapter 5, Building and Consuming RESTful APIs with Go*
- *Chapter 6, Working with gRPC and Microservices Architecture*

1

Developing Command-Line Interfaces with Go

In today's DevOps ecosystem, **command-line interfaces (CLIs)** are more than just helpful utilities; they're core tools that empower engineers to streamline workflows, manage infrastructure, and orchestrate complex deployments with precision and speed.

A well-designed CLI tool enables seamless automation, giving DevOps teams the agility they need to handle everything from routine tasks to high-stakes production issues. For any DevOps professional, mastering the creation of CLI tools can open doors to greater efficiency, reliability, and control over infrastructure.

This chapter focuses on building robust and elegant CLI applications with Go, a language well suited for DevOps needs. Go brings specific strengths that make it an ideal choice for developing CLIs that need to perform reliably across diverse environments, scale with demands, and operate efficiently under heavy workloads.

In this chapter, we will cover the following topics:

- Understanding and processing user input through command parsing and argument handling
- Formatting and structuring CLI output for clear user feedback
- Implementing networking techniques for CLI tools, including TCP, SSH, concurrency, and configuration management with YAML
- Applying best practices for maintainable, testable, and reliable CLI development
- Building a complete, real-world CLI application from start to finish

Why Go is the perfect match for CLI development in DevOps

CLIs play an important role in DevOps by helping teams automate tasks, interact with infrastructure, and manage systems more efficiently. Whether it's deploying services, configuring environments, or pulling logs, CLI tools give engineers precision and speed at the keyboard. In DevOps, where repeatability and automation are essential, building custom CLI tools allows teams to tailor workflows to their exact needs.

Go is particularly well suited for building CLI tools that meet these demands. It combines performance, portability, and simplicity in a way that supports the fast-paced and often complex nature of DevOps work.

Here are a few key reasons why Go is a great choice for CLI development:

- **Cross-compilation**: Go's built-in cross-compilation capabilities allow developers to build executables for multiple operating systems, such as Linux, macOS, and Windows, from a single code base. This flexibility is especially useful in DevOps, where tools must often work across different environments. With Go, you write your code once, build it for any platform, and ensure it runs smoothly everywhere it's needed.
- **Concurrency**: Go's unique approach to concurrency, powered by **goroutines**, is very important for applications that need to handle multiple tasks in parallel. Whether a CLI tool is pulling data from various APIs, managing multiple cloud resources, or performing intensive data processing, Go's concurrency model allows it to handle demands smoothly without complexity, making it ideal for high-performance applications.
- **Streamlined tooling and minimal dependencies**: Go emphasizes simplicity, and its powerful standard library means you often don't need many third-party packages to build a complete, feature-rich CLI tool. This minimal dependency approach means fewer compatibility issues, reduced maintenance overhead, and an overall smoother experience.

- **Fast build times and static binaries**: Go compiles quickly and produces self-contained binaries with no runtime dependencies. This makes distribution easy and ensures consistent behavior across environments – qualities that DevOps teams highly value.

Taken together, these features make Go a practical and powerful choice for building CLI tools that are fast, reliable, and easy to distribute. Later in this chapter, we'll explore how to put these strengths into practice by learning about command parsing and argument handling, formatting output for users, following best practices for robust CLI development, and so on. This will give a solid foundation for developing high-quality CLI tools tailored to real-world DevOps workflows.

Building reliable, user-friendly, and efficient CLI tools in Go

In this section, you will learn how to build a well-structured, practical CLI application in Go that meets the demands of real-world DevOps scenarios. You'll learn how to organize commands, handle arguments and flags, and output information in a way that's user-friendly and polished. We'll also cover CLI best practices, such as error handling, code organization, and maintaining consistent behavior across environments, ensuring your application is as robust as it is functional.

Through hands-on examples and step-by-step guidance, this section aims to give you the skills to develop, test, and refine Go-based CLIs that are effective, efficient, and ready for deployment.

Command parsing and argument handling

Command parsing and argument handling are key parts of any command-line application. These features allow a CLI tool to understand what action the user wants to perform and what data they want to provide.

Commands define the available operations (such as `init`, `deploy`, or `delete`), while arguments (such as `-expires 7d` or `-query "id"`) and flags (such as `-verbose` or `-debug`) help fine-tune how those commands behave. Understanding how to handle these inputs properly is the foundation for building flexible and user-friendly CLI tools.

The `os.Args` slice is Go's most basic tool for accessing command-line arguments. `os.Args[0]` always holds the name of the command, while `os.Args[1:]` contains the arguments passed by the user. This approach is perfect for small, single-command applications where complexity is minimal.

Here's a simple example that demonstrates how to handle basic commands using `os.Args`:

```
package main

import (
    "fmt"
    "os"
)

func main() {
    if len(os.Args) < 2 {
        fmt.Println("Expected 'hello' subcommand")
        return
    }

    command := os.Args[1]

    switch command {
    case "hello":
        name := "world"
        if len(os.Args) > 2 {
            name = os.Args[2]
        }
        fmt.Printf("Hello, %s!\n", name)
    default:
        fmt.Printf("Unknown command: %s\n", command)
    }
}
```

The `flag` package enables simple parsing of command-line options such as `-name` or `-age`. Flags provide more flexible argument handling and are especially useful for CLI tools that require optional settings:

```
package main

import (
    "flag"
    "fmt"
)
```

```go
func main() {
    name := flag.String("name", "world", "specify the name to greet")
    age := flag.Int("age", 0, "specify the age")

    flag.Parse() // Parse all flags

    fmt.Printf("Hello, %s! You are %d years old.\n", *name, *age)
}
```

Building CLI applications often requires support for features such as subcommands, flags, and configuration handling – especially when the tool needs to manage complex interactions or multiple actions. These features are essential for creating flexible and well-structured command-line tools, similar to how tools such as `kubectl` and `git` are organized. One of the most popular Go libraries that provides all of these capabilities is the `cobra` package. `cobra` is widely used for developing powerful CLI applications in Go and makes it easy to define commands, handle user input, and organize logic cleanly.

Setting up cobra

To install `cobra`, we first need to run the following command in the terminal:

```
go get -u github.com/spf13/cobra
```

This command fetches the `cobra` package and adds it to the Go project.

Creating the root command

The `root` command is the base command for the application. We define it using `cobra.Command`, which includes basic configurations such as `Use` (the command name) and `Short` (a brief description):

```go
package main

import (
    "fmt"
    "github.com/spf13/cobra"
    "os"
)

func main() {
```

```
    rootCmd := &cobra.Command{
        Use:   "app",
        Short: "A simple CLI application",
        Run: func(cmd *cobra.Command, args []string) {
            fmt.Println("Welcome to the app!")
        },
    }

    if err := rootCmd.Execute(); err != nil {
        fmt.Println(err)
        os.Exit(1)
    }
}
```

This code creates a basic command-line application using the `cobra` library. It starts by defining the main command, called `app`, which users can run from the terminal. When the command is executed, it prints a simple message: **Welcome to the app!**. This is done using `cobra`'s `Command` struct, where the `Use` field defines the command name, `Short` gives a brief description, and `Run` contains the code to execute when the command is called.

After setting up the command, the program calls `rootCmd.Execute()` to actually run the CLI. If there's an error while running the command – such as a typo or unexpected input – it prints the error and exits with a non-zero status, indicating that something went wrong.

Let's build and run the program:

```
go run main.go
```

The output will be as follows:

```
Welcome to the app!
```

Adding subcommands

Subcommands allow users to perform specific tasks, such as `app hello` or `app goodbye`. Each subcommand can have its own flags and arguments.

The following example shows how to add a simple "`hello`" subcommand using `cobra`:

```
helloCmd := &cobra.Command{
    Use:   "hello",
    Short: "Greet the user",
    Run: func(cmd *cobra.Command, args []string) {
        name := "world"
        if len(args) > 0 {
            name = args[0]
        }
        fmt.Printf("Hello, %s!\n", name)
    },
}
rootCmd.AddCommand(helloCmd)
```

This code creates a new subcommand called `hello`. When the user runs the command, if they provide a name (for example, `app hello Ege`), the program greets them using that name. If no name is provided, it defaults to greeting "world." Finally, the `hello` subcommand is attached to the `root` command using the `AddCommand()` method.

Let's run it in the terminal:

```
go run main.go hello
```

The output will be as follows:

```
Hello, world!
```

Let's pass a name:

```
go run main.go hello Ada
```

The output will be as follows:

```
Hello, Ada!
```

`cobra` supports both persistent and local flags:

- **Persistent flags**: Available to the root command and all subcommands
- **Local flags**: Specific to a single command

In this example, we're enhancing the `hello` subcommand by adding a custom flag. This allows users to change the greeting message using the `--greeting` (or `-g`) flag when they run the command. Before, the greeting was always fixed as `Hello`, but with this update, users can now customize it. For instance, someone could run `app hello Mert --greeting Hi` and the output would be `Hi, Mert!` instead of the default `Hello, Mert!`. Let's take a look at how this is implemented in code:

```
var greeting string
helloCmd.Flags().StringVarP(
    &greeting, "greeting", "g", "Hello", "custom greeting"
)

helloCmd.Run = func(cmd *cobra.Command, args []string) {
    name := "world"
    if len(args) > 0 {
        name = args[0]
    }
    fmt.Printf("%s, %s!\n", greeting, name)
}
```

Best practices

When building CLI applications with `cobra`, it's important to follow a few best practices to make the tool easier to use, more reliable, and easier to maintain:

- **Organize commands clearly**: Use subcommands to divide functionality, making it easier for users to explore features
- **Documentation**: Provide short and long descriptions for each command to make `cobra help` output informative
- **Error handling**: Use the `cmd.MarkFlagRequired()` function to enforce necessary flags and improve error messages

Output formatting and user feedback

Designing effective output and user feedback is essential to creating intuitive and user-friendly CLI applications. A well-designed CLI tool provides information in a structured, readable format, helping users understand both the outcome of their actions and any errors encountered.

The Go `fmt` package serves as the foundation for most output in CLI applications. It provides the common `Print()`, `Printf()`, and `Println()` functions for generating basic text output. For instance, `fmt.Printf()` can be particularly helpful in formatting data into structured, readable lines with specific spacing and alignment, using verbs such as `%d` for integers, `%s` for strings, and `%f` for floating-point numbers. Using these formatting verbs effectively helps ensure that numbers, dates, and other elements align consistently, which enhances readability in tables and logs.

The following example shows how to use `fmt.Printf()` to print structured table-like output:

```
package main

import "fmt"

func main() {
    fmt.Printf("%-20s %10s %10s\n", "Name", "Age", "Score")
    fmt.Printf("%-20s %10d %10.2f\n", "Alice", 30, 85.6)
    fmt.Printf("%-20s %10d %10.2f\n", "Bob", 24, 92.3)
    fmt.Printf("%-20s %10d %10.2f\n", "Charlie", 29, 88.1)
}
```

This example aligns text and numbers into columns by specifying the width for each field. In this case, `%20s` reserves 20 characters for the `Name` column, `%10d` reserves 10 characters for the integer `Age` column, and `%10.2f` reserves 10 characters for a floating-point number with two decimal places in the `Score` column. Using `fmt` in this way can transform simple print statements into clean, organized tables that convey structured information efficiently.

Beyond basic formatting, Go's ecosystem offers libraries to create even more dynamic and user-friendly output. The popular `github.com/olekukonko/tablewriter` library, for instance, provides specialized tools for generating table-based output that includes borders, alignment, and automatic column width adjustments. Here's how to use it to display structured data in a tabular format:

```
package main

import (
    "github.com/olekukonko/tablewriter"
    "os"
)
```

```
func main() {
    data := [][]string{
        {"Alice", "30", "85.6"},
        {"Bob", "24", "92.3"},
        {"Charlie", "29", "88.1"},
    }

    table := tablewriter.NewWriter(os.Stdout)
    table.SetHeader([]string{"Name", "Age", "Score"})

    for _, v := range data {
        table.Append(v)
    }
    table.Render()
}
```

This code produces a table with headers, borders, and automatically adjusted column widths. `tablewriter` also provides customization options, such as changing the header style, row colors, and cell alignment. This type of well-formatted table output can be incredibly useful in applications that manage data records, display lists, or report aggregated information. The output will look like this:

```
+---------+-----+-------+
| NAME    | AGE | SCORE |
+---------+-----+-------+
| Alice   | 30  | 85.6  |
| Bob     | 24  | 92.3  |
| Charlie | 29  | 88.1  |
+---------+-----+-------+
```

Another key element of output formatting is color. Colors can help users quickly identify different types of information, such as warnings, errors, or success messages. For example, green might indicate a successful operation, while red could denote an error. Although Go's standard library doesn't provide built-in color support, third-party libraries such as `github.com/fatih/color` make it easy to add color to CLI outputs.

Consider the following example, which uses color to add emphasis to success, error, and informational messages:

```
package main

import (
    "fmt"
    "github.com/fatih/color"
)

func main() {
    success := color.New(color.FgGreen).SprintFunc()
    warning := color.New(color.FgYellow).SprintFunc()
    error := color.New(color.FgRed).SprintFunc()

    fmt.Println(success("Operation completed successfully!"))
    fmt.Println(warning("This is a warning message."))
    fmt.Println(error("An error occurred during the operation."))
}
```

In this code, the `SprintFunc()` method from the `color` package allows us to create functions that wrap strings in the specified color. We can apply green for success messages, yellow for warnings, and red for errors. This color-coded output can greatly improve usability, as users can instantly recognize the nature of each message.

For longer-running tasks, such as file downloads or data processing, providing users with a visual indication of progress can improve their experience and understanding of the task's duration. A CLI application without progress indicators may leave users uncertain of whether it's actively working or stalled. One effective solution is the `progressbar` package, which lets developers implement customizable progress bars.

The following example shows how to use the `progressbar` package to display progress during a task:

```
package main

import (
    "github.com/schollz/progressbar/v3"
    "time"
)
```

```
func main() {
    bar := progressbar.NewOptions(100,
        progressbar.OptionSetDescription("Downloading..."),
        progressbar.OptionShowBytes(true),
        progressbar.OptionSetWidth(20),
    )

    for i := 0; i < 100; i++ {
        bar.Add(1)
        time.Sleep(50 * time.Millisecond)
    }
}
```

In this example, the progress bar displays a count of completed steps, a description, and updates at each step. The bar updates dynamically, giving users a sense of real-time progress. This feature is invaluable in CLI tools that handle extensive tasks, such as downloading files, backing up data, or processing large datasets.

Networking best practices

Networking is a crucial component for many CLI applications, especially in DevOps contexts where tools often interact with remote servers, databases, cloud services, and APIs. Developing efficient, reliable, and secure networked applications involves several best practices that can prevent common pitfalls and make applications more resilient. Go provides a robust standard library for network programming, covering HTTP, TCP, and UDP protocols, as well as support for asynchronous communication and concurrent request handling.

Go's goroutines make it easy to execute network requests concurrently, which is ideal for applications that need to retrieve multiple resources or perform batch operations. For example, if a CLI tool retrieves information from several endpoints, each request can be executed in its own goroutine, enabling the tool to complete the task more quickly than sequential processing. Here's an example that demonstrates concurrent HTTP requests using goroutines:

```
package main

import (
    "fmt"
    "net/http"
```

```
    "sync"
    "time"
)

func fetchURL(url string, wg *sync.WaitGroup) {
    defer wg.Done()
    resp, err := http.Get(url)
    if err != nil {
        fmt.Println("Error fetching:", url, err)
        return
    }
    defer resp.Body.Close()
    fmt.Println("Fetched", url, "with status", resp.Status)
}

func main() {
    urls := []string{
        "https://golang.org", "https://go.dev", "https://godoc.org"
    }
    var wg sync.WaitGroup

    for _, url := range urls {
        wg.Add(1)
        go fetchURL(url, &wg)
    }

    wg.Wait()
    fmt.Println("All URLs fetched")
}
```

In this code, each `fetchURL` call runs as a separate goroutine, fetching a URL concurrently and printing the status. `sync.WaitGroup` ensures that the `main` function waits for all goroutines to complete before exiting. Using concurrency effectively in Go minimizes idle time and enables CLI tools to handle network operations with high efficiency.

While concurrency is powerful, it's essential to handle errors and implement retries, especially when dealing with network operations. Network failures are common, and ensuring reliability in your CLI application involves detecting failures and retrying requests as necessary.

Error handling and retries

Network communication is inherently unreliable, and connections can fail for reasons ranging from temporary server issues to network timeouts. It's a best practice to implement retry logic for network requests to ensure robustness. This practice is especially useful when interacting with APIs or cloud services where occasional errors, such as rate limiting or service outages, are common.

Go's standard library doesn't include a built-in retry mechanism, but retries can be implemented using a simple loop or a helper function. Here's an example of retry logic that makes multiple attempts to fetch a URL with a delay between retries:

```
package main

import (
    "fmt"
    "net/http"
    "time"
)

func fetchWithRetry(url string, attempts int, delay time.Duration) error {
    for i := 0; i < attempts; i++ {
        resp, err := http.Get(url)
        if err == nil {
            resp.Body.Close()
            fmt.Println("Fetched", url, "on attempt", i+1)
            return nil
        }
        fmt.Println("Attempt", i+1, "failed; retrying in", delay)
        time.Sleep(delay)
    }
    return fmt.Errorf(
        "failed to fetch %s after %d attempts", url, attempts
    )
}

func main() {
    err := fetchWithRetry("https://golang.org", 3, 2*time.Second)
    if err != nil {
        fmt.Println("Error:", err)
```

```
        } else {
            fmt.Println("Successfully fetched URL")
        }
    }
```

In this code, the `fetchWithRetry` function makes multiple attempts to fetch a URL, pausing between attempts. The function returns an error if it exhausts all retries. By adding retry logic, CLI applications can recover from transient network errors and reduce failures.

Securing connections

Security is paramount when CLI tools handle sensitive data or interact with protected resources. Ensuring secure connections via HTTPS and properly handling certificates are foundational practices for networked CLI applications. Go's `http` package automatically enforces HTTPS connections when URLs start with `https://`, but additional measures may be needed for certificate validation or when working with self-signed certificates.

In cases where self-signed certificates are necessary (for example, testing environments), the Go HTTP client can be configured to skip certificate verification. However, be cautious, as this practice should never be used in production. Here's an example of how to skip certificate verification (for development only):

```
package main

import (
    "crypto/tls"
    "net/http"
    "fmt"
)

func main() {
    http.DefaultTransport.(*http.Transport).TLSClientConfig = &tls.Config{
        InsecureSkipVerify: true
    }
    resp, err := http.Get("https://self-signed.badssl.com/")
    if err != nil {
        panic(err)
    }
    defer resp.Body.Close()
    fmt.Println("Response status:", resp.Status)
}
```

Setting `InsecureSkipVerify` to `true` disables certificate verification, allowing connections to proceed. However, this approach introduces security risks and should only be used in controlled environments where certificate validation is impractical, such as development and testing.

For production, always ensure certificates are properly validated. Use trusted **certificate authorities (CAs)** and avoid storing sensitive data in plain text over the network. Go's `crypto/tls` package provides extensive features for managing certificates, encryption, and **Secure Sockets Layer (SSL)** configurations.

Handling timeouts

Network timeouts are a vital component of resilient CLI applications, preventing indefinite waits for unresponsive servers. Without timeouts, a CLI tool could hang if a network request stalls, creating a poor user experience. Go's `http.Client` allows setting timeouts for both connection establishment and response retrieval, providing fine-grained control over network operations.

To set a timeout, configure the `Timeout` field of the HTTP client. Here's how you can set a five-second timeout on an HTTP request:

```
package main

import (
    "fmt"
    "net/http"
    "time"
)

func main() {
    client := http.Client{
        Timeout: 5 * time.Second,
    }

    resp, err := client.Get("https://golang.org")
    if err != nil {
        fmt.Println("Request timed out:", err)
        return
    }
    defer resp.Body.Close()
    fmt.Println("Response status:", resp.Status)
}
```

In this example, if the request takes longer than five seconds, it will automatically terminate, returning a timeout error. This practice prevents CLI tools from waiting indefinitely for responses, enhancing responsiveness and user experience. For applications with multiple requests, you can set timeouts based on the type of request or service being accessed, balancing efficiency with reliability.

Rate limiting

For CLI applications that make frequent network requests, especially those that interact with public APIs, implementing rate limiting is essential. Many APIs have rate limits in place to prevent abuse and manage traffic. If a CLI tool exceeds these limits, it may be temporarily blocked or denied access, causing inconvenience for users. By implementing rate limiting on the client side, you can prevent overloading APIs and ensure smooth interaction.

A basic rate-limiting approach is to delay each request by a small interval. Alternatively, you can use a more sophisticated method, such as token bucket algorithms, to enforce request limits dynamically. Here's an example using a simple rate limiter in Go:

```
package main

import (
    "fmt"
    "time"
)

func main() {
    rate := time.Second / 5 // 5 requests per second
    ticker := time.NewTicker(rate)
    defer ticker.Stop()

    for i := 0; i < 20; i++ {
        <-ticker.C
        fmt.Println("Request", i+1)
    }
}
```

This code limits requests to five per second, controlling the rate at which requests are made. By implementing such controls, your CLI tool avoids overwhelming APIs and aligns with usage limits, ensuring continued access and compliance with rate restrictions.

Best practices for building robust CLIs

Building robust CLI applications requires more than just functionality; it demands attention to design, usability, security, and maintainability. CLI tools are used in varied environments, often under unpredictable conditions, and must handle errors gracefully, provide clear feedback, and offer intuitive interactions.

Designing intuitive command structures

A well-designed command structure is critical to the usability of CLI applications. Users should be able to intuitively understand the flow of commands and subcommands without needing extensive documentation. A good CLI should provide a logical organization of commands that can easily be discovered and navigated. Here are some best practices:

- **Subcommand organization**: Use subcommands to organize related commands hierarchically. For instance, if a CLI tool interacts with cloud resources, the top-level command could be `cloud`, with subcommands such as `create`, `delete`, `list`, and `update`. This structure not only makes it easier for users to find specific commands but also supports extensibility as the tool grows.

  The following is an example:

  ```
  $ mycli cloud create --name example
  $ mycli cloud delete --id 123
  ```

  In Go, libraries such as `cobra` provide a straightforward way to implement such nested command structures, allowing developers to focus on functionality while ensuring the application is easy to use.

- **Descriptive command and flag names**: Commands and flags should be concise but descriptive. Avoid abbreviations that might be unclear to users. For instance, `--config` is more intuitive than `--cfg`, as it clearly communicates the purpose of the flag. Additionally, providing both long-form and short-form flags (such as `-h` and `--help`) can improve usability, as users often expect both.
- **Consistent flag and argument order**: Consistency in flag and argument ordering helps users avoid errors and reduces the learning curve. For example, if one command requires the `--name` flag before `--id`, this order should be maintained across the tool.

These practices help make the CLI tool easier to use, more consistent, and more intuitive for users to understand and work with. By following a clear structure and using descriptive names, you ensure that users can navigate the CLI confidently and perform tasks with minimal confusion.

Effective error handling and feedback

CLI applications must provide clear, actionable feedback, especially in error scenarios. Users rely on CLI feedback to understand what went wrong and how to resolve issues. Effective error handling and feedback mechanisms ensure the tool behaves predictably and helps users correct errors without frustration. Here are some best practices:

- **User-friendly error messages**: When errors occur, error messages should be clear and specific. Instead of displaying a generic "*invalid input*" message, indicate precisely what was wrong. For example, a message such as **Invalid argument: '--mode' must be one of [full, basic]** is far more helpful. Go's errors package and the enhanced `fmt.Errorf()` function allow custom error messages, making it easy to provide informative feedback.
- **Exit codes**: Use appropriate exit codes to communicate the nature of the error, as follows:
    - `0` for success
    - `1` for general errors
    - `2` for command misuse or syntax errors
    - `3` and above for specific application errors, such as network or authentication issues

  Exit codes help integrate CLI tools into larger automation workflows by signaling success or failure explicitly, allowing other tools or scripts to respond accordingly.
- **Error logging for debugging**: For complex applications, detailed error logs are valuable for debugging. Error logs that include timestamps, error codes, and stack traces (when appropriate) allow developers to diagnose issues effectively. You can use Go's `log` package to handle this, creating logs with adjustable verbosity to provide insights while maintaining usability.

By following these practices, the CLI tool will not only be easier to troubleshoot but will also provide a smoother experience for users. Clear feedback, consistent exit codes, and helpful logs all contribute to building reliable and user-friendly CLI applications.

Testing for reliability

Testing is essential for building reliable CLI applications, especially those intended for use in production environments. Proper testing ensures that commands behave as expected, even in edge cases, and that updates don't introduce regressions. Here are some best practices:

- **Unit testing command functions**: Unit tests verify that individual command functions behave correctly. Testing frameworks such as `testing` (Go's built-in testing package) make it simple to write test cases for each command and subcommand, checking that expected inputs produce correct outputs.

- **Mocking external dependencies**: CLI applications often interact with external services, such as APIs or databases. To test these functions without relying on actual network calls, use mocking frameworks such as `gomock` to simulate external dependencies. Mocking allows you to control responses from external services, ensuring tests are fast, reliable, and isolated from external factors.
- **Integration testing for full command execution**: In addition to unit tests, integration tests ensure that commands work together as expected, verifying the entire execution path. Use a tool such as go `test` with shell scripts or Docker containers to create environments that mirror production setups, allowing you to test command interactions, environment variables, and other runtime factors. Integration testing is particularly useful for complex tools that operate across multiple systems.

Together, these testing strategies help ensure the CLI tool is dependable, well structured, and ready for real-world use. By covering both individual functions and the overall behavior of the application, you can confidently deliver a robust experience to the users.

Configuration management and flexibility

Flexibility in configuration is a hallmark of well-built CLI applications. Users often need to customize behavior or change environment settings, especially when running tools in different contexts. Go's configuration options, including environment variables and configuration files, make it easy to create adaptable CLI tools. Here are some best practices:

- **Environment variables for global settings**: Environment variables are useful for settings that apply across sessions or contexts, such as authentication tokens or default server URLs. For example, if a CLI tool interacts with a web API, the base URL might be stored in an environment variable:

```
apiURL := os.Getenv("API_BASE_URL")
if apiURL == "" {
    apiURL = "https://default.api.com"
}
```

- **Configuration files for user-specific settings**: Configuration files offer persistent, user-specific settings. Libraries such as `viper` make it easy to work with configuration files in JSON, YAML, or TOML formats. Config files can store user preferences, default options, and other settings that personalize the tool.

- **Command-line flags for immediate overrides**: While configuration files set defaults, command-line flags let users override specific options instantly. This layered approach to configuration (environment variables, config files, and flags) maximizes flexibility, allowing users to adjust settings based on immediate needs.

By combining these configuration methods, you give users the power to tailor the CLI tool to their environment and preferences. This flexibility helps ensure the tool remains useful and adaptable in a variety of scenarios.

Documentation and help messages

Clear documentation is essential to user experience, guiding users in setting up, using, and troubleshooting the CLI tool. Help messages and detailed documentation improve usability and reduce support requests. Here are some best practices:

- **Comprehensive help messages**: The `cobra` library provides an easy way to include help messages in Go CLI applications. Each command and flag should have descriptive help text that explains its purpose, expected input, and usage examples. A good help message system allows users to get quick insights without needing to reference external documentation.

  For example, a well-documented help message might look like this:

```
$ mycli deploy --help

Usage:
  mycli deploy [flags]

Flags:
  -f, --file string      Path to deployment configuration file
  -t, --timeout int      Maximum wait time (default 60)
  -v, --verbose          Enable verbose output

Examples:
  mycli deploy -f config.yaml
  mycli deploy --timeout 120
```

- **Clear usage examples**: Including usage examples in help messages and documentation can significantly reduce the learning curve. Examples should cover common tasks and complex scenarios, showing users how to leverage the tool fully.

- **Comprehensive README and wiki documentation**: Beyond in-app help, maintain a detailed `README` file and wiki for your CLI project. Include installation steps, common commands, and troubleshooting tips. For more complex tools, a separate documentation site (using tools such as MkDocs) can provide an organized, searchable reference.

Providing thorough documentation across help messages, `README` files, and wikis ensures users can quickly find the information they need. This improves user satisfaction and encourages adoption by making the CLI tool easier to learn and use.

Summary

In this chapter, we explored the essentials of developing CLIs using Go, a language well suited for DevOps needs. We started by understanding the importance of CLIs in the DevOps ecosystem and why Go is an ideal choice for building these tools.

We then delved into various methods for parsing commands and handling arguments, from basic approaches using the `os` and `flag` packages to more advanced techniques with the `cobra` package. Additionally, we covered the best practices for organizing commands, error handling, and providing user-friendly output.

We also examined how to enhance CLI applications with effective output formatting, including the use of tables and color for better readability and user feedback. Networking best practices were discussed, emphasizing concurrency, error handling, secure connections, and rate limiting to build robust and reliable tools.

Finally, we highlighted the importance of intuitive command structures, comprehensive documentation, and thorough testing to ensure the CLI applications are user-friendly, maintainable, and efficient in real-world DevOps scenarios.

In the next chapter, we'll shift focus to managing the life cycle of CLI tools. You will learn how to version your applications, handle releases, and implement update mechanisms to keep your tools current and reliable.

2

Packaging and Distributing Go CLIs

Packaging and distributing Go CLI applications is important for ensuring that these tools – Go-based command line interfaces – are easily accessible, deployable, and consistent across different environments.

Proper packaging, including building platform-specific binaries and containerizing applications, simplifies the deployment process, enhances the user experience, and minimizes configuration issues.

By adopting best practices in distribution, developers can ensure their CLI applications are reliable, maintainable, and ready for production, ultimately improving efficiency and scalability in both development and operational contexts.

In this chapter, we will cover the following topics:

- How to package and distribute Go CLI applications effectively
- How to build executable files for different operating systems (Windows, macOS, Linux)
- How to create Docker images for CLI tools for easy sharing and consistent deployment
- How these steps help prepare your application for real-world use and make it easier to deploy and maintain

Building executable binaries for different platforms

When developing CLI applications in Go, it's essential to ensure they are easily distributable and executable across various operating systems. One of Go's strengths is its ability to compile code into standalone binaries that can run on different platforms without requiring additional dependencies.

This section explores how to build these executables for multiple operating systems, including techniques for cross-compilation, handling platform-specific nuances, and automating the build process for consistent results.

Understanding Go's compilation model

Go's compiler is designed to produce statically linked binaries, meaning the resulting executables include everything needed to run the application, except for a small runtime dependency on the operating system. This model simplifies distribution, as users don't need to install a separate runtime or manage dependencies.

To compile a Go application, use the `go build` command:

```
$ go build -o mycli
```

This command generates an executable named `mycli` in the current directory. By default, the binary is built for the platform (OS and architecture) on which the `go build` command is executed.

In many Go projects, especially larger ones, the entry point (`main.go`) is placed in a subdirectory, such as `cmd/mycli/`, to organize code better. In such cases, you can pass the path to the entry point when building:

```
$ go build -o mycli ./cmd/mycli
```

This convention helps separate the CLI entry point from library packages and is commonly used in production-grade Go applications.

Cross-compilation basics

Cross-compilation is the process of building executables for different platforms from a single development environment. Go's toolchain supports cross-compilation out of the box, making it straightforward to build binaries for various operating systems and architectures.

To cross-compile a Go application, you need to set the `GOOS` and `GOARCH` environment variables to specify the target operating system and architecture. For example, here's how to compile a binary for Windows on a Linux machine:

```
$ GOOS=windows GOARCH=amd64 go build -o mycli.exe
```

Similarly, here's how to build for macOS:

```
$ GOOS=darwin GOARCH=amd64 go build -o mycli
```

And the following code is for Linux:

```
$ GOOS=linux GOARCH=amd64 go build -o mycli
```

Common `GOOS` values:

- `darwin` (macOS)
- `linux` (Linux)
- `windows` (Windows)

Common `GOARCH` values:

- `amd64` (64-bit x86)
- `386` (32-bit x86)
- `arm` (32-bit ARM)
- `arm64` (64-bit ARM)

Handling platform-specific differences

While Go abstracts many platform-specific details, there are cases where behavior can differ across operating systems. Handling these differences ensures your CLI tool works reliably on all target platforms.

To ensure the CLI tool works seamlessly across different platforms, there are a few key considerations. Here are some best practices for handling platform-specific differences:

- **File paths**: Use the `filepath` package to manage file paths in a platform-agnostic way. The `filepath.Join()` function automatically uses the correct path separator (/ on Unix-like systems and \ on Windows).

```
import "path/filepath"

func getConfigPath() string {
    return filepath.Join("config", "settings.json")
}
```

- **Environment variables**: The way environment variables are accessed and used can vary. Use the os package to interact with environment variables in a consistent manner:

```
import "os"

func getEnvVar(key string) string {
    return os.Getenv(key)
}
```

- **Line endings**: Text files might have different line endings (`\n` for Unix-like systems and `\r\n` for Windows). Use Go's `bufio` package to handle line endings when reading or writing text files, ensuring compatibility across platforms.

By handling these platform-specific differences properly, the CLI application will behave reliably no matter where it runs. This ensures a smooth experience for users on any operating system.

Building tags for platform-specific code

Go provides a powerful feature called **build tags** that lets us include or exclude files or code blocks during compilation based on the target platform, architecture, or custom conditions.

This is especially useful when the CLI uses OS-specific system calls, file operations, or third-party integrations.

File-level build tags

We can create separate files for different platforms using naming conventions (`_windows.go`, `_linux.go`, and so on) or use a build tag comment at the top of a file:

Here's the Windows platform-specific code:

```
//go:build windows
// +build windows

package main
import "fmt"

func sayHello() {
    fmt.Println("Hello from Windows")
}
```

This is the Linux platform-specific code:

```
//go:build linux
// +build linux

package main
import "fmt"

func sayHello() {
    fmt.Println("Hello from Linux")
}
```

The compiler will include the appropriate file depending on the target platform when you run `go build`.

Inline build tags

Alternatively, we can use `//go:build` within a single file to conditionally compile code blocks based on the environment.

Build tags offer a clean, idiomatic way to separate platform-specific logic and keep the code base maintainable and portable. This approach avoids cluttering the logic with runtime OS checks and ensures platform correctness at compile time.

External dependencies and tooling

In more advanced CLI tools, we may rely on external tools or services, such as open source CLI utilities, databases such as Redis, or other services. While Go modules allow direct integration with tools written in Go, external dependencies written in other languages or provided only as binaries require extra care for cross-platform compatibility.

Here are a few strategies to manage such dependencies:

- **Use containers for consistency**: If the CLI depends on tools such as Redis, Postgres, or non-Go CLIs, we can package these in Docker containers and manage their lifecycle (for example, spin them up during development or integration tests). This provides a uniform setup across platforms.
- **Fallback to prebuilt binaries**: If a dependency offers binaries for multiple platforms (for example, `jq` or `ffmpeg`), include logic in the CLI to detect the OS/architecture and download the correct binary if it's missing.

- **Add dependency checks**: Proactively check whether external tools are installed using functions such as `exec.LookPath()` and display informative messages to the user or trigger automated installation when safe.

```
import (
    "fmt"
    "os/exec"
)

func checkDependency(tool string) error {
    _, err := exec.LookPath(tool)
    if err != nil {
        return fmt.Errorf("%s not found in PATH", tool)
    }
    return nil
}
```

Managing external dependencies carefully ensures the CLI tool behaves predictably and is easier to set up on any system.

Optimizing binaries for distribution

When building binaries for distribution, it's important to optimize them for size and performance. Go provides flags to strip debug information and reduce binary size.

When optimizing binaries for distribution, it's essential to consider different methods for reducing their size and improving performance. The following are some effective techniques to achieve this:

- **Stripping debug information**: Use the `-ldflags` flag to remove debugging information, which reduces the size of the binary:

```
$ go build -ldflags="-s -w" -o mycli
```

  - `-s`: Omit the symbol table, which includes information such as function names, variable names, and line number mappings. These symbols are useful for debugging but unnecessary in production builds.
  - `-w`: Omit the DWARF symbol table, which is used for debuggers and profilers to provide stack traces, variable inspection, and other runtime metadata.

- **UPX compression**: Another way to reduce binary size is to compress the executable using upx (Ultimate Packer for eXecutables). Install upx and then compress your binary:

  ```
  $ upx mycli
  ```

  While upx can significantly reduce the size of binaries, it may have a slight impact on startup time due to decompression.

Another useful flag to consider is `-trimpath`, which removes file system paths from the compiled binary. This is particularly helpful for improving build reproducibility and protecting sensitive or system-specific paths in distributed binaries:

```
$ go build -trimpath -ldflags="-s -w" -o mycli
```

Here, `-trimpath` removes all file system paths from the compiled binary, replacing them with module or import paths.

Using `-trimpath` in combination with `-s` and `-w` is a common practice in CI pipelines or public distributions, as it helps create cleaner, more portable builds.

> **Important note**
>
> While Go offers other advanced flags for tuning inlining or garbage collection, they are generally recommended only in highly specialized performance scenarios and are not typically necessary for standard CLI tooling.

Automating the build process

Automating the build process ensures consistency and reduces the risk of human error, especially when targeting multiple platforms. This can be achieved using `shell scripts`, `Makefiles`, or Go tools such as `goreleaser`.

- **Using shell scripts**: Create a shell script to automate the build process for multiple platforms:

  ```
  #!/bin/bash

  platforms=("windows/amd64" "darwin/amd64" "linux/amd64")
  output="mycli"

  for platform in "${platforms[@]}"
  do
  ```

```
    GOOS=${platform%/*}
    GOARCH=${platform#*/}
    output_name=$output'-'$GOOS'-'$GOARCH
    if [ $GOOS = "windows" ]; then
        output_name+='.exe'
    fi
    env GOOS=$GOOS GOARCH=$GOARCH go build -o $output_name
done
```

- **Using Makefiles**: Makefiles offer a structured approach to defining build rules:

```
BINARY_NAME=mycli

all: windows macos linux

windows:
    GOOS=windows GOARCH=amd64 go build -o $(BINARY_NAME).exe

macos:
    GOOS=darwin GOARCH=amd64 go build -o $(BINARY_NAME)

linux:
    GOOS=linux GOARCH=amd64 go build -o $(BINARY_NAME)
```

Run the `make` command to build for all platforms:

```
$ make
```

- **Using Goreleaser**: `goreleaser` simplifies cross-platform builds, packaging, and releasing binaries. Install `goreleaser` and create a configuration file (`.goreleaser.yml`):

```
version: 2

builds:
  - binary: mycli
    goos:
      - windows
      - darwin
      - linux
    goarch:
      - amd64
```

By default, this configuration requires environment variables (such as `GITHUB_TOKEN`) to publish a release. To disable this publishing behavior, add the following section to the `.goreleaser.yml` file:

```
release:
  disable: true
```

Run `goreleaser` to automate the entire release process:

```
$ goreleaser release
```

Use the `--snapshot` flag to build locally without triggering the full release process:

```
$ goreleaser release --snapshot
```

This creates versioned and platform-specific binaries in the `dist/` directory without needing authentication tokens or remote release permissions.

By automating the build process, we can save time, ensure consistent results across different platforms, and focus more on improving the application instead of managing repetitive build tasks.

Testing built binaries

After building binaries, it's crucial to test them on each target platform to ensure they function correctly. You can use virtual machines, cloud services like Azure or AWS, or platform-specific tools such as **Windows Subsystem for Linux** (**WSL**) on Windows for testing. Always verify that the binaries work as expected, handle errors gracefully, and perform well under real-world conditions.

Dockerizing CLI applications

Docker has revolutionized the way applications are packaged, distributed, and run across different environments. By containerizing CLI applications, developers ensure that their software runs consistently, regardless of the underlying system. This section covers the fundamentals of Docker, the process of creating Docker images for Go-based CLI applications, and best practices for optimizing and managing these images.

Introduction to Docker and its benefits

Docker is an open source platform that automates the deployment of applications within lightweight, portable containers. Containers bundle an application with all its dependencies, configurations, and libraries, enabling it to run consistently across various environments.

Here are the key benefits of Docker for CLI applications:

- **Consistency**: Docker ensures that CLI applications behave the same way in development, testing, and production environments.
- **Isolation**: Containers isolate the application from the host system, reducing conflicts with other applications.
- **Portability**: Docker images can be easily shared and deployed on any system with Docker installed.
- **Simplified deployment**: Docker images can be deployed on cloud platforms, CI/CD pipelines, and local machines with minimal configuration.

Creating a Dockerfile for a Go CLI application

A Dockerfile is a script that contains a series of instructions on how to build a Docker image. Let's create a Dockerfile for a sample Go CLI application called `mycli`.

Step 1: Start with a lightweight base image that includes Go. For most CLI applications, the `golang:alpine` image is a popular choice because it is small and efficient.

```
# Use the official Golang image as a base
FROM golang:alpine
```

Step 2: Set the working directory inside the container where the application's source code will be copied and compiled.

```
# Set the working directory
WORKDIR /app
```

Step 3: Copy the application's source code from the host machine to the container.

```
# Copy the source code to the working directory
COPY . .
```

Step 4: Run the go `build` command to compile the application inside the container.

```
# Build the Go application
RUN go build -o mycli
```

Step 5: Specify the command that should run when the container starts. In this case, it's the compiled CLI application.

```
# Define the entry point for the container
ENTRYPOINT ["./mycli"]
```

Here's a full Dockerfile example:

```
FROM golang:alpine
WORKDIR /app
COPY . .
RUN go build -o mycli
ENTRYPOINT ["./mycli"]
```

Building the Docker image

Once the Dockerfile is ready, the next step is to build the Docker image. Use the `docker build` command, specifying a tag for the image.

```
$ docker build -t mycli-image .
```

This command creates a Docker image named `mycli-image` using the instructions in the `Dockerfile`.

Running the Dockerized CLI application

To run the CLI application inside a container, use the `docker run` command, passing the image name and any necessary arguments for the application.

```
$ docker run --rm mycli-image --help
```

The `--rm` flag removes the container after it exits, keeping the system clean.

Optimizing the Docker image

Docker images can become large, especially when they include development tools and dependencies. To optimize the image size, consider the following techniques:

1. **Multi-stage builds**: Multi-stage builds allow you to use multiple `FROM` statements in a `Dockerfile`, where each stage can have its own base image. This approach helps in building the application in one stage and copying only the necessary files to a minimal base image in the final stage.

   ```
   # First stage: Build the application
   FROM golang:alpine AS builder
   WORKDIR /app
   COPY . .
   RUN go build -o mycli
   ```

```
# Second stage: Create a smaller image for the final executable
FROM alpine
WORKDIR /root/
COPY --from=builder /app/mycli .
ENTRYPOINT ["./mycli"]
```

2. **Using a scratch image**: For minimal Go applications, you can use the `scratch` base image, which is an empty image with nothing pre-installed. This drastically reduces the image size.

```
FROM golang:alpine AS builder
WORKDIR /app
COPY . .
RUN go build -o mycli

FROM scratch
COPY --from=builder /app/mycli .
ENTRYPOINT ["./mycli"]
```

3. **Removing unnecessary files**: Ensure that only the necessary files and binaries are copied into the final image. Use `.dockerignore` to exclude files that are not needed, similar to `.gitignore` in Git.

   Sample `.dockerignore` file:

```
# Exclude the vendor directory
/vendor

# Ignore local binaries
/bin
```

By applying these techniques, you can significantly reduce the image size and improve performance.

Using Docker Compose for local development

When building CLI tools in Go, it's often helpful to simulate the environment in which the application will run. For instance, if the CLI tool depends on a database or a service, you can use `Docker Compose` to spin up those dependencies alongside the Go CLI tool. This allows you to create a consistent local development setup where everything is containerized and can run together smoothly.

What is Docker Compose?

Docker Compose is a tool for defining and running multi-container Docker applications. With a `docker-compose.yml` file, you can configure multiple services (such as a database, a web service, or other dependencies) and specify how they should interact. This simplifies the management of the local development environment and allows you to simulate a real-world setup without installing complex services on the local machine.

Instead of running each service individually with `docker run`, Docker Compose lets you define everything in one file and bring everything up with a single command.

Let's walk through setting up Docker Compose for a Go CLI application that interacts with a simple PostgreSQL database. Here is some simple Go code that connects to a PostgreSQL database:

```
package main

import (
    "database/sql"
    "fmt"
    "log"
    "os"
    _ "github.com/lib/pq"
)

func main() {
    connStr := os.Getenv("DATABASE_URL")
    if connStr == "" {
        log.Fatal("DATABASE_URL environment variable is not set")
    }
    db, err := sql.Open("postgres", connStr)
    if err != nil {
        log.Fatal(err)
    }
    defer db.Close()

    // Interact with the database
    rows, err := db.Query(
        "SELECT usesysid, usename FROM pg_catalog.pg_user;"
    )
```

```
    if err != nil {
        log.Fatal(err)
    }
    defer rows.Close()

    for rows.Next() {
        var id int
        var name string
        if err := rows.Scan(&id, &name); err != nil {
            log.Fatal(err)
        }
        fmt.Printf("User ID: %d, Name: %s\n", id, name)
    }
}
```

DATABASE_URL is an environment variable that the code requires in order to connect to the PostgreSQL database.

Let's create the docker-compose.yml file that will run both the Go CLI application and a PostgreSQL database.

```
version: '3.8'

services:
  cli:
    build: .
    container_name: cli-container
    environment:
      - DATABASE_URL=postgres://user:password@db:5432/db?sslmode=disable
    depends_on:
      - db

  db:
    image: postgres:13
    container_name: db
    environment:
      POSTGRES_USER: user
      POSTGRES_PASSWORD: password
      POSTGRES_DB: db
```

```
    volumes:
      - postgres_data:/var/lib/postgresql/data
    ports:
      - "5432:5432"

volumes:
  postgres_data:
    driver: local
```

In this configuration, we have the following:

- **cli**: This service builds the Go CLI application using the Dockerfile in the current directory (`.`). It also sets the `DATABASE_URL` environment variable, which the Go tool will use to connect to the database.
- **db**: This service runs a PostgreSQL container. It sets up the database with a user, password, and the database name. It also persists the database data using a Docker volume.

With the `docker-compose.yml` file in place, we can now build and run both the Go CLI tool and PostgreSQL together.

To start the services, simply run this:

```
$ docker compose up
```

If the required images are not yet built, `docker-compose up` will automatically build them. However, if there are changes to the Dockerfile or application code and you want to ensure the image is rebuilt, it's recommended to run the following:

```
$ docker compose build
```

This explicitly rebuilds the images to reflect the latest changes. Once the services are up, the Go CLI tool container and the PostgreSQL database container will be running and ready for interaction.

To stop the containers and clean up the environment after testing, run this:

```
$ docker compose down
```

Benefits of using Docker Compose

Using Docker Compose in the development workflow brings several practical advantages that improve productivity, collaboration, and reliability:

- **Simplicity**: You don't have to manually configure and manage each service. Docker Compose handles the dependencies for you.

- **Reproducibility**: Docker Compose ensures that the local development environment is consistent every time you run it. Developers on different machines will have the same setup.
- **Portability**: By using containers, you can easily move the setup between different systems, such as your local machine, CI/CD pipelines, or cloud environments.
- **Isolation**: Docker containers provide a clean, isolated environment for the services, avoiding conflicts with other applications on your system.

Overall, Docker Compose makes it easy to set up, share, and run your development environment in a consistent and reliable way.

Managing environment variables and configuration

When containerizing CLI applications, it's essential to manage environment variables and configuration files correctly. Docker provides mechanisms to pass environment variables and mount volumes.

- Here's how to pass environment variables:

```
$ docker run --rm -e ENV_VAR=value mycli-image
```

- Use the os package in Go to access these variables:

```
import "os"

func main() {
    envVar := os.Getenv("ENV_VAR")
    fmt.Println("Environment Variable:", envVar)
}
```

- Here's how to mount configuration files:

```
$ docker run --rm -v $(pwd)/config.yaml:/app/config.yaml mycli-image
```

  This command mounts the `config.yaml` file from the host into the container at the specified path.

Best practices for Dockerizing CLI applications

When Dockerizing CLI applications, it's important to follow best practices to ensure that the images are efficient, secure, and easy to manage. The following tips can help to optimize the Docker images and improve the overall quality of the Dockerized CLI applications.

- **Use minimal base images**: Start with the smallest possible base image to reduce the attack surface and image size.
- **Keep Dockerfiles simple**: Use clear, concise instructions and avoid unnecessary complexity.
- **Leverage multi-stage builds**: Build the application in a more feature-rich environment and then copy the result to a minimal image.
- **Optimize build cache**: Structure the Dockerfile to take advantage of Docker's caching mechanism, reducing build times.
- **Regularly update base images**: Keep base images up to date with security patches and updates.
- **Document Docker usage**: Provide clear documentation for users on how to build, run, and use the Dockerized CLI application.
- By following these best practices, you can ensure that the Dockerized CLI applications are efficient, secure, and maintainable. Proper optimization and clear documentation will help improve both the performance and user experience of the tool.

By combining Docker with best practices for building and running CLI applications, developers can achieve a powerful and reliable toolchain. Docker's flexibility in managing dependencies, isolating environments, and ensuring consistent behavior across platforms makes it an ideal solution for both development and deployment workflows. Whether we are building simple utilities or complex distributed tools, Dockerizing projects ensures scalability, portability, and ease of maintenance.

Summary

In this chapter, we explored the critical aspects of packaging and distributing Go CLI applications, focusing on building executable binaries and Dockerizing these applications for various platforms. We began by discussing how to compile Go applications into executable binaries tailored for different operating systems, emphasizing cross-compilation techniques and the use of Go's toolchain to ensure that applications run seamlessly on diverse environments. This approach enhances the portability of CLI tools, making them easily distributable to a wide audience.

Next, we dived into Dockerizing CLI applications, highlighting the advantages of containerization, such as consistency, isolation, and simplified deployment. We walked through creating a Dockerfile, building Docker images, and running containerized applications. Additionally, we covered optimization strategies such as multi-stage builds and using minimal base images to reduce image size and enhance security. This section provided practical insights into managing environment variables and configurations, and adhering to best practices for containerizing CLI applications.

In the next chapter, we will delve deeper into integrating Prometheus for monitoring and observability in Go applications. We will focus on advanced techniques for metric collection, monitoring, and setting up alerting to ensure applications are performing optimally and are easily traceable in production.

3

Integrating Go Applications with Prometheus

In software development, monitoring and observability are very important for maintaining the health and performance of applications. Integrating Prometheus allows developers to track critical metrics in real time, identify performance bottlenecks, and quickly respond to issues before they impact end users. By implementing Prometheus, developers get access to deep insights into application behavior, resource usage, and overall system health, which are very important for optimizing performance and ensuring high availability.

Also, the integration of Prometheus with visualization tools such as Grafana enhances the ability to interpret data through customizable dashboards and alerts. As Go continues to be a popular choice for building high-performance and scalable applications, leveraging Prometheus for monitoring ensures that these applications remain resilient and responsive in production environments.

In this chapter, we will cover the following topics:

- Learn why monitoring and observability are important and how Prometheus and Grafana help you understand what's happening in your Go applications
- Set up Prometheus and Grafana so you can collect and visualize performance data from your Go programs
- Add monitoring to your Go code by exposing custom metrics that Prometheus can track
- Create alerts based on metrics so you can get notified when something goes wrong in your application
- Use Go libraries for easier integration to simplify the way you add metrics and connect to Grafana dashboards

Introduction to monitoring and observability with Prometheus and Grafana

In today's fast-changing software world, keeping an eye on how applications perform is more important than ever. As software systems become bigger and more complex, older monitoring methods no longer provide enough information to manage them well. This is where tools such as Prometheus and Grafana help, making it easier to track performance and keep applications running smoothly.

The role of monitoring and observability

Monitoring involves the continuous collection, processing, and analysis of data to ensure that applications are running as expected. It provides real-time feedback on the state of the system, such as CPU usage, memory consumption, request latency, and error rates. Monitoring answers the question, *Is the system working properly right now?* and helps in detecting issues before they escalate into major problems.

Observability, on the other hand, is a broader concept that refers to the ability to infer the internal state of a system from its external outputs. It focuses on understanding why something is happening in the system by leveraging three main types of data—metrics, logs, and traces:

- **Metrics** are numerical data points, such as CPU usage or request counts, that show how the system is performing over time
- **Logs** are detailed records of events that happen in the system, often used to track what actions were taken or where errors occurred
- **Traces** follow the path of a request as it moves through different parts of the system, helping to pinpoint slowdowns or failures in complex flows

Observability enables developers and operators to explore and understand the behavior of their systems, especially in diagnosing complex issues and improving overall system performance.

Prometheus: a robust monitoring solution

Prometheus is an open source monitoring and alerting toolkit designed for reliability and scalability in cloud-native environments. It is known for its powerful time-series database, flexible query language (PromQL), and efficient data collection and storage mechanisms. Prometheus excels in monitoring highly dynamic environments where instances may frequently come and go, such as containerized applications orchestrated by Kubernetes.

Some of the standout features of Prometheus include the following:

- **Multi-dimensional data model**: Prometheus stores all data as time series identified by metric names and key/value pairs, allowing for rich and flexible querying
- **Pull-based data collection**: Prometheus scrapes metrics from configured endpoints, which simplifies the process of integrating with various services
- **Built-in alerting**: Prometheus supports alerting based on the metrics collected, enabling proactive incident response
- **Support for service discovery**: Prometheus can automatically discover targets through integrations with service discovery systems like Kubernetes, Consul, and others

Grafana: visualization and dashboarding

While Prometheus handles the collection and storage of metrics, Grafana complements it by providing a powerful and flexible platform for visualizing and analyzing these metrics. Grafana allows users to create dynamic and interactive dashboards that can display metrics in various formats, including graphs, tables, and heatmaps.

Some of the standout features of Grafana include the following:

- **Customizable dashboards**: Grafana's intuitive interface makes it easy to create, modify, and share dashboards tailored to specific use cases
- **Wide range of data sources**: In addition to Prometheus, Grafana supports numerous other data sources, making it a versatile tool for unified monitoring
- **Alerting and notifications**: Grafana can be configured to send alerts based on threshold conditions, integrating with various notification channels such as email, Slack, and PagerDuty
- **Annotations and event overlays**: Users can annotate dashboards with events or changes in the system, providing context to the visualized data

The synergy between Prometheus and Grafana

When used together, Prometheus and Grafana offer a comprehensive monitoring and observability solution. Prometheus excels in collecting and storing metrics efficiently, while Grafana provides an intuitive interface for visualizing these metrics and gaining actionable insights. This combination empowers teams to quickly detect, diagnose, and resolve issues, leading to more resilient and high-performing applications.

By integrating Prometheus and Grafana into their monitoring stack, developers and operators can ensure that they have the tools needed to maintain the health and performance of their Go applications, even in the most demanding environments. The insights gained through effective monitoring and observability not only help in troubleshooting but also in making informed decisions about system improvements and optimizations.

Setting up Prometheus and Grafana for Go applications

Setting up Prometheus and Grafana ensures that you can collect, store, and visualize metrics effectively. In this section, we will guide you through the setup process, including installing Prometheus and Grafana, configuring Prometheus to scrape metrics from your Go application, and setting up Grafana dashboards to visualize these metrics.

Installing Prometheus

Prometheus is available as a standalone binary that can be downloaded from the official Prometheus website:

```
$ wget https://github.com/prometheus/prometheus/releases/download/v3.5.0/
prometheus-3.5.0.linux-amd64.tar.gz
```

Once the download is complete, extract the `tar.gz` archive:

```
$ tar xvfz prometheus-3.5.0.linux-amd64.tar.gz
```

> **Important note**
>
> At the time of writing, version 3.5.0 is the latest LTS release of Prometheus. However, before installing, it's recommended to check the official Prometheus GitHub releases page (`https://github.com/prometheus/prometheus/releases`) to see whether a newer version is available. Updates may include critical security patches or important bug fixes, so staying up to date is essential for production environments.

Navigate to the extracted directory and run Prometheus using the following command:

```
$ ./prometheus --config.file=prometheus.yml
```

By default, Prometheus will start on port `9090`. You can verify it by visiting `http://localhost:9090` in your web browser.

Configuring Prometheus

Prometheus uses a configuration file (`prometheus.yml`) to define its scraping targets and other settings.

Edit the `prometheus.yml` file to include your Go application as a scrape target:

```
scrape_configs:
  - job_name: 'go_app'
    static_configs:
      - targets: ['localhost:8080']
```

In this example, Prometheus will scrape metrics from `localhost:8080`, where your Go application is expected to expose its metrics endpoint.

If you make changes to the `prometheus.yml` file while Prometheus is running, you need to reload the configuration. This can be done by sending a `SIGHUP` signal to the Prometheus process or through the Prometheus web interface:

```
$ kill -HUP <prometheus_pid>
```

Instrumenting Go applications

To expose metrics from your Go application, you need to instrument your code using the Prometheus Go client library.

Add the Prometheus client library to your Go project using `go get`:

```
$ go get github.com/prometheus/client_golang/prometheus
$ go get github.com/prometheus/client_golang/prometheus/promhttp
```

Import the necessary packages and set up a simple HTTP server to expose the `metrics` endpoint:

```
package main

import (
    "math/rand"
    "net/http"
    "time"
    "github.com/prometheus/client_golang/prometheus"
    "github.com/prometheus/client_golang/prometheus/promhttp"
)
```

```
func main() {
    http.Handle("/metrics", promhttp.Handler())
    http.ListenAndServe(":8080", nil)
}
```

You can also define custom metrics such as counters, gauges, and histograms:

```
// Define a counter
var opsProcessed = prometheus.NewCounter(prometheus.CounterOpts{
    Name: "myapp_processed_ops_total",
    Help: "The total number of processed events",
})

// Define a gauge
var currentUsers = prometheus.NewGauge(prometheus.GaugeOpts{
    Name: "myapp_current_users",
    Help: "Current number of active users",
})

// Define a histogram
var requestDuration = prometheus.NewHistogram(prometheus.HistogramOpts{
    Name: "myapp_request_duration_seconds",
    Help: "Histogram of response time for handler",
    Buckets: prometheus.DefBuckets,
})


func init() {
    prometheus.MustRegister(opsProcessed)
    prometheus.MustRegister(currentUsers)
    prometheus.MustRegister(requestDuration)
}

func process() {
    start := time.Now()

    // Increment counter
    opsProcessed.Inc()
```

```
    // Simulate random user count for gauge
    currentUsers.Set(float64(rand.Intn(100)))

    // Simulate request duration
    requestDuration.Observe(time.Since(start).Seconds())
}
```

Now that the Go application is exposing metrics, the next step is to visualize them using a powerful tool such as Grafana.

Installing Grafana

Grafana can be downloaded from the Grafana website. Choose the version that matches your operating system:

```
$ wget https://dl.grafana.com/oss/release/grafana-12.1.0.linux-amd64.tar.
gz
```

Extract the downloaded `tar.gz` archive:

```
$ tar -zxvf grafana-12.1.0.linux-amd64.tar.gz
```

> **Important note**
>
> At the time of writing, version 12.1.0 is the latest release of Grafana. However, before installing, it's recommended to check the official Grafana GitHub releases page (`https://github.com/grafana/grafana/releases`) to see whether a newer version is available. Updates may include critical security patches or important bug fixes, so staying up to date is essential for production environments.

Navigate to the extracted directory and start Grafana:

```
$ ./bin/grafana-server
```

By default, Grafana runs on port `3000`. Access it by visiting `http://localhost:3000` in your browser.

Setting up Grafana dashboards

Follow these steps to set up Grafana with Prometheus and create your first dashboard:

1. Log in to Grafana using the default credentials (`admin` for both username and password). You will be prompted to change the password upon the first login.
2. Go to **Connections** | **Data Sources**.
3. Click on **Add data source** and select **Prometheus**.
4. In the URL field, enter `http://localhost:9090` and click **Save & Test**.
5. Go to **Dashboards** and click on **Create Dashboard**.
6. Click **Add new panel** and use PromQL to query metrics from Prometheus.
7. Here is an example query to display the total number of processed operations:

```
myapp_processed_ops_total
```

8. You can also customize the appearance of your panels by adjusting the **Visualization** options, including graph type, axis labels, and color schemes.
9. Click on **Alert** in the panel editor to create an alert rule based on your metric.
10. Configure the conditions under which the alert should trigger and specify notification channels such as email or Slack.

Once the panels and alerts are set up, you'll have a live dashboard that gives real-time insights into the Go application's behavior. This makes it easier to spot issues quickly and take action before they affect users.

Exposing metrics: instrumenting Go code

Instrumenting your Go code to expose metrics is a crucial step in integrating your application with Prometheus for monitoring. By adding instrumentation, you can collect meaningful data about your application's behavior, performance, and resource usage. In this section, we will cover the process of instrumenting Go applications with Prometheus client libraries, creating various types of metrics, and organizing your code to facilitate effective monitoring.

Installing the Prometheus client library for Go

Before you can start instrumenting your Go code, you need to install the Prometheus client library. This library provides the necessary tools to define and register metrics in your application.

Use go get to install the Prometheus client library:

```
$ go get github.com/prometheus/client_golang/prometheus
$ go get github.com/prometheus/client_golang/prometheus/promhttp
```

These commands will add the Prometheus client library to your project, allowing you to use its functions and types.

Defining metrics

Metrics in Prometheus are divided into several types, each suited for different kinds of measurements. The primary types are counters, gauges, histograms, and summaries. We will explore each type and provide examples of how to define them in Go.

Counters

Counters are metrics that only increase. They are ideal for counting events such as the number of requests handled or errors encountered. Here is an example:

```
var requestsProcessed = prometheus.NewCounter(
    prometheus.CounterOpts{
        Name: "myapp_requests_processed_total",
        Help: "The total number of processed requests",
    })
```

After defining a counter, you must register it with Prometheus:

```
prometheus.MustRegister(requestsProcessed)
```

You can increment the counter using the `Inc()` method:

```
requestsProcessed.Inc()
```

Gauges

Gauges are metrics that can go up and down. They are useful for measuring values that fluctuate, such as memory usage or the number of active users. Here is an example:

```
var currentMemoryUsage = prometheus.NewGauge(
    prometheus.GaugeOpts{
        Name: "myapp_memory_usage_bytes",
        Help: "Current memory usage in bytes",
    })
```

Register the gauge with Prometheus:

```
prometheus.MustRegister(currentMemoryUsage)
```

Update the gauge with the `Set()` method:

```
currentMemoryUsage.Set(float64(memoryUsage))
```

Histograms

Histograms measure the distribution of values over a range. They are ideal for recording response times or sizes of requests. Here is an example:

```
var requestDuration = prometheus.NewHistogram(
    prometheus.HistogramOpts{
        Name:    "myapp_request_duration_seconds",
        Help:    "Histogram of response times for handler in seconds",
        Buckets: prometheus.DefBuckets,
    })
```

Register the histogram:

```
prometheus.MustRegister(requestDuration)
```

Observe a value with the `Observe()` method:

```
start := time.Now()
// Handle request
requestDuration.Observe(time.Since(start).Seconds())
```

Summaries

Summaries are similar to histograms but provide a quantile-based view. They are less commonly used due to their complexity and the overhead they introduce. Here is an example:

```
var requestLatency = prometheus.NewSummary(
    prometheus.SummaryOpts{
        Name:       "myapp_request_latency_seconds",
        Help:       "Summary of request latencies in seconds",
        Objectives: map[float64]
float64{0.5: 0.05, 0.9: 0.01, 0.99: 0.001},
    })
```

Register the summary:

```
prometheus.MustRegister(requestLatency)
```

Record a value using the `Observe()` method:

```
requestLatency.Observe(latency.Seconds())
```

Organizing metrics in your application

As the application grows, the number of metrics can increase significantly. Organizing metrics properly ensures maintainability and clarity.

Encapsulating metrics

Encapsulate metric definitions and registrations in dedicated functions and keep them in a separate package or file (for example, `metrics/metrics.go`). This approach improves the separation of concerns and keeps the main application logic clean.

Use Go's `init()` function to register metrics automatically when the package is imported, eliminating the need to manually invoke an initialization function from `main()`:

```
// metrics/metrics.go
package metrics

import (
    "github.com/prometheus/client_golang/prometheus"
)

var (
    RequestsProcessed = prometheus.NewCounter(prometheus.CounterOpts{
    Name: "requests_processed_total",
    Help: "Total number of processed HTTP requests",
})

CurrentMemoryUsage = prometheus.NewGauge(prometheus.GaugeOpts{
    Name: "current_memory_usage_bytes",
    Help: "Current memory usage in bytes",
})

)

func init() {
    prometheus.MustRegister(RequestsProcessed)
```

```
    prometheus.MustRegister(CurrentMemoryUsage)
}
```

Then, in the `main` package, simply import the `metrics` package:

```
package main

import (
    _ "mycli/metrics"
)
func main() {
    // Start the application
}
```

This pattern ensures automatic registration, better encapsulation, and a cleaner `main()` function.

Using middleware

Middleware can automatically instrument the HTTP handlers, reducing the need for manual metric updates in each handler function.

For example, we can create a middleware that tracks the number of requests and measures the time each request takes. This middleware wraps the existing handlers and updates the relevant metrics before and after the request is processed:

```
// metrics/middleware.go
package metrics

import (
    "net/http"
    "time"
)

func MetricsMiddleware(next http.Handler) http.Handler {
    return http.HandlerFunc(func(w http.ResponseWriter, r *http.Request) {
        RequestsProcessed.Inc()
        start := time.Now()

        next.ServeHTTP(w, r)
```

```
        duration := time.Since(start).Seconds()
        RequestDuration.Observe(duration)
    })
}
```

We can also define a histogram for request durations in the `metrics.go` file:

```
RequestDuration = prometheus.NewHistogram(prometheus.HistogramOpts{
    Name: "http_request_duration_seconds",
    Help: "Duration of HTTP requests in seconds",
    Buckets: prometheus.DefBuckets,
})
```

The `/metrics` endpoint is a special HTTP endpoint that Prometheus will scrape. It automatically exposes all registered metrics in plain text format, following the Prometheus exposition format.

We don't have to manually serialize metrics; `promhttp.Handler()` takes care of converting in-memory metric values into a format that Prometheus understands:

```
http.Handle("/metrics", promhttp.Handler())
```

Then, in the `main` application, we can set up HTTP routes and wrap them with the middleware:

```
package main

import (
    "fmt"
    "net/http"

    "mycli/metrics" // Register metrics and imports the middleware

    "github.com/prometheus/client_golang/prometheus/promhttp"
)

func testHandler(w http.ResponseWriter, r *http.Request) {
    fmt.Fprintln(w, "Hello from test handler!")
}

func main() {
    // Application endpoints
    http.Handle(
```

```
        "/test",
        metrics.MetricsMiddleware(
            http.HandlerFunc(testHandler)
        )
    )

    // Endpoint for Prometheus to scrape
    http.Handle("/metrics", promhttp.Handler())

    http.ListenAndServe(":8080", nil)
}
```

With this setup, every time `/test` is accessed, the middleware automatically increases the request counter and records the request's duration, while `/metrics` exposes all collected metrics in the Prometheus format.

This approach also ensures that every request to the handler is automatically tracked for both count and duration, which helps to monitor application performance without adding metric logic to every single handler.

This pattern makes it easier to maintain monitoring logic as the application grows.

Best practices

To get the most value from the monitoring setup, it's important to follow some common best practices. These guidelines will help you create metrics that are useful, efficient, and easy to manage:

- **Naming conventions**: Follow Prometheus naming conventions to ensure consistency. Metric names should be descriptive and use underscores to separate words.
- **Documentation**: Document each metric's purpose and how it should be interpreted. This helps maintainers and new team members understand your monitoring setup.
- **Avoid over-instrumentation**: Instrumenting every function or variable can lead to performance issues and cluttered dashboards. Focus on key metrics that provide valuable insights.
- **Testing metrics**: Write tests to verify that your metrics are being recorded correctly. Use Prometheus' test utilities or create mock metrics to simulate various scenarios. Here are some examples of what to test:

- **Naming conventions**: Ensure that all counter metrics follow the Prometheus convention of ending in `_total`. This helps with consistency and automatic parsing in tools such as Grafana.
- **Presence of key metrics**: Verify that expected metrics are registered, especially for critical paths such as HTTP request durations or error counts.
- **Value assertions**: Check that metrics record expected values during test scenarios (for example, when a handler is called, the request count increases).

By following these best practices, you can keep your monitoring setup clean and effective. This makes it easier to spot problems, track performance, and maintain the system over time.

Introduction to alerting and incident response

In any production environment, it is essential to have a robust system in place for alerting and incident response. Monitoring applications and infrastructure provides valuable insights, but without a proper alerting mechanism, critical issues may go unnoticed until they escalate into significant problems. Prometheus offers a powerful alerting system that, when combined with incident response strategies, helps maintain the reliability and availability of your services.

Setting up alertmanager

Alertmanager is a component of Prometheus that handles alerts, including deduplication, grouping, and routing to the appropriate receiver channels such as email, Slack, or PagerDuty.

Download and install Alertmanager from the Prometheus website or use a package manager such as **Homebrew** or **apt**:

```
$ brew install alertmanager
```

Configure Alertmanager by creating an `alertmanager.yml` file with the desired routes and receivers.

```
route:
 receiver: 'default'
 group_wait: 30s
 group_interval: 5m
 repeat_interval: 4h
receivers:
 - name: 'default'
 slack_configs:
 - api_url: 'https://hooks.slack.com/services/xxx'
 channel: '#alerts'
```

This configuration file sets up a basic Alertmanager setup that sends all alerts to a Slack channel. The route section defines the default behavior for handling alerts. The `group_wait: 30s` setting means Alertmanager waits 30 seconds before sending the first notification, giving time for related alerts to arrive so they can be grouped together. The `group_interval: 5m` ensures that if new alerts arrive after the initial notification, they'll be batched together and sent every 5 minutes rather than immediately. The `repeat_interval: 4h` prevents notification fatigue by only re-sending alerts every 4 hours if they remain active.

The receivers section defines where alerts should be sent. In this case, all alerts go to a Slack channel names #alerts using a webhook URL. We'll need to replace the api_url with the actual Slack webhook URL, which we can generate from the Slack workspace settings.

Once the configuration file is ready, we can start Alertmanager and point it to the configuration:

```
alertmanager --config.file=alertmanager.yml
```

Alertmanager will now listen for alerts from Prometheus and route them to the Slack channel. We can access the Alertmanager web interface at `http://localhost:9093` to view active alerts, silences, and notification status. This setup ensures that the team is notified about issues promptly through Slack, with intelligent grouping to avoid overwhelming them with too many notifications at once.

Configuring alert rules in Prometheus

We can define alert rules in Prometheus using YAML configuration files. These rules specify the conditions under which alerts should be triggered:

```
groups:
- name: example
  rules:
  - alert: HighMemoryUsage
    expr: node_memory_Active_bytes > 4e+09
    for: 2m
    labels:
      severity: warning
    annotations:
      summary: "High memory usage detected"
```

Reload Prometheus to apply the new alert rules:

```
$ curl -X POST http://localhost:9090/-/reload
```

Integrating Alertmanager with Prometheus

In Prometheus' `prometheus.yml` configuration file, specify the `alertmanager` service URL:

```
alerting:
  alertmanagers:
  - static_configs:
    - targets:
      - localhost:9093
```

Best practices

When building robust monitoring and alerting systems, it's not enough to simply detect problems; we also need to respond effectively. The following best practices help ensure that the team can act quickly and confidently when issues arise:

- **Incident response strategies**: Having alerts in place is only the first step. An effective incident response strategy ensures that the right actions are taken promptly when an alert is triggered.
- **Defining incident response procedures**: Document clear procedures for responding to different types of incidents. Include steps for diagnosing the issue, mitigating the impact, and communicating with stakeholders.
- **Automating responses**: Automate repetitive response tasks where possible. Use tools such as Ansible or Terraform to apply fixes quickly.
- **Conducting post-incident reviews**: After resolving an incident, perform a post-incident review to analyze the root cause, what went well, and what could be improved. Update documentation and processes accordingly.
- **Training and drills**: Regularly train your team on incident response procedures and conduct drills to simulate real incidents. This practice helps ensure everyone is prepared to handle emergencies effectively.

Following these steps helps teams respond to incidents more efficiently and learn from them. Over time, this leads to more stable systems and quicker recovery when things go wrong.

Utilizing Go libraries for Prometheus and Grafana integration

Integrating Go applications with Prometheus and Grafana can be greatly simplified by using various Go libraries. These libraries provide abstractions and utilities that make it easier to instrument your code, expose metrics, and interact with Prometheus and Grafana. In this section, we will explore the key Go libraries available for Prometheus and Grafana integration, their features, and how to use them effectively in your applications.

Prometheus client Go library

The Prometheus client Go library (`client_golang`) is the official Go client library for Prometheus. It is widely used for instrumenting Go applications to expose metrics in a format that Prometheus can scrape.

Installing the library

To install the library, use the following go get command:

```
$ go get github.com/prometheus/client_golang/prometheus
$ go get github.com/prometheus/client_golang/prometheus/promhttp
```

These commands add the Prometheus client library to your Go project, allowing you to start defining and exposing metrics.

Defining metrics

The library supports various types of metrics such as counters, gauges, histograms, and summaries. Here's an example of how to define and register a counter metric:

```
var requestsProcessed = prometheus.NewCounter(
    prometheus.CounterOpts{
        Name: "myapp_requests_processed_total",
        Help: "The total number of processed requests",
    })
prometheus.MustRegister(requestsProcessed)
```

You can increment the counter using the `Inc()` method:

```
requestsProcessed.Inc()
```

Exposing Metrics

To expose the metrics for Prometheus to scrape, use the `promhttp` package to create an HTTP handler:

```
http.Handle("/metrics", promhttp.Handler())
log.Fatal(http.ListenAndServe(":8080", nil))
```

This handler will serve the metrics at the `/metrics` endpoint.

Grafana libraries for visualization

While Prometheus handles the collection and storage of metrics, Grafana is used for visualizing these metrics. Although Grafana itself doesn't have a specific Go library for integration, you can use APIs and JSON models to programmatically create and manage Grafana dashboards.

Grafana API

Grafana provides a REST API that allows you to automate various tasks, such as creating dashboards, panels, and data sources. You can use any HTTP client in Go to interact with this API.

Here is an example using the `net/http` package:

```
func createGrafanaDashboard(apiURL, apiKey string, dashboardData []
byte) error {
    req, err := http.NewRequest(
        "POST",
        apiURL,
        bytes.NewBuffer(dashboardData)
    )
    if err != nil {
        return err
    }
    req.Header.Set("Content-Type", "application/json")
    req.Header.Set("Authorization", "Bearer "+apiKey)

    client := &http.Client{}
    resp, err := client.Do(req)
    if err != nil {
        return err
    }
    defer resp.Body.Close()
```

```
    if resp.StatusCode != http.StatusOK {
        return fmt.Errorf(
            "failed to create dashboard, status code: %d",
            resp.StatusCode
        )
    }
    return nil
}
```

Here is an example of the minimal JSON structure we can pass as the dashboard data (`dashboardData`):

```
{
  "dashboard": {
    "id": null,
    "uid": "example-dashboard",
    "title": "Example Dashboard",
    "tags": ["automation"],
    "timezone": "browser",
    "schemaVersion": 36,
    "version": 0,
    "panels": []
  },
  "folderId": 0,
  "overwrite": true
}
```

The base URL for Grafana instance should be something like `http://localhost:3000` or the public Grafana URL. The full endpoint for dashboard creation is as follows:

```
POST http://localhost:3000/api/dashboards/db
```

To authenticate the API requests, it's recommended to use a service account token rather than a user API key. Here's how to create one:

1. Log in to Grafana as an admin.
2. Go to **Administration | Service Accounts**.
3. Click **Add service account**, enter a name, and select the appropriate role (for example, **Admin** or **Editor**).

4. After the service account is created, open its details page.
5. Click **Add service account token**, provide a name, and copy the token shown.
6. Use this token as the apiKey parameter in the API request.

Using the Grafana API can save time and reduce manual effort when managing dashboards. It also makes it easier to keep your monitoring setup consistent across different environments.

Using Grafana Terraform provider

For those using infrastructure as code, the Grafana Terraform provider can be a powerful tool to manage Grafana resources declaratively. This approach can be integrated into your CI/CD pipelines for automated provisioning and updates:

```
provider "grafana" {
  url  = "https://grafana.example.com"
  auth = "Bearer your_api_token"
}

resource "grafana_dashboard" "example" {
  config_json = file("./dashboard.json")
}
```

Using the Grafana Terraform provider helps you manage dashboards and other resources in a repeatable and version-controlled way. This makes the monitoring setup easier to maintain and scale as the infrastructure grows.

Additional libraries and tools

Several other libraries and tools can complement your integration of Go applications with Prometheus and Grafana. Here are a few notable ones:

- **promauto**: The promauto package simplifies the creation and registration of metrics, reducing boilerplate code. Here's how to use it:

```
var requestsProcessed = promauto.NewCounter(prometheus.CounterOpts{
    Name: "myapp_requests_processed_total",
    Help: "The total number of processed requests",
})
```

- **logrus and zap for structured logging**: Libraries such as `logrus` and `zap` provide structured logging capabilities that can be integrated with Prometheus for enhanced observability. For instance, you can log key metrics and events that are not suitable for Prometheus metrics but still important for monitoring and debugging.
- **opentelemetry-go**: OpenTelemetry is an observability framework that integrates with Prometheus for metrics collection. Using the `opentelemetry-go` library, you can collect and export traces alongside metrics, providing a comprehensive view of your application's performance:

```
import (
    "log"
    "go.opentelemetry.io/otel"
    "go.opentelemetry.io/otel/exporters/prometheus"
)

func init() {
    exporter, err := prometheus.New()
    if err != nil {
        log.
Fatalf("failed to initialize prometheus exporter: %v", err)
    }
    otel.SetMeterProvider(exporter.MeterProvider())
}
```

These tools can help to extend the observability setup beyond basic metrics. Choosing the right combination based on the application's needs can make monitoring more effective and easier to manage.

Best practices for using Go libraries

Here are some best practices to keep in mind when using Go libraries:

- **Choosing the right libraries**: Select libraries that are well-maintained and widely used in the community. This ensures you get timely updates and support.
- **Minimizing dependencies**: Be mindful of the number of dependencies you introduce. Each new library adds potential complexity and maintenance overhead.
- **Contributing back**: If you find issues or want to add features to a library, consider contributing back to the project. Open source contributions help improve the ecosystem for everyone.

Keeping these best practices in mind can help to write cleaner, more maintainable Go code. They also make it easier to manage the project in the long run.

Summary

In this chapter, we learned about the importance of integrating Go applications with Prometheus and Grafana to achieve robust monitoring and observability. We began by understanding the foundational concepts of monitoring and observability and how they are crucial in maintaining the performance and reliability of software applications. Through the exploration of Prometheus and Grafana, we experienced how to set up these tools to collect, store, and visualize metrics effectively.

We then learned how to expose custom metrics by instrumenting Go code, allowing Prometheus to scrape and analyze these metrics. This hands-on approach provided us with the skills to track the behavior and performance of our Go applications comprehensively. Additionally, we explored various alerting mechanisms and incident response strategies, understanding the importance of timely detection and resolution of issues. Lastly, we utilized Go libraries that simplify the integration with Prometheus and Grafana, enhancing the observability framework and ensuring that the applications are well-monitored and maintainable.

The next chapter will explore how to build custom Go exporters for Prometheus. It will guide you through designing, implementing, and deploying exporters to collect application-specific metrics with accuracy and performance in mind.

4

Writing Go Exporters for Prometheus

Writing Go exporters for Prometheus is important because it allows developers to collect and share specific data about their applications. While Prometheus can monitor many standard metrics, some applications have unique data that needs to be tracked. By creating custom exporters, developers can expose important information such as system performance, request counts, or error rates in a way that Prometheus understands. This helps teams monitor their applications more effectively and respond quickly to any issues.

Custom exporters also improve the overall health and performance of applications by providing accurate and detailed insights. Instead of relying only on general system metrics, developers can track exactly what matters most for their software. This makes troubleshooting easier and helps teams make better decisions to optimize performance. With well-designed exporters, businesses can ensure their applications run smoothly, reduce downtime, and improve user experience.

In this chapter, we will cover the following topics:

- Understand what Prometheus exporters are and how they help expose custom metrics
- Learn how to design exporters that are efficient, scalable, and aligned with your application's needs
- Implement different types of metrics such as counters, gauges, and histograms in Go
- Test and deploy exporters so they are reliable in production environments

Understanding exporters and their role in Prometheus

Prometheus is a powerful monitoring tool that collects and analyzes metrics from various applications and systems. However, not all applications expose their metrics in a format that Prometheus can read. This is where exporters come in. An exporter is a tool that collects data from an application or system and converts it into a format that Prometheus understands. It acts as a bridge between the application and Prometheus, ensuring that important metrics are available for monitoring and analysis.

Exporters are particularly useful when dealing with third-party applications, legacy systems, or custom software that does not natively support Prometheus. By using an exporter, developers and system administrators can monitor critical aspects of their applications without modifying the original software. This makes exporters a key component of the Prometheus ecosystem.

What is an exporter?

An exporter is a small program or script that collects specific data from an application, processes it, and then exposes it in a way that Prometheus can scrape. The data is usually provided via an HTTP endpoint, allowing Prometheus to collect it at regular intervals. The exporter translates raw data into meaningful metrics, making it easier for teams to monitor and analyze their applications.

For example, consider a database system that does not provide Prometheus-compatible metrics. A database exporter can be created to connect to the database, retrieve important information such as query counts, error rates, and connection status, and then expose these metrics in a structured format. Prometheus can then scrape these metrics and store them for analysis.

Exporters follow a pull-based model, meaning that Prometheus requests data from the exporter rather than the exporter pushing data to Prometheus. This approach allows for better scalability and control, as Prometheus decides when and how often to collect metrics.

Types of exporters

There are two main types of exporters: official and custom exporters.

Official exporters

These are developed and maintained by the Prometheus community or software vendors. They are widely used and tested, ensuring reliability and accuracy. The following are examples:

- **Node exporter** (for monitoring system metrics such as CPU and memory usage)

- **MySQL exporter** (for monitoring MySQL databases)
- **Blackbox exporter** (for probing network endpoints)

Custom exporters

Sometimes, applications do not have an official exporter available. In such cases, developers create custom exporters tailored to their specific needs. Custom exporters are useful when monitoring proprietary applications or unique business logic that is not covered by existing exporters.

How exporters work

The process of using an exporter involves several steps:

1. **Data collection**: The exporter gathers raw data from an application, system, or service. This can involve making API calls, querying databases, or reading log files.
2. **Metric conversion**: The raw data is processed and converted into a structured format that Prometheus understands, such as counters, gauges, or histograms.
3. **Exposing metrics**: The exporter provides an HTTP endpoint (usually `/metrics`), which Prometheus scrapes at predefined intervals.
4. **Prometheus scraping**: Prometheus collects the exposed metrics and stores them in its time-series database.
5. **Data visualization and alerts**: The collected data can be visualized in Grafana or used to trigger alerts based on predefined thresholds.

Each exporter must be carefully designed to ensure that it collects accurate data, performs efficiently, and does not overload the system it is monitoring.

Why use exporters?

Exporters play an important role in the Prometheus ecosystem, as follows:

- **Extend Prometheus' capabilities**: Exporters allow Prometheus to monitor a wider range of applications, including those that do not natively support Prometheus
- **Minimize changes to applications**: Instead of modifying existing applications to expose Prometheus metrics, an exporter can be used to collect data externally
- **Improve observability**: Exporters provide deeper insights into application performance, system health, and potential issues
- **Enhance scalability**: Prometheus can handle multiple exporters across different applications, making it easier to scale monitoring efforts

Challenges of using exporters

While exporters are powerful tools, they come with some challenges:

- **Performance overhead**: Poorly optimized exporters can consume excessive resources, affecting application performance
- **Data accuracy**: If an exporter does not collect data correctly, it can lead to misleading or incomplete metrics
- **Security considerations**: Exporters expose data over HTTP, so proper authentication and access controls should be implemented to prevent unauthorized access
- **Maintenance effort**: Custom exporters require ongoing updates and maintenance to keep them working with changes in the monitored application

Besides these challenges, exporters remain a valuable part of a robust monitoring setup. With careful design and regular maintenance, their benefits often outweigh the challenges.

Design principles for custom metrics exporters

Creating a custom metrics exporter for Prometheus requires careful planning and design. A well-designed exporter ensures that data is collected accurately, efficiently, and in a way that benefits monitoring and analysis. In this section, we will cover the key design principles that developers should follow when building custom metrics exporters.

Keep it simple and focused

A good exporter should be simple and focused on its purpose. It should collect only the necessary metrics and avoid unnecessary complexity. Adding too many features or collecting excessive data can slow down the exporter and impact system performance. Instead, the exporter should focus on providing meaningful metrics that help in monitoring key aspects of an application.

For example, if an exporter is designed to monitor a database, it should only collect relevant metrics, such as query counts, error rates, and connection status, rather than gathering every possible detail about the system.

Use Prometheus metric types correctly

Prometheus supports different types of metrics, including counters, gauges, and histograms. Each metric type has a specific use case, and choosing the right one is important:

- **Counters** should be used for metrics that only increase over time, such as the number of requests processed or errors encountered

- **Gauges** are for metrics that can go up and down, such as the number of active connections or memory usage
- **Histograms** are useful for measuring distributions, such as response times or request sizes

Using the correct metric type ensures that the collected data is meaningful and can be analyzed effectively.

Minimize performance impact

An exporter should be designed to run efficiently without consuming too many system resources. If an exporter takes up too much CPU, memory, or disk space, it can negatively impact the application or system it is monitoring. To reduce performance impact, do the following:

- Avoid collecting metrics too frequently unless necessary
- Use caching to store frequently accessed data and reduce redundant computations
- Optimize database queries or API calls to minimize response time and resource usage
- By keeping the exporter lightweight, it can operate smoothly without interfering with the monitored application

Ensure data accuracy and consistency

Metrics must be collected accurately to provide useful insights. Inaccurate data can lead to incorrect analysis and misleading alerts. To ensure accuracy, do the following:

- Collect data from reliable sources
- Validate and filter metrics before exposing them
- Test the exporter with sample data to verify correctness

Consistency is also important. Metric names, labels, and data formats should follow Prometheus best practices to make the metrics easy to understand and use.

Make the exporter configurable

Different environments may require different configurations for an exporter. Providing configuration options makes it easier to customize the exporter for different use cases. A good exporter should allow users to configure:

- The port and endpoint where metrics are exposed
- The frequency of data collection
- Authentication settings for secure access
- Filters to enable or disable specific metrics

Using a configuration file or environment variables can make it easier to adjust settings without modifying the code.

Implement proper error handling

Errors can occur when collecting data, such as API failures, missing resources, or connection timeouts. Proper error handling ensures that the exporter does not crash and continues to function even when issues arise. Best practices for error handling include the following:

- Logging errors for debugging purposes
- Retrying failed requests with a backoff strategy
- Providing default values when data is unavailable
- Gracefully handling unexpected conditions instead of exiting abruptly

Handling errors correctly makes the exporter more reliable and reduces downtime.

Secure the exporter

Since exporters expose metrics over an HTTP endpoint, security is an important consideration. Unauthorized access to metrics can reveal sensitive information about an application. To secure the exporter, do the following:

- Restrict access to the metrics endpoint using authentication or network policies
- Use HTTPS to encrypt data transmission
- Avoid exposing unnecessary system details in the metrics
- Regularly update the exporter to fix security vulnerabilities

Taking these security measures helps prevent potential risks and protects the monitored system.

Document and maintain the exporter

A well-documented exporter is easier to use, maintain, and troubleshoot. Documentation should include the following:

- A description of the metrics collected and their meanings
- Instructions on how to install, configure, and run the exporter
- Examples of how to use the exporter with Prometheus
- Guidelines for troubleshooting common issues

Maintaining the exporter involves regularly checking for bugs, optimizing performance, and updating it to support changes in the monitored application or Prometheus itself.

By following these design principles, you can create exporters that are efficient, reliable, and easy to maintain. A well-designed exporter not only improves observability but also reduces the operational burden over time. Paying attention to performance, accuracy, and security ensures your exporter can be trusted in production environments.

Now that we've covered how to design custom exporters, the next step is to learn how to implement the actual metric types. In the following section, we will explore how to use counters, gauges, and histograms to represent different kinds of application data.

Implementing metric types: Counters, gauges, and histograms

Metrics play a crucial role in monitoring applications, and Prometheus provides different metric types to capture various kinds of data. The three most commonly used metric types are the following:

- **Counters**: Used for counting events that only increase (e.g., number of requests)
- **Gauges**: Used for values that can go up and down (e.g., memory usage)
- **Histograms**: Used for tracking distributions of values over time (e.g., request durations)

In this section, we will explore how to implement these metric types in a Go application with practical examples.

Implementing counters

Counters are useful when you need to track the number of occurrences of an event. A common use case is counting HTTP requests:

```
package main

import (
    "github.com/prometheus/client_golang/prometheus"
    "github.com/prometheus/client_golang/prometheus/promhttp"
    "net/http"
    "log"
)

// Define a Counter metric
var requestCounter = prometheus.NewCounter(
    prometheus.CounterOpts{
```

```
        Name: "http_requests_total",
        Help: "Total number of HTTP requests",
    },
)

func handler(w http.ResponseWriter, r *http.Request) {
    requestCounter.Inc() // Increment counter
    w.Write([]byte("Hello, World!"))
}

func main() {
    // Register the metric
    prometheus.MustRegister(requestCounter)

    http.Handle("/metrics", promhttp.Handler())
    http.HandleFunc("/", handler)

    log.Println("Server is running on port 8080...")
    log.Fatal(http.ListenAndServe(":8080", nil))
}
```

In this example, every time an HTTP request hits the root endpoint, the counter increments. This allows Prometheus to track how many requests the server has received since it started. The metric is registered with Prometheus using `prometheus.MustRegister`, and the `/metrics` endpoint is exposed so that Prometheus can scrape and collect the data at regular intervals.

Implementing gauges

Gauges represent values that fluctuate, such as memory usage or active users:

```
package main

import (
    "github.com/prometheus/client_golang/prometheus"
    "github.com/prometheus/client_golang/prometheus/promhttp"
    "net/http"
    "log"
    "math/rand"
    "time"
```

```
)

// Define a Gauge metric
var activeUsers = prometheus.NewGauge(
    prometheus.GaugeOpts{
        Name: "active_users",
        Help: "Current number of active users",
    },
)

func simulateUserActivity() {
    for {
        time.Sleep(2 * time.Second)
        // Simulating user count fluctuation
        activeUsers.Set(float64(rand.Intn(100)))
    }
}

func main() {
    // Register the metric
    prometheus.MustRegister(activeUsers)

    // Start simulating user activity
    go simulateUserActivity()

    http.Handle("/metrics", promhttp.Handler())

    log.Println("Server is running on port 8080...")
    log.Fatal(http.ListenAndServe(":8080", nil))
}
```

Here, the active user count is updated randomly every two seconds, mimicking real-world behavior.

Implementing histograms

Histograms help track value distributions, such as request durations or response sizes:

```
package main

import (
    "github.com/prometheus/client_golang/prometheus"
    "github.com/prometheus/client_golang/prometheus/promhttp"
    "net/http"
    "log"
    "math/rand"
    "time"
)

// Define a Histogram metric
var requestDuration = prometheus.NewHistogram(
    prometheus.HistogramOpts{
        Name:    "http_request_duration_seconds",
        Help:    "Histogram of response durations",
        Buckets: prometheus.LinearBuckets(0.1, 0.2, 5),
    },
)

func handler(w http.ResponseWriter, r *http.Request) {
    start := time.Now()
    // Simulating response time
    time.Sleep(time.Duration(rand.Intn(500)) * time.Millisecond)
    duration := time.Since(start).Seconds()
    requestDuration.Observe(duration)
    w.Write([]byte("Request completed."))
}

func main() {
    // Register the metric
    prometheus.MustRegister(requestDuration)

    http.Handle("/metrics", promhttp.Handler())
```

```
    http.HandleFunc("/", handler)

    log.Println("Server is running on port 8080...")
    log.Fatal(http.ListenAndServe(":8080", nil))
}
```

This code tracks how long each HTTP request takes to complete and records the duration using a **histogram**. The histogram groups the durations into predefined buckets, making it easier to see how requests are distributed over time. For example, you can find out how many requests took less than 0.1 seconds, between 0.1 and 0.3 seconds, and so on. This helps to understand the overall performance of the application and identify slow or inconsistent response times.

Ensuring data accuracy and performance

Ensuring accurate and efficient data collection is crucial when developing Prometheus exporters. Poorly implemented metrics can lead to incorrect insights, excessive resource consumption, and performance issues in production environments. In this section, we will explore techniques to improve data accuracy and optimize performance for Go exporters.

Avoiding missing or incomplete data

One of the biggest challenges in metric collection is ensuring that no data points are lost or missed. Here's how you can prevent missing data:

- **Regular data collection**: Ensure that metrics are updated at consistent intervals
- **Use default values**: Avoid null values by initializing metrics with default values
- **Monitor exporter logs**: Log errors and warnings to detect any failures in data collection

The following example shows how to define and register a new gauge metric using Prometheus. A gauge is useful for tracking values that can go up or down, such as active connections or resource usage:

```
package main

import (
    "github.com/prometheus/client_golang/prometheus"
    "github.com/prometheus/client_golang/prometheus/promhttp"
    "net/http"
    "log"
    "time"
```

```
)

var requestCount = prometheus.NewGauge(prometheus.GaugeOpts{
    Name: "http_requests_total",
    Help: "Total number of HTTP requests",
})

func recordMetrics() {
    for {
        time.Sleep(2 * time.Second)
        requestCount.Inc() // Ensuring data is updated periodically
    }
}

func main() {
    prometheus.MustRegister(requestCount)
    go recordMetrics()

    http.Handle("/metrics", promhttp.Handler())
    log.Println("Exporter running on port 8080...")
    log.Fatal(http.ListenAndServe(":8080", nil))
}
```

This code defines a Prometheus gauge metric named `http_requests_total`, registers it with Prometheus, and updates it periodically in a separate `goroutine` to simulate changing values; it also exposes the metric on the `/metrics` HTTP endpoint so that Prometheus can scrape and collect the data at regular intervals.

Reducing memory and CPU usage

Large-scale monitoring systems can generate massive amounts of data, which can degrade system performance. To optimize efficiency, do the following:

- **Use batching**: Instead of updating metrics on every request, batch updates periodically
- **Minimize labels**: Labels increase memory usage; use them only when necessary
- **Optimize histogram buckets**: Choosing too many buckets increases memory consumption, while too few buckets reduces accuracy

It is important to understand how to reduce memory and CPU usage when working with Prometheus metrics. Efficient use of resources helps keep the monitoring system responsive and stable, especially at scale. The following code demonstrates how to define and use a histogram with optimized buckets to balance accuracy and resource consumption:

```
package main

import (
	"github.com/prometheus/client_golang/prometheus"
	"github.com/prometheus/client_golang/prometheus/promhttp"
	"net/http"
	"log"
	"math/rand"
	"time"
)

var requestDuration = prometheus.NewHistogram(prometheus.HistogramOpts{
	Name:    "http_request_duration_seconds",
	Help:    "Request duration histogram",
	Buckets: prometheus.ExponentialBuckets(0.1, 2, 5),
})

func handler(w http.ResponseWriter, r *http.Request) {
	start := time.Now()
	time.Sleep(time.Duration(rand.Intn(500)) * time.Millisecond)
	duration := time.Since(start).Seconds()
	requestDuration.Observe(duration) // Using optimized histogram buckets

	w.Write([]byte("Request completed"))
}

func main() {
	prometheus.MustRegister(requestDuration)

	http.Handle("/metrics", promhttp.Handler())
	http.HandleFunc("/", handler)

	log.Println("Exporter running on port 8080...")
	log.Fatal(http.ListenAndServe(":8080", nil))
}
```

Using exponential buckets in a histogram helps reduce memory and CPU usage while still providing useful information about request durations. In this example, the histogram uses fewer buckets that grow in size exponentially, which means short and long requests can both be tracked without storing too many details. This approach lowers the amount of memory needed and reduces the processing load on the exporter. It is a practical way to monitor performance without overwhelming the system. This technique is especially helpful when dealing with high volumes of traffic or running the exporter in resource-constrained environments.

Handling high traffic load

When dealing with high-traffic environments, exporters should be designed to handle thousands of requests per second efficiently:

- **Use asynchronous metric collection**: Avoid blocking requests when updating metrics
- **Leverage caching**: Store calculated values and refresh periodically instead of computing on every request
- **Scale exporters horizontally**: Run multiple instances behind a load balancer if necessary

Exporters need to handle traffic efficiently when requests come in at a very high rate. One way to improve performance is to update metrics in the background using separate threads. This avoids delays in responding to incoming requests. The following code shows how to safely update a counter metric using a mutex and a `goroutine` to keep the main request handler fast and responsive:

```
package main

import (
    "github.com/prometheus/client_golang/prometheus"
    "github.com/prometheus/client_golang/prometheus/promhttp"
    "net/http"
    "log"
    "math/rand"
    "sync"
    "time"
)

var (
    requestCount = prometheus.NewCounter(prometheus.CounterOpts{
        Name: "http_requests_total",
        Help: "Total number of HTTP requests",
```

```
    })
    mutex sync.Mutex
)

func recordMetrics() {
    for {
        time.Sleep(time.Second)
        mutex.Lock()
        requestCount.Inc() // Using a mutex to ensure thread safety
        mutex.Unlock()
    }
}

func handler(w http.ResponseWriter, r *http.Request) {
    // Using a goroutine to handle metric updates asynchronously
    go recordMetrics()
    w.Write([]byte("Request received"))
}

func main() {
    prometheus.MustRegister(requestCount)

    http.Handle("/metrics", promhttp.Handler())
    http.HandleFunc("/", handler)

    log.Println("Exporter running on port 8080...")
    log.Fatal(http.ListenAndServe(":8080", nil))
}
```

This code shows how to update a Prometheus counter metric in a way that does not slow down the HTTP server. When a request is received, a new background task is started to update the metric. This background task uses a mutex to safely increase the counter without causing conflicts between multiple threads. By running the metric update in the background and protecting the shared counter with a mutex, the code ensures that the main request handler remains fast and can handle many incoming requests. This approach helps the exporter perform well even under heavy traffic by keeping metric updates quick and safe.

Testing and deploying exporters

Testing and deploying Prometheus exporters are crucial steps in ensuring their reliability and stability in production environments. A well-tested exporter helps maintain accurate monitoring, while proper deployment strategies ensure smooth integration with Prometheus and other monitoring tools. This section covers how to test exporters effectively and the best practices for deploying them in real-world scenarios.

Unit testing exporters

Unit testing ensures that individual functions within an exporter work correctly. The `prometheus/testutil` package provides utilities for verifying metric collection:

```
package main

import (
    "testing"
    "github.com/prometheus/client_golang/prometheus"
    "github.com/prometheus/client_golang/prometheus/testutil"
)

func TestCounterMetric(t *testing.T) {
    counter := prometheus.NewCounter(prometheus.CounterOpts{
        Name: "test_counter",
        Help: "A test counter",
    })
    counter.Inc()

    if testutil.ToFloat64(counter) != 1 {
        t.Errorf(
            "Expected counter to be 1, got %f", testutil.ToFloat64(
                counter
            )
        )
    }
}
```

This code is a unit test that checks whether a Prometheus counter metric works as expected. It creates a new counter and increases its value by 1. Then it uses the `testutil.ToFloat64` function to read the current value of the counter. The test compares the actual value to the expected value of 1. If the values do not match, it reports an error. This helps confirm that the metric logic is working correctly and the counter behaves as intended.

Integration testing with Prometheus

Integration testing verifies that the exporter correctly exposes metrics in a format that Prometheus can scrape:

```
$ # Start the exporter locally
$ ./my_exporter &

$ # Use curl to check the exposed metrics
$ curl http://localhost:8080/metrics
```

Containerizing the exporter

Using Docker simplifies deployment and ensures consistency across environments:

```
FROM golang:1.23 AS builder
WORKDIR /app
COPY . .
RUN go build -o exporter .

FROM alpine:latest
WORKDIR /root/
COPY --from=builder /app/exporter .
CMD ["./exporter"]
```

Build and run the Docker container:

```
$ docker build -t my_exporter .
$ docker run -p 8080:8080 my_exporter
```

Automating deployment with Kubernetes

For scalable deployments, exporters should be deployed in Kubernetes clusters:

```
apiVersion: apps/v1
kind: Deployment
```

```
metadata:
  name: my-exporter
spec:
  replicas: 2
  selector:
    matchLabels:
      app: my-exporter
  template:
    metadata:
      labels:
        app: my-exporter
    spec:
      containers:
      - name: my-exporter
        image: my_exporter:latest
        ports:
        - containerPort: 8080
```

Apply the configuration:

```
$ kubectl apply -f exporter-deployment.yaml
```

This YAML file shows how to deploy a Prometheus exporter to a Kubernetes cluster. It creates a deployment named `my-exporter` with two replicas to ensure high availability. The selector field matches Pods with the label `app: my-exporter`, and the template section defines how those Pods should be created. Each Pod runs a container named `my-exporter` using the `my_exporter:latest` image. The container exposes port `8080` so Prometheus can scrape metrics from it. After saving this configuration to a file named `exporter-deployment.yaml`, you can use the `kubectl apply` command to deploy it to the cluster.

This setup makes it easier to manage, scale, and update the exporter across different environments.

Summary

In this chapter, we learned about the importance of exporters in the Prometheus ecosystem and how they help collect and expose metrics for monitoring. We explored the role of exporters, understanding when to use them and how they integrate with Prometheus. We also discussed key design principles for building efficient exporters, including structuring code properly, reducing overhead, and ensuring scalability. These best practices help developers create exporters that are reliable and optimized for performance.

We then focused on implementing different metric types, such as counters, gauges, and histograms. Through practical examples, we saw how each metric type is used for tracking various aspects of application performance, such as request counts, memory usage, and response times. Additionally, we covered strategies for ensuring data accuracy and optimizing performance, including using efficient data structures, handling high traffic loads, and minimizing resource consumption.

Finally, we looked at testing and deploying exporters to ensure they work correctly in real-world environments. We explored unit testing, integration testing, and best practices for validating exporter behavior. We also covered deployment techniques using Docker and Kubernetes, making it easier to run exporters in production. By applying these concepts, developers can build robust and efficient exporters that provide valuable monitoring insights for their applications.

The next chapter introduces how to build and use RESTful APIs with Go. You'll learn how to set up an API server, handle requests, manage routes, and work with data from other APIs. It's a hands-on guide to creating real-world web services using Go.

5

Building and Consuming RESTful APIs with Go

Building and consuming RESTful APIs with Go is very important for developing modern web applications that communicate efficiently over the internet. UIs allow user-system interactions while APIs allow system-system interactions. In more detail, APIs allow different software systems to interact, enabling data exchange between services, mobile apps, and web applications. Go is a great choice for building APIs because it is fast and lightweight and has excellent built-in support for handling HTTP requests. By using Go, developers can create scalable and high-performance APIs that serve data quickly and reliably, making it easier to build interconnected systems.

Consuming APIs is just as important as building them, as many applications rely on external data sources to function. With Go's powerful HTTP packages, developers can easily make requests to external APIs, process responses, and integrate the data into their applications. This ability allows developers to connect their Go applications with third-party services such as payment gateways, weather data providers, and social media platforms. Understanding both API creation and consumption ensures that developers can build flexible, data-driven applications that seamlessly interact with the broader web ecosystem.

In this chapter, we will cover the following topics:

- Learn how to build a basic API server using Go's standard library
- Understand how to handle different types of HTTP requests and send responses, including JSON output and error messages
- Set up routing to handle different API paths and use middleware for things such as logging and authentication

- Build practical, API-based applications that are scalable and easy to maintain

Setting up a basic API server with Go

In this section, we will set up a simple API server using Go, focusing on building a URL shortener. A URL shortener takes a long URL and returns a shorter, easy-to-share version. The API will provide endpoints to create short URLs and retrieve the original URLs. We will use Go's built-in `net/http` package and `gorilla/mux` for routing.

Setting up a project

First, create a new Go project and initialize a module:

```
$ mkdir go-url-shortener
$ cd go-url-shortener
$ go mod init github.com/<yourusername>/go-url-shortener
```

Next, install the `gorilla/mux` package for routing:

```
$ go get -u github.com/gorilla/mux
```

Creating the API server

Now, create a `main.go` file and set up a basic HTTP server:

```
package main

import (
    "fmt"
    "log"
    "net/http"
    "github.com/gorilla/mux"
)

func main() {
    r := mux.NewRouter()
    r.HandleFunc("/", homeHandler).Methods("GET")

    fmt.Println("Server running on port 8080")
    log.Fatal(http.ListenAndServe(":8080", r))
}
```

```
func homeHandler(w http.ResponseWriter, r *http.Request) {
    w.Write([]byte("Welcome to the URL shortener API!"))
}
```

Run the server:

```
$ go run main.go
```

Open your browser and go to `http://localhost:8080`. You should see the message **Welcome to the URL shortener API!**.

Creating the URL shortening logic

To store short URLs, we will use an in-memory map. Create a file named `handlers.go`.

Before we can build our URL shortener, we need to import the necessary Go packages. These include libraries for handling HTTP requests, encoding and decoding JSON, generating random values, and ensuring safe concurrent access to shared data:

```
package main

import (
    "encoding/json"
    "math/rand"
    "net/http"
    "sync"
)
```

To represent both the input and output of our URL shortener service, we define a simple struct. This struct holds the original long URL and the generated short URL:

```
type URL struct {
    Short string `json:"short_url"`
    Long  string `json:"long_url"`
}
```

We use a map to store short URLs and their corresponding long URLs. Since this map could be accessed by multiple users at the same time, we also define a mutex to make those accesses safe:

```
var (
    urlStore = make(map[string]string)
    mutex    = &sync.Mutex{}
)
```

Next, we create a function to generate a short, random string. This will serve as the unique code for each shortened URL. It picks six random characters from a predefined set of letters and numbers:

```
func generateShortURL() string {
    const letters = "abcdefghijklmnopqrstuvwxyzABCDEFGHIJKLMNOPQRSTUVWXYZ0
    123456789"
    short := make([]byte, 6)
    for i := range short {
        short[i] = letters[rand.Intn(len(letters))]
    }
    return string(short)
}
```

The following function handles requests to shorten a long URL. It decodes the input JSON, generates a short code, stores the mapping safely, and responds with the full shortened URL in JSON format:

```
func createShortURLHandler(w http.ResponseWriter, r *http.Request) {
    var request URL
    if err := json.NewDecoder(r.Body).Decode(&request); err != nil {
        http.Error(w, "Invalid request", http.StatusBadRequest)
        return
    }

    short := generateShortURL()
    mutex.Lock()
    urlStore[short] = request.Long
    mutex.Unlock()

    response := URL{
        Short: "http://localhost:8080/" + short,
        Long: request.Long
    }
    w.Header().Set("Content-Type", "application/json")
    json.NewEncoder(w).Encode(response)
}
```

The `getOriginalURLHandler` function handles requests to a short URL. It extracts the short code from the URL path, looks it up in the map, and, if found, redirects the user to the original long URL. If not found, it returns an error:

```
func getOriginalURLHandler(w http.ResponseWriter, r *http.Request) {
    vars := mux.Vars(r)
    short := vars["short"]

    mutex.Lock()
    longURL, exists := urlStore[short]
    mutex.Unlock()

    if !exists {
        http.Error(w, "Short URL not found", http.StatusNotFound)
        return
    }

    http.Redirect(w, r, longURL, http.StatusFound)
}
```

With these functions in place, we now have the basic logic for a working URL shortener. The `createShortURLHandler` function accepts a long URL, generates a short version, and stores the mapping. The `getOriginalURLHandler` function looks up the short code and redirects users to the original link. The use of a mutex ensures that multiple users can safely access and update the in-memory store at the same time. Together, these pieces demonstrate how Go can be used to build efficient and reliable web services.

Adding routes

Now, update `main.go` to include these routes:

```
package main

import (
    "fmt"
    "log"
    "net/http"
    "github.com/gorilla/mux"
)

func main() {
    r := mux.NewRouter()
    r.HandleFunc("/", homeHandler).Methods("GET")
```

```
    r.HandleFunc("/shorten", createShortURLHandler).Methods("POST")
    r.HandleFunc("/{short}", getOriginalURLHandler).Methods("GET")

    fmt.Println("Server running on port 8080")
    log.Fatal(http.ListenAndServe(":8080", r))
}
```

Restart the server.

To run the application, make sure all relevant `.go` files are compiled together. All Go files (`main.go`, `handlers.go`, etc.) are in the same directory, so we can use the following:

```
$ go run .
```

Alternatively, we can specify the exact files:

```
$ go run main.go handlers.go
```

Important note

The `go run main.go` command alone will not work correctly, because `main.go` relies on functions defined in `handlers.go` (such as `createShortURLHandler` and `getOriginalURLHandler`). Omitting them will result in an `undefined` error.

Testing the API

Use `curl` or Postman to shorten a URL:

```
$ curl -X POST "http://localhost:8080/shorten" -H "Content-Type: application/json" -d '{"long_url": "https://example.com"}'
```

The following is an example response:

```
{
  "short_url": "http://localhost:8080/abc123",
  "long_url": "https://example.com"
}
```

Visit `http://localhost:8080/abc123` in your browser, and it should redirect you to `https://example.com`.

Now that our routes are set up and the server is running, we can send requests and see the URL shortener in action. This gives us a working foundation to build on.

Next, we will improve how our application handles requests and responses to make it more reliable and user-friendly.

Handling requests and responses

In this section, we will enhance our URL shortener by processing incoming data correctly, handling errors, and structuring responses in a clear and user-friendly way. We will use Go's `net/http` package along with `gorilla/mux` for better request handling.

Understanding HTTP methods and JSON handling

Before we dive into handling data, it is important to understand how web APIs work with different types of HTTP methods. These methods define what kind of action the client wants the server to perform:

- `GET`: Retrieve data from the server
- `POST`: Send data to the server to create a resource
- `PUT`: Update an existing resource
- `DELETE`: Remove a resource from the server

Go provides the `encoding/json` package to encode and decode JSON data in API requests and responses.

Validating incoming data

To make our URL shortener more reliable, we should ensure the input from users is valid. The updated version of the `createShortURLHandler` function adds basic validation to check that the incoming request is correctly formatted and includes a valid `long_url` value.

We start by importing standard Go libraries for handling JSON, HTTP, random values, synchronization, and routing:

```
package main

import (
    "encoding/json"
    "math/rand"
    "net/http"
    "sync"
    "github.com/gorilla/mux"
)
```

We define a URL struct that will be used to hold both the original long URL and the generated short URL. This helps with both decoding incoming JSON and encoding outgoing responses. We use a map to store the mappings from short URLs to long URLs. A mutex is also used to ensure thread-safe access when multiple requests are handled at the same time:

```
type URL struct {
    Short string `json:"short_url"`
    Long  string `json:"long_url"`
}

var (
    urlStore = make(map[string]string)
    mutex    = &sync.Mutex{}
)
```

This function generates a six-character random string using letters and numbers, which will act as the short URL path:

```
func generateShortURL() string {
    const letters = "abcdefghijklmnopqrstuvwxyzABCDEFGHIJKLMNOPQRSTUVWXYZ0
    123456789"
    short := make([]byte, 6)
    for i := range short {
        short[i] = letters[rand.Intn(len(letters))]
    }
    return string(short)
}
```

The `createShortURLHandler` function processes incoming `POST` requests to create a shortened URL. It includes three main steps:

1. Decode the JSON request body.
2. Validate that the `long_url` field is present.
3. Generate and store the shortened URL (`short_url`), and send a JSON response back to the client.

Here's how `createShortURLHandler` is implemented in Go:

```
func createShortURLHandler(w http.ResponseWriter, r *http.Request) {
    var request URL
```

```
    // Decode JSON request body
    if err := json.NewDecoder(r.Body).Decode(&request); err != nil {
        http.Error(w, "Invalid JSON format", http.StatusBadRequest)
        return
    }

    // Validate URL input
    if request.Long == "" {
        http.Error(w, "Missing long_url field", http.StatusBadRequest)
        return
    }

    // Generate short URL and store it
    short := generateShortURL()
    mutex.Lock()
    urlStore[short] = request.Long
    mutex.Unlock()

    // Response with JSON
    response := URL{
        Short: "http://localhost:8080/" + short,
        Long: request.Long
    }
    w.Header().Set("Content-Type", "application/json")
    json.NewEncoder(w).Encode(response)
}
```

By adding input validation, we make sure our API handles bad data more gracefully and returns helpful error messages to the user. This makes the application more robust and user-friendly.

Next, we will focus on improving how our API handles different kinds of responses and provides better feedback to clients.

Improving error responses

Instead of using `http.Error`, we can create a helper function to format errors as JSON responses:

```
func respondWithError(w http.ResponseWriter, code int, message string) {
    w.Header().Set("Content-Type", "application/json")
```

```
    w.WriteHeader(code)
    json.NewEncoder(w).Encode(map[string]string{"error": message})
}
```

Modify the `createShortURLHandler()` function to use this helper:

```
if err := json.NewDecoder(r.Body).Decode(&request); err != nil {
    respondWithError(w, http.StatusBadRequest, "Invalid JSON format")
    return
}

if request.Long == "" {
    respondWithError(w, http.StatusBadRequest, "Missing long_url field")
    return
}
```

These changes make our error responses more consistent and easier to understand. It also prepares the code for future improvements, such as adding error codes or more detailed messages.

Handling GET requests and redirects

Now, let's improve our function for retrieving the original URL and handling cases where the short URL doesn't exist:

```
func getOriginalURLHandler(w http.ResponseWriter, r *http.Request) {
    vars := mux.Vars(r)
    short := vars["short"]

    mutex.Lock()
    longURL, exists := urlStore[short]
    mutex.Unlock()

    if !exists {
        respondWithError(w, http.StatusNotFound, "Short URL not found")
        return
    }

    http.Redirect(w, r, longURL, http.StatusFound)
}
```

This update ensures that users get a clear message if the short URL is invalid or missing. It also helps make the redirection behavior more reliable and user-friendly.

Enhancing response structure

For better API responses, let's create a function to format successful responses:

```
func respondWithJSON(w http.ResponseWriter, code int, payload interface{})
{
    w.Header().Set("Content-Type", "application/json")
    w.WriteHeader(code)
    json.NewEncoder(w).Encode(payload)
}
```

Modify `createShortURLHandler()` to use `respondWithJSON()`:

```
response := URL{
    Short: "http://localhost:8080/" + short,
    Long: request.Long
}
respondWithJSON(w, http.StatusCreated, response)
```

Using a helper function such as `respondWithJSON` makes the code easier to read and keeps the response format consistent across the API. This also helps when the API grows, and more endpoints are added later.

Adding routes to main.go

Finally, update `main.go` to use the improved handlers:

```
package main

import (
    "fmt"
    "log"
    "net/http"
    "github.com/gorilla/mux"
)

func main() {
    r := mux.NewRouter()
    r.HandleFunc("/", homeHandler).Methods("GET")
```

```
    r.HandleFunc("/shorten", createShortURLHandler).Methods("POST")
    r.HandleFunc("/{short}", getOriginalURLHandler).Methods("GET")

    fmt.Println("Server running on port 8080")
    log.Fatal(http.ListenAndServe(":8080", r))
}
```

Now the server is ready to handle requests using the updated handlers. With the routes in place, the API is structured and easy to test.

Testing the API

Use `curl` to test the API:

```
$ curl -X POST "http://localhost:8080/shorten" -H "Content-Type:
application/json" -d '{"long_url": "https://example.com"}'
```

The following is an example response:

```
{
  "short_url": "http://localhost:8080/abc123",
  "long_url": "https://example.com"
}
```

To get redirected to the original URL, use the following:

```
$ curl -L http://localhost:8080/abc123
```

These commands show how to shorten a URL and follow the redirect using `curl`. With this, it can be quickly tested and confirmed that the URL shortener works as expected.

Managing routing and middleware

Middleware is a key component in web applications, acting as a layer between the request and response cycle. It allows developers to process requests before they reach the main handlers, making it easier to handle cross-cutting concerns such as logging, authentication, rate limiting, and error handling.

For example, in a URL shortener API, middleware can do the following:

- Log incoming requests for debugging
- Check API keys to restrict access
- Handle **Cross-Origin Resource Sharing** (**CORS**) to allow requests from different domains

- Rate limit requests to prevent abuse
- Standardize error responses

In this section, we will learn how to use middleware to improve the structure and behavior of a Go web application. Middleware helps handle tasks such as logging, authentication, and rate limiting before the main logic of a request is run. We will start by understanding how middleware works, then build and apply different types of middleware to our routes. By the end, you will know how to combine and test middleware to make your application more secure, efficient, and easier to manage.

How middleware works

Middleware functions are executed in the order they are defined, processing requests before they reach the main handler and modifying responses before they are sent back. Middleware in Go typically takes `http.Handler` as input, wraps around it, and returns another `http.Handler`.

Let's explore different types of middleware by integrating them into our URL shortener API.

Logging middleware

Logging middleware helps track API activity by logging request details such as method, path, and response time. The following is a sample implementation:

```
package main

import (
    "log"
    "net/http"
    "time"
)

func LoggingMiddleware(next http.Handler) http.Handler {
    return http.HandlerFunc(func(w http.ResponseWriter, r *http.Request) {
        start := time.Now()
        next.ServeHTTP(w, r)
        duration := time.Since(start)
        log.Printf("%s %s took %v", r.Method, r.URL.Path, duration)
    })
}
```

Update `main.go` to use this middleware:

```
r := mux.NewRouter()
r.Use(LoggingMiddleware) // Apply logging middleware globally
```

Start the server and make some requests:

```
$ curl http://localhost:8080/
```

Check the logs:

```
GET / took 200ms
```

This logging middleware gives useful information about each request that hits the server. It helps to monitor how the API is being used and how long requests are taking. This is especially helpful when debugging issues or analyzing performance.

Adding authentication middleware

To restrict API access, we can implement a simple form of authentication and authorization middleware that checks for an API key before allowing requests. While this is not a secure or scalable solution for production use, it demonstrates the core idea of protecting endpoints with access control.

Before we start writing the authentication code, it is important to understand the difference between authentication and authorization. These two concepts are closely related but serve different purposes in controlling access to an API:

- Authentication confirms who the requester is
- Authorization determines what the requester is allowed to do

In this example, we'll check for an API key in the request header and validate it against a predefined map of users and their roles.

Let's create a file named `auth.go`:

```
package main

import (
    "net/http"
)

// A simple user-role mapping with API keys
```

```
var apiKeys = map[string]string{
    "key-admin-123": "admin",
    "key-user-456":  "user",
}

func AuthenticationMiddleware(next http.Handler) http.Handler {
    return http.HandlerFunc(func(w http.ResponseWriter, r *http.Request) {
        apiKey := r.Header.Get("X-API-Key")

        role, ok := apiKeys[apiKey]
        if !ok {
            http.Error(w, "Forbidden", http.StatusForbidden)
            return
        }

        // Store the role in the request context (could be used for RBAC
        // later)
        r.Header.Set("X-User-Role", role)
        next.ServeHTTP(w, r)
    })
}
```

Now, let's apply middleware:

```
r := mux.NewRouter()
r.Use(AuthenticationMiddleware) // Apply authentication middleware
```

Make a request without an API key:

```
$ curl http://localhost:8080/shorten
```

The following is the response:

```
{
  "error": "Forbidden"
}
```

Now, make a request with the API key:

```
$ curl -H "X-API-Key: key-admin-123" http://localhost:8080/shorten
```

Using authentication middleware helps protect the API from unauthorized access by checking for a valid API key. It ensures only trusted clients can use the endpoints. This is a simple but effective way to add a basic layer of security to the application.

This example combines authentication and basic authorization using hardcoded API keys and roles. While useful for demonstration purposes, this is not secure or maintainable for production. For real-world applications, consider using the following:

- OAuth2 with providers such as Auth0, Microsoft Entra ID (formerly Azure AD), or Google Identity
- **JSON Web Tokens** (**JWTs**) to securely encode identity and claims
- API gateways with built-in authentication/authorization mechanisms
- **Role-Based Access Control** (**RBAC**) for fine-grained access control

Avoid hardcoding secrets or access control logic in real applications. Use secure, configurable solutions that can be updated without changing code.

Rate-limiting middleware

Rate limiting prevents abuse by restricting the number of requests for a certain amount of time from a user:

```
package main

import (
    "net/http"
    "sync"
    "time"
)

var (
    requests      = make(map[string]int)
    requestsMutex sync.Mutex
)

func RateLimitMiddleware(next http.Handler) http.Handler {
    return http.HandlerFunc(func(w http.ResponseWriter, r *http.Request) {
        ip, _, err := net.SplitHostPort(r.RemoteAddr)
        if err != nil {
```

```
            ip = r.RemoteAddr // fallback if parsing fails
        }
        requestsMutex.Lock()
        requests[ip]++
        count := requests[ip]
        requestsMutex.Unlock()

        if count > 5 {
            http.Error(w, "Too many requests", http.StatusTooManyRequests)
            return
        }

        time.AfterFunc(time.Minute, func() {
            requestsMutex.Lock()
            requests[ip]--
            requestsMutex.Unlock()
        })

        next.ServeHTTP(w, r)
    })
}
```

Apply Middleware:

```
r.Use(RateLimitMiddleware)
```

Make multiple requests quickly:

```
for i in {1..6}; do curl http://localhost:8080/shorten; done
```

The sixth request should return the following:

```
{
  "error": "Too many requests"
}
```

Rate limiting helps ensure that the API remains stable and fair for all users by blocking excessive traffic from a single source. This approach can reduce server overload and discourage misuse. By using middleware, it's possible to apply rate limiting consistently across all routes in the application.

Combining middleware

Middleware functions can be chained together by applying multiple `.Use()` calls:

```
r := mux.NewRouter()
r.Use(LoggingMiddleware)
r.Use(AuthenticationMiddleware)
r.Use(RateLimitMiddleware)
```

This ensures the following:

- Every request is logged
- Only authorized users can access the API
- Users cannot send too many requests in a short period

Combining middleware helps to build a safer and more reliable API by layering different protections and features. Each middleware takes care of a specific task, and together they work like a filter for all incoming requests. This setup makes the application easier to manage and scale over time.

Testing middleware in Go

Testing middleware is very important to ensure it behaves as expected. We can use the `net/http/httptest` package to simulate requests:

```
package main

import (
    "net/http"
    "net/http/httptest"
    "testing"
)

func TestAuthenticationMiddleware(t *testing.T) {
    handler := AuthenticationMiddleware(
        http.HandlerFunc(func(w http.ResponseWriter, r *http.Request) {
            w.WriteHeader(http.StatusOK)
        })
    )

    req, _ := http.NewRequest("GET", "/", nil)
```

```
    // Test without API key
    rec := httptest.NewRecorder()
    handler.ServeHTTP(rec, req)

    if rec.Code != http.StatusUnauthorized {
        t.Errorf("expected status 401, got %d", rec.Code)
    }

    // Test with API key
    req.Header.Set("X-API-Key", "my-secret-key")
    rec = httptest.NewRecorder()
    handler.ServeHTTP(rec, req)

    if rec.Code != http.StatusOK {
        t.Errorf("expected status 200, got %d", rec.Code)
    }
}
```

Run the tests:

```
go test
```

Testing middleware helps catch problems early and ensures the logic is working correctly. By simulating different scenarios, it's possible to verify that all of the middleware behaves as intended. This gives confidence in the API's reliability and makes future changes easier to manage.

Consuming external APIs and integrating data

In modern software systems, external APIs play a very important role in integrating services. Whether you're dealing with data from third-party services, interacting with a microservice, or just consuming external resources, interacting with APIs is a common task. In this chapter, we'll explore how to interact with external APIs, particularly focusing on consuming URL data, validating it, and integrating monitoring with Prometheus in middleware.

We'll use the `httpstatus.io` API, a service that provides URL status codes, to demonstrate how you can make API calls, parse responses, and integrate Prometheus metrics to track URL validation.

Creating the middleware for URL validation

We need middleware to ensure that the URL provided in the request body is valid. The URL will be sent to the `httpstatus.io` API to validate its availability and retrieve metadata.

In `main.go`, we create the middleware that will check the URL:

```
package main

import (
    "bytes"
    "encoding/json"
    "fmt"
    "io"
    "log"
    "net/http"
    "os"
    "strings"
    "github.com/gorilla/mux"
)
```

Before shortening a URL, we want to make sure it's valid and reachable. This middleware checks whether the request includes a proper URL, then calls an external service (`httpstatus.io`) to confirm that the URL is available:

```
type URL struct {
    Short string `json:"short_url"`
    Long  string `json:"long_url"`
}
// Middleware for validating the URL
func validateURLMiddleware(next http.Handler) http.Handler {
    return http.HandlerFunc(func(w http.ResponseWriter, r *http.Request) {
        // Read the full body once
        data, err := io.ReadAll(r.Body)
        if err != nil {
            http.Error(
                w, "Unable to read request body",
                http.StatusInternalServerError
            )
            return
```

```
        }

        // Restore the body so it can be read again later
        r.Body = io.NopCloser(bytes.NewReader(data))

        // Check URL in request body
        var urlReq URL
        err = json.Unmarshal(data, &urlReq)
        if err != nil || urlReq.Long == "" {
            http.Error(
                w, "Invalid JSON or empty URL", http.StatusBadRequest
            )
            return
        }
```

If the URL is valid, the middleware lets the request continue to the next handler. If it's not valid, it returns an error without moving forward:

```
        // Call httpstatus.io API to validate URL
        if !isValidURL(urlReq.Long) {
            http.Error(w, "Invalid URL", http.StatusBadRequest)
            return
        }

        // Call the next handler if URL is valid
        next.ServeHTTP(w, r)
    })
}
```

The `isValidURL` function sends a request to `https://api.httpstatus.io/v1/status` using the URL from the request body. It passes the URL in the JSON body and includes a token for authentication. If the response status is `200 OK`, the URL is considered valid:

```
// Function to check URL using httpstatus.io
func isValidURL(url string) bool {
    requestBody := map[string]string{
        "requestUrl": url,
    }

    body, _ := json.Marshal(requestBody)
```

```
    req, err := http.NewRequest(
        "POST", "https://api.httpstatus.io/v1/status", bytes.NewBuffer(
            body
        )
    )
    if err != nil {
        log.Println("Error creating request:", err)
        return false
    }

    req.Header.Set("Content-Type", "application/json")
    billingToken := os.Getenv("HTTPSTATUS_TOKEN")
    if billingToken == "" {
        log.Println("HTTPSTATUS_TOKEN environment variable not set")
        return false
    }
    req.Header.Set("X-Billing-Token", billingToken)

    // Send the request to validate the URL
    client := &http.Client{}
    resp, err := client.Do(req)
    if err != nil {
        log.Println("Error sending request:", err)
        return false
    }
    defer resp.Body.Close()

    // We only care about the status code to check URL validity
    return resp.StatusCode == http.StatusOK
}
```

This middleware helps catch bad URLs early, so the service only processes valid ones. It also improves reliability by using a trusted service to check that URLs are working.

While the check (`resp.StatusCode == http.StatusOK`) is fine for a simplified use case, it's important to know that some APIs may return `200 OK` even when it failed to process the request. The response body may contain more detailed information that we should check for accurate validation.

An example is APIs that return a response in the following schema:

```
{
  "errorMessage": "",
  "data": {}
}
```

We need to check the `errorMessage` field and confirm that there is no error message.

Best practice: Don't hardcode secrets!

Storing sensitive data such as API tokens directly in the source code (for example, in `Set("X-Billing-Token", "...")`) is considered a security risk. Anyone with access to the code base, either by accident or via a breach, could potentially access the credentials and misuse them. Instead consider using environment variables, or secret managers, such as Azure Key Vault, HashiCorp Vault, or Google Secret Manager.

Adding this validation step helps protect the API from invalid or broken links and improves the overall experience for users.

In earlier examples, we applied middleware globally using `r.Use()`. In this case, we may want to apply the URL validation only to the `/shorten` endpoint. Here's how:

```
r := mux.NewRouter()
r.Handle(
    "/shorten",
    validateURLMiddleware(http.HandlerFunc(createShortURLHandler))
).Methods("POST")
```

This way, only `POST` requests to `/shorten` will pass through the validation middleware.

For larger applications, grouping related endpoints using subrouters is a cleaner approach. We can attach middleware at the group level:

```
r := mux.NewRouter()

// Create a subrouter for /shorten routes
shortenSubrouter := r.PathPrefix("/shorten").Subrouter()
shortenSubrouter.Use(validateURLMiddleware)
shortenSubrouter.HandleFunc("", createShortURLHandler).Methods("POST")

// We can still define other routes on the main router
r.HandleFunc("/info", getStatsHandler).Methods("GET")
```

Using subrouters improves code organization and allows us to apply middleware selectively to route groups.

Creating the URL shortener with metrics integration

Now, let's create the actual URL shortener and integrate Prometheus metrics in a middleware to track analytics such as HTTP status codes, response times, and content lengths.

We import libraries for handling HTTP requests, routing with **gorilla/mux**, and working with **Prometheus** metrics:

```
package main

import (
    "encoding/json"
    "log"
    "net/http"
    "time"

    "github.com/gorilla/mux"
    "github.com/prometheus/client_golang/prometheus"
    "github.com/prometheus/client_golang/prometheus/promhttp"
)
```

We define three Prometheus metrics: one to count requests, one to track how long they take, and one to measure the size of the response. These will be used to monitor the API's behavior in real time:

```
// Prometheus metrics
var (
    httpRequestsTotal = prometheus.NewCounterVec(
        prometheus.CounterOpts{
            Name: "http_requests_total",
            Help: "Total number of HTTP requests.",
        },
        []string{"method", "route", "status_code"},
    )

    httpDuration = prometheus.NewHistogramVec(
        prometheus.HistogramOpts{
```

```
            Name:        "http_duration_seconds",
            Help:        "Histogram of HTTP request durations.",
            Buckets: prometheus.DefBuckets,
        },
        []string{"method", "route"},
    )

    httpContentLength = prometheus.NewHistogramVec(
        prometheus.HistogramOpts{
            Name:        "http_content_length_bytes",
            Help:        "Histogram of HTTP response content lengths.",
            Buckets: prometheus.DefBuckets,
        },
        []string{"method", "route"},
    )
)
```

We register the metrics with Prometheus so that they become available for tracking:

```
func init() {
    // Register metrics with Prometheus
    prometheus.MustRegister(httpRequestsTotal)
    prometheus.MustRegister(httpDuration)
    prometheus.MustRegister(httpContentLength)
}
```

This handler is called when a user wants to shorten a URL. For now, it just returns a sample message. It also logs request metrics such as status code and duration:

```
// Handler to create short URL
func createShortURLHandler(w http.ResponseWriter, r *http.Request) {
start := time.Now()
// Short URL creation logic (stub for this example)
    w.WriteHeader(http.StatusCreated)
    w.Write([]byte("Shortened URL"))
    logRequestMetrics(r, http.StatusCreated, time.Since(start))
}
```

This function logs the metrics for each request. It tracks the request method, route, response time, and a fake content length (as a placeholder):

```
// Function to log request metrics
func logRequestMetrics(
    r *http.Request,
    statusCode int,
    duration time.Duration
) {
    route := mux.CurrentRoute(r).GetName()

    httpRequestsTotal.WithLabelValues(
        r.Method, route, fmt.Sprintf("%d", statusCode)).Inc()
    httpDuration.WithLabelValues(r.Method, route).Observe(
        duration.Seconds())

    // Here, we'd normally calculate the actual content length
    contentLength := 700 // Stubbed content length for this example
    httpContentLength.WithLabelValues(r.Method, route).Observe(
        float64(contentLength)
    )
}
```

In `main`, we define the routes and handlers. We also add the URL validation middleware to the `/shorten` route and expose the `/metrics` endpoint so Prometheus can scrape the data:

```
func main() {
    // Create router and register routes
    r := mux.NewRouter()
    r.HandleFunc("/", homeHandler).Methods("GET")
    r.HandleFunc("/shorten", createShortURLHandler).Methods("POST")
    r.HandleFunc("/{short}", getOriginalURLHandler).Methods("GET")

    // Attach the validateURLMiddleware to the /shorten route
    r.Handle("/shorten", validateURLMiddleware(http.
HandlerFunc(createShortURLHandler)))

    // Metrics endpoint
    r.Handle("/metrics", promhttp.Handler())
```

```
    // Start server
    log.Fatal(http.ListenAndServe(":8080", r))
}
```

This code sets up the core of a working URL shortener that is also production-ready when it comes to monitoring. Prometheus metrics allow developers and system administrators to track how the API is performing under load and whether it's responding correctly and efficiently.

Adding monitoring support like this is an important step in building reliable backend systems. It helps detect problems early and gives confidence when deploying to production.

Integrating Prometheus metrics

We already added Prometheus metrics to the handlers and created the relevant counter and histogram. When you visit the `/metrics` route, it will expose the metrics in Prometheus format. Here are the metrics we're tracking:

- `http_requests_total`: Tracks the total number of HTTP requests, including method, route, and status code
- `http_duration_seconds`: Tracks the duration of HTTP requests in seconds
- `http_content_length_bytes`: Tracks the size of the HTTP responses in bytes

The URL validation middleware, `validateURLMiddleware()`, checks whether a given URL is valid before allowing the request to proceed. If the URL is invalid, it returns **400 Bad Request**. If valid, it passes control to the next handler.

Use a tool such as Postman or `curl` to make a `POST` request to `/shorten` with a `requestUrl` in the body.

Make sure to use a valid or invalid URL to see how the middleware handles it:

```
$ curl -X POST http://localhost:8080/shorten \
-H "Content-Type: application/json" \
-d '{"requestUrl": "https://example.com"}'
```

Visit `/metrics` to view Prometheus metrics.

This gives a basic setup where every request is tracked and measured. It's possible now to monitor how the application is performing and catch problems early by looking at the metrics.

Summary

In this chapter, we focused on getting started with Go to build a simple web server. We explored how to use Go's `net/http` package to create an HTTP server, define routes, and handle basic requests. The chapter introduced the essentials of building an API server, such as writing handlers that process incoming HTTP requests and send appropriate responses, allowing you to interact with users through a web API.

We also built an API server by introducing more complex routing with the `gorilla/mux` router. This router allows for flexible route matching, making it easier to manage URL patterns and parameters. We also covered middleware functions, which act as a way to process requests before they reach their respective handlers. Middleware is useful for tasks such as logging, authentication, and validation, and it can be easily integrated into the routing system. By chaining multiple middleware functions, you can ensure your application is more maintainable and organized while handling different concerns separately.

We also focused on how your Go application can interact with external services. We learned how to make HTTP requests to external APIs, process the data returned from these APIs, and integrate it into applications. Using the `httpstatus.io` API as an example, we validated URLs and retrieved useful metadata such as response times and content lengths. The chapter also demonstrated how to send analytics data, such as performance metrics, using tools such as Prometheus to monitor API requests, response times, and content sizes.

In the next chapter, you'll learn how to secure microservices and APIs. It will cover important topics such as authentication, authorization, and how to keep the data and services safe when they communicate with each other.

6

Working with gRPC and Microservices Architecture

In modern software development, applications are often built using a microservices architecture where different services handle different tasks and communicate with each other. gRPC is a powerful tool that helps these services communicate efficiently. Unlike traditional REST APIs, gRPC uses **Protocol Buffers (Protobuf)** to serialize data in a compact binary format, making data transfer faster and reducing bandwidth usage. This is especially useful in microservices environments where performance and reliability are critical. By using gRPC, services can communicate with low latency, making applications more responsive and scalable.

gRPC also provides advanced features such as bidirectional streaming, allowing continuous data exchange between clients and servers in real time. This is beneficial for applications that need to handle large volumes of data or require instant updates. Additionally, gRPC supports strong typing and automatic code generation, reducing the risk of errors and making it easier to maintain service contracts.

As a result, using gRPC in a microservices architecture improves the overall performance, security, and reliability of distributed applications.

In this chapter, we will cover the following topics:

- Understanding what gRPC is and how it helps microservices communicate efficiently
- Learning how to define service contracts using Protocol Buffers
- Setting up a gRPC server and client in Go
- Implementing client-side and server-side streaming in gRPC

- Following best practices for using gRPC in microservices, such as handling errors and securing communication

Defining service contracts with Protocol Buffers

In this section, we will learn how to define service contracts using Protobuf for a URL shortener application. Protobuf is a lightweight and efficient way to serialize structured data, making it an ideal choice for microservices communication. It is like XML or JSON, but smaller, faster, and more efficient.

Protobuf allows us to define the structure of the data exchanged between services and automatically generate the necessary code for communication in multiple programming languages. This makes it perfect for defining service contracts in a gRPC-based microservices architecture.

Before writing our `.proto` file, let's set up a clean project layout so the rest of the examples work as expected:

```
url-shortener/
├── go.mod
├── proto/
│   └── url_shortener.proto
├── server/
│   └── server.go
└── client/
    └── client.go
```

Let's initialize the Go module:

```
go mod init url-shortener
```

A Protobuf definition file has a `.proto` extension that describes the following:

- **Messages**: Data structures exchanged between services
- **Services:** Functions (RPCs) that clients can call

To get started, create the `url_shortener.proto` file in the `proto/` folder:

```
syntax = "proto3";

package urlshortener;

option go_package = "url-shortener/proto;proto";
```

```
// Define the URL shortening service
service URLShortener {
  // Shorten a URL
  rpc ShortenURL (ShortenRequest) returns (ShortenResponse);

  // Retrieve original URL
  rpc GetOriginalURL (GetRequest) returns (GetResponse);
}

// Request to shorten a URL
message ShortenRequest {
  string original_url = 1;
}

// Response with shortened URL
message ShortenResponse {
  string short_url = 1;
}
// Request to retrieve original URL
message GetRequest {
  string short_url = 1;
}

// Response with original URL
message GetResponse {
  string original_url = 1;
}
```

We are using `proto3`, the latest version of Protobuf.

The package name groups related definitions and prevents name conflicts:

- The `URLShortener` service defines a gRPC service with two RPC methods:
  - `ShortenURL` to shorten a URL
  - `GetOriginalURL` to retrieve the original URL
- The `ShortenRequest` message carries the original URL

- The `ShortenResponse` message returns the shortened URL
- The `GetRequest` message carries the shortened URL to get the original one
- The `GetResponse` message returns the original URL

To generate Go code from `.proto` files, we need the **Protocol Buffer Compiler** (`protoc`) installed on the system:

```
sudo apt update

sudo apt install -y protobuf-compiler
```

Install the Go plugins for `protoc`:

```
go install google.golang.org/protobuf/cmd/protoc-gen-go@latest
go install google.golang.org/grpc/cmd/protoc-gen-go-grpc@latest
```

Verify the installation:

```
protoc --version
protoc-gen-go --version
protoc-gen-go-grpc --version
```

Generate the Go code from the `.proto` files;

```
protoc --go_out=. --go-grpc_out=. proto/url_shortener.proto
```

This will generate two files:

- `url_shortener.pb.go`: Contains Go structs and methods for the Protobuf messages
- `url_shortener_grpc.pb.go`: Contains gRPC service definitions

We can now use the generated code to create a gRPC server and client:

```
import (
    "context"
    pb "url-shortener/proto"
)
```

Accessing generated types and methods

Once the `.proto` files are compiled, Go generates code that includes all the necessary types and service methods. These generated types make it easy to work with structured request and response data in the gRPC application:

- `pb.ShortenRequest`: Request struct for shortening a URL
- `pb.ShortenResponse`: Response struct for shortened URL
- `pb.GetRequest`: Request struct for retrieving a URL
- `pb.GetResponse`: Response struct for original URL

With the code now generated, we are ready to build the gRPC server and client. These generated types and methods will help us send and receive structured data between services. In the next steps, we will use them to handle real gRPC requests and responses.

Creating a gRPC server

To build a working gRPC service, we need to create a server that implements the methods defined in the `.proto` file. The following code sets up `URLShortenerServer`, which can shorten URLs and retrieve the original URLs using an in-memory map. It also starts a gRPC server that listens for requests on port `50051`.

First, import the required Go libraries, including standard packages for networking and logging, and the generated Protobuf code (`pb`):

```
package main

import (
    "context"
    "fmt"
    "io"
    "log"
    "net"

    pb "url-shortener/proto"
    "google.golang.org/grpc"
)
```

Define a struct that implements the URL shortening gRPC service. It also contains a map to store short URLs and their corresponding original URL mappings:

```
type URLShortenerServer struct {
    pb.UnimplementedURLShortenerServer
    urlMap map[string]string
}
```

Add a function that takes a long URL and generates a short one using a simple counter-based approach (`short.ly/1`, `short.ly/2`, etc.). It stores the mapping in `urlMap` and returns the short URL to the client:

```
func (s *URLShortenerServer) ShortenURL(
    ctx context.Context,
    req *pb.ShortenRequest
) (*pb.ShortenResponse, error) {
    shortURL := fmt.Sprintf("short.ly/%d", len(s.urlMap)+1)
    s.urlMap[shortURL] = req.OriginalUrl
    return &pb.ShortenResponse{ShortUrl: shortURL}, nil
}
```

This logic is basic and not suitable for production, but it's perfect for demonstrating gRPC method implementation.

Add a function that accepts a short URL and looks it up in `urlMap`. If found, it returns the original URL. Otherwise, it returns an error:

```
func (s *URLShortenerServer) GetOriginalURL(
    ctx context.Context,
    req *pb.GetRequest
) (*pb.GetResponse, error) {
    originalURL, exists := s.urlMap[req.ShortUrl]
    if !exists {
        return nil, fmt.Errorf("URL not found")
    }
    return &pb.GetResponse{OriginalUrl: originalURL}, nil
}
```

This is how the client can reverse a short URL back into the original one.

Finally, we write the `main()` function to start the gRPC server on port `50051`. It listens for requests and registers the URL shortener service:

```
func main() {
    listener, err := net.Listen("tcp", ":50051")
    if err != nil {
        log.Fatalf("Failed to listen: %v", err)
    }
```

```
    server := grpc.NewServer()
    pb.RegisterURLShortenerServer(
        server,
        &URLShortenerServer{urlMap: make(map[string]string)}
    )

    log.Println("gRPC server is running on port 50051...")
    if err := server.Serve(listener); err != nil {
        log.Fatalf("Failed to serve: %v", err)
    }
}
```

With this setup, we now have a basic but functional gRPC server that can shorten URLs and retrieve the original ones using in-memory storage. While this example keeps things simple to focus on the core ideas, we can continue building on it by adding persistence, validation, or a frontend interface to turn it into a more complete application.

Creating a gRPC client

The following code shows how to build a gRPC client that connects to the URL shortener server. It first establishes a connection, then sends a request to shorten a URL, and prints the shortened version. After that, it sends another request to retrieve the original URL using the shortened one and prints the result.

First, import the packages we need. This includes `context` to manage request timeouts, `log` and `fmt` for printing messages, and the generated gRPC code under `pb`. We also bring in the `grpc` library:

```
package main

import (
    "context"
    "fmt"
    "log"
    "time"

    pb "url-shortener/proto"
    "google.golang.org/grpc"
)
```

Now, create a connection to the gRPC server running on `localhost` at port `50051`. Use the `grpc.WithInsecure()` option to skip encryption, which is fine for testing. We use `defer` to make sure the connection is closed when we're done:

```
conn, err := grpc.Dial(
    "localhost:50051",
    grpc.WithInsecure(),
    grpc.WithBlock()
)
if err != nil {
    log.Fatalf("Failed to connect: %v", err)
}
defer conn.Close()
```

After the connection is ready, we use it to create a client that can talk to the URL shortening service:

```
client := pb.NewURLShortenerClient(conn)
```

Now, let's call the `ShortenURL` method, passing in a long URL. If the request succeeds, the server returns a shortened URL, which we print to the terminal:

```
    shortenResponse, err := client.ShortenURL(
        context.Background(),
        &pb.ShortenRequest{OriginalUrl: "https://example.com"}
    )
if err != nil {
    log.Fatalf("Failed to shorten URL: %v", err)
}
fmt.Println("Shortened URL:", shortenResponse.ShortUrl)
```

Finally, we send the shortened URL back to the server using `GetOriginalURL` to fetch the original link. The result is printed so we can see that the service works as expected:

```
getResponse, err := client.GetOriginalURL(
    context.Background(),
    &pb.GetRequest{ShortUrl: shortenResponse.ShortUrl}
)
if err != nil {
    log.Fatalf("Failed to get original URL: %v", err)
}
fmt.Println("Original URL:", getResponse.OriginalUrl)
```

This example shows how a basic gRPC client works and helps to understand how to send requests, receive responses, and interact with a remote service.

Now that we've seen both the server and the client in action, we should have a good foundation to build more advanced features or integrate gRPC into other projects.

Best practices for defining Protobuf files

Here are some best practices to follow when defining `.proto` files:

- **Use meaningful names**: Choose clear and descriptive names for services and messages
- **Add comments**: Add comments in the `.proto` file to document the functionality
- **Group related services**: If you have multiple services, group them logically under a common package

In this section, we learned how to define service contracts using Protobuf in a gRPC-based URL shortener. We defined services and messages in a `.proto` file, generated Go code from those definitions, and used it to implement a gRPC server and client. Clear, well-structured Protobuf contracts ensure efficient and reliable communication between microservices.

Implementing streaming with gRPC

In this section, we will explore how to implement gRPC streaming in a URL shortener application. Streaming allows continuous data exchange between the client and server, enabling real-time processing and high-performance communication.

gRPC supports three types of streaming:

- **Server streaming**: The server sends multiple responses to a single client request
- **Client streaming**: The client sends multiple requests and receives a single response
- **Bidirectional streaming**: Both the client and the server send a stream of messages to each other

In this section, we will do the following:

- Implement server-side streaming to send a list of shortened URLs
- Implement client-side streaming to batch shorten multiple URLs
- Implement bidirectional streaming to send and receive real-time URL statistics

Overview of gRPC streaming

Streaming is useful when you need to send or receive a continuous flow of data, instead of waiting for everything at once. This can be great for real-time updates, processing batches of data, or transferring large files more efficiently.

Here's how it works, step by step:

1. **Connection established**: The client and server open a connection and keep it open for the stream.
2. **Data sent in chunks**: Instead of sending all the data at once, they send pieces (chunks) as needed.
3. **Connection closed**: Once everything is sent and received, the connection is closed.

You might use streaming if you need live updates, for example, tracking how many times a short URL is clicked. It also helps when sending large or multiple items at once without overwhelming the server or client.

Defining gRPC streaming methods

We will add streaming methods to our `url_shortener.proto` Protobuf file.

Let's start by defining the syntax and package for our service:

```
syntax = "proto3";

package urlshortener;
```

Now, we define the `URLShortener` service. This is where we list all the operations our service supports:

```
service URLShortener {
  rpc ShortenURL (ShortenRequest) returns (ShortenResponse);
  rpc GetOriginalURL (GetRequest) returns (GetResponse);
  rpc ListShortenedURLs (ListRequest) returns (stream ShortenResponse);
  rpc BatchShortenURLs (stream ShortenRequest) returns (BatchResponse);
  rpc MonitorURLStats (stream StatsRequest) returns (stream StatsResponse);
}
```

Each method in the service has a specific purpose and uses a different type of gRPC communication. Before we implement them, let's take a quick look at what each method does. This will help to understand how and when to use them:

- `ShortenURL`: A simple request-response to shorten a single URL
- `GetOriginalURL`: Fetches the original URL from a shortened one
- `ListShortenedURLs`: Server-side streaming to return a list of all shortened URLs
- `BatchShortenURLs`: Client-side streaming to shorten multiple URLs in one request
- `MonitorURLStats`: Bidirectional streaming to monitor real-time stats for each URL:

```
// Request to shorten a URL
message ShortenRequest {
  string original_url = 1;
}

// Response with shortened URL
message ShortenResponse {
  string short_url = 1;
}

// Request to get original URL
message GetRequest {
  string short_url = 1;
}

// Response with original URL
message GetResponse {
  string original_url = 1;
}

// Request for listing URLs
message ListRequest {}

// Response with list of shortened URLs
message BatchResponse {
  int32 count = 1;
}

// Request for URL statistics
message StatsRequest {
  string short_url = 1;
```

```
}

// Response with URL stats
message StatsResponse {
  string short_url = 1;
  int32 clicks = 2;
}
```

Run the following command to regenerate the Go code:

```
protoc --go_out=. --go-grpc_out=. proto/url_shortener.proto
```

This will update the `url_shortener.pb.go` and `url_shortener_grpc.pb.go` files.

With these updates, the `.proto` file now supports different types of gRPC streaming methods. You are now ready to build more powerful and flexible communication patterns between your services. In the next steps, we will implement these methods on the server and client sides.

Implementing server-side streaming

To begin, open the `server/server.go` file and update it to include the server-side streaming method:

```
// ListShortenedURLs streams all shortened URLs to the client
func (s *URLShortenerServer) ListShortenedURLs(
    req *pb.ListRequest,
    stream pb.URLShortener_ListShortenedURLsServer
) error {
    for shortURL, _ := range s.urlMap {
        resp := &pb.ShortenResponse{
            ShortUrl: shortURL,
        }
        // Send the response to the client
        if err := stream.Send(resp); err != nil {
            return err
        }
    }
    return nil
}
```

Implementing the client for server streaming

To use the server-side stream, update the `client/client.go` file to receive and process the streamed responses from the server:

```
func listShortenedURLs(client pb.URLShortenerClient) {
    ctx, cancel := context.WithTimeout(context.Background(), 5*time.
Second)
    defer cancel()

    stream, err := client.ListShortenedURLs(ctx, &pb.ListRequest{})
    if err != nil {
        log.Fatalf("Failed to list URLs: %v", err)
    }

    for {
        resp, err := stream.Recv()
        if err == io.EOF {
            break
        }
        if err != nil {
            log.Fatalf("Error receiving stream: %v", err)
        }
        fmt.Println("Shortened URL:", resp.ShortUrl)
    }
}
```

This function connects to the server and asks for a list of all shortened URLs. It listens to the stream of responses coming from the server and prints each shortened URL as it arrives. The loop continues until all the data has been received or an error occurs.

Implementing client-side streaming

Let's update the `server/server.go` file to handle client-side streaming by implementing the `BatchShortenURLs` method:

```
// BatchShortenURLs shortens multiple URLs
func (s *URLShortenerServer) BatchShortenURLs(
    stream pb.URLShortener_BatchShortenURLsServer
) error {
```

```
    count := 0
    for {
        req, err := stream.Recv()
        if err == io.EOF {
            return stream.SendAndClose(
                &pb.BatchResponse{
                    Count: int32(count)
                }
            )
        }
        if err != nil {
            return err
        }
        shortURL := fmt.Sprintf("short.ly/%d", len(s.urlMap)+1)
        s.urlMap[shortURL] = req.OriginalUrl
        count++
    }
}
```

Implementing the client for client streaming

Update `client/client.go` to send a stream of URLs:

```
func batchShortenURLs(client pb.URLShortenerClient) {
    ctx, cancel := context.WithTimeout(context.Background(), 5*time.
Second)
    defer cancel()

    stream, err := client.BatchShortenURLs(ctx)
    if err != nil {
        log.Fatalf("Failed to create stream: %v", err)
    }

    urls := []string{
        "https://example1.com",
        "https://example2.com",
        "https://example3.com",
    }
```

```
    for _, url := range urls {
        req := &pb.ShortenRequest{OriginalUrl: url}
        if err := stream.Send(req); err != nil {
            log.Fatalf("Failed to send URL: %v", err)
        }
    }

    resp, err := stream.CloseAndRecv()
    if err != nil {
        log.Fatalf("Error receiving response: %v", err)
    }
    fmt.Printf(
        "Batch shortening completed. %d URLs shortened.\n",
        resp.Count
    )
}
```

Implementing bidirectional streaming

Now, let's update the `server/server.go` file to support bidirectional streaming by implementing the `MonitorURLStats` method:

```
// MonitorURLStats streams real-time statistics
func (s *URLShortenerServer) MonitorURLStats(
    stream pb.URLShortener_MonitorURLStatsServer
) error {
    for {
        req, err := stream.Recv()
        if err == io.EOF {
            return nil
        }
        if err != nil {
            return err
        }

        stats := &pb.StatsResponse{
            ShortUrl: req.ShortUrl,
            Clicks:   int32(len(req.ShortUrl) * 10), // Simulated clicks
                                                     // for demo
```

```
        }

        // Send stats back to the client
        if err := stream.Send(stats); err != nil {
            return err
        }
    }
}
```

Implementing the client for bidirectional streaming

Let's now implement the client-side logic to support bidirectional streaming. In this code, the client will send a list of shortened URLs to the server and receive real-time statistics for each of them. This allows the client to send and receive data at the same time over a single connection:

```
func monitorURLStats(client pb.URLShortenerClient) {
    ctx, cancel := context.WithTimeout(context.Background(), 5*time.
Second)
    defer cancel()

    stream, err := client.MonitorURLStats(ctx)
    if err != nil {
        log.Fatalf("Failed to create stream: %v", err)
    }

    urls := []string{
        "short.ly/1",
        "short.ly/2",
    }

    // Send URLs and receive stats
    waitc := make(chan struct{})
    go func() {
        for _, url := range urls {
            req := &pb.StatsRequest{ShortUrl: url}
            if err := stream.Send(req); err != nil {
                log.Fatalf("Failed to send stats request: %v", err)
            }
        }
```

```
        stream.CloseSend()
    }()

    go func() {
        for {
            resp, err := stream.Recv()
            if err == io.EOF {
                break
            }
            if err != nil {
                log.Fatalf("Error receiving stats: %v", err)
            }
            fmt.Printf("Stats for %s: %d clicks\n", resp.ShortUrl, resp.
Clicks)
        }
        close(waitc)
    }()
    <-waitc
}
```

This implementation shows how bidirectional streaming can help build interactive and responsive applications. As you can see, the client sends multiple requests using a goroutine, while another goroutine listens for server responses. This concurrent setup enables the client to receive real-time updates without waiting for the entire input to be sent. It is especially useful in scenarios where both the client and server need to continuously exchange information, such as live analytics or chat systems.

Running the gRPC server and client

To run the gRPC server and client successfully, follow these detailed steps.

Running the gRPC server

The gRPC server is responsible for handling incoming client requests, processing them, and sending responses or streaming data back to the client:

```
go run server/server.go
```

When the server starts, it should display a message similar to the following:

```
Starting gRPC server on port :50051
```

This means that the server is listening for incoming gRPC requests on port `50051`, and it is ready to process the methods defined in the `url_shortener.proto` file.

Running the gRPC client

The client is responsible for sending requests to the server and handling the responses:

```
go run client/client.go
```

What to expect for each streaming type

Let's see what happens when you run the client and use each of the gRPC streaming methods. These examples will help you understand how data flows between the client and server in different streaming scenarios.

Server-side streaming: ListShortenedURLs

In server-side streaming, the client sends a single request, and the server responds by sending back a stream of results, one at a time. This is useful when the server needs to return a list of items:

- The client sends a request to list all shortened URLs
- The server streams each shortened URL back to the client

You should see output similar to the following:

```
Shortened URL: short.ly/1
Shortened URL: short.ly/2
Shortened URL: short.ly/3
```

This output confirms that the server is streaming the list of shortened URLs to the client one by one.

Client-side streaming: BatchShortenURLs

In client-side streaming, the client sends a stream of data to the server, and when it's done, the server sends back one response. This is helpful when sending a batch of inputs to be processed together:

- The client sends multiple URLs to be shortened as a stream
- Once all URLs are sent, the server processes them and returns the number of URLs shortened

Expected output is similar to the following:

```
Batch shortening completed. 3 URLs shortened.
```

This confirms that the client successfully sent a stream of URLs and received a summary from the server.

Bidirectional Streaming: MonitorURLStats

In bidirectional streaming, both the client and server send data streams at the same time. This is great for real-time use cases such as live monitoring or chat apps:

- The client sends URLs to monitor for statistics
- The server continuously streams real-time statistics for each URL back to the client

Expected output is similar to the following:

```
Stats for short.ly/1: 100 clicks
Stats for short.ly/2: 120 clicks
```

This confirms that both the client and server are sending and receiving streams of data simultaneously.

Best practices for gRPC in microservices

When working with gRPC in a microservices architecture, it's essential to follow best practices to ensure high performance, security, and maintainability.

Efficient connection management and load balancing

In a microservices environment, multiple gRPC clients may connect to the same server. To avoid opening and closing connections repeatedly, it's best to use connection pooling and implement load balancing when working with multiple instances.

Connection pooling

Instead of creating a new connection for every request, reuse a single connection for multiple requests:

```
package main

import (
    "context"
    "log"
    "time"
    pb "url-shortener/proto"
    "google.golang.org/grpc"
```

```
)

var conn *grpc.ClientConn
var client pb.URLShortenerClient

func init() {
    var err error
    conn, err = grpc.Dial(
        "localhost:50051",
        grpc.WithInsecure(),
        grpc.WithBlock()
    )
    if err != nil {
        log.Fatalf("Failed to connect: %v", err)
    }
    client = pb.NewURLShortenerClient(conn)
}

func shortenURL(url string) {
    ctx, cancel := context.WithTimeout(context.Background(), time.Second)
    defer cancel()

    res, err := client.ShortenURL(
        ctx,
        &pb.ShortenRequest{OriginalUrl: url}
    )
    if err != nil {
        log.Fatalf("Error while shortening URL: %v", err)
    }
    log.Printf("Short URL: %s", res.ShortUrl)
}

func main() {
    shortenURL("https://example.com")
}
```

Reusing a single connection instead of creating a new one each time helps reduce overhead and improve performance. This is especially useful when the client makes many requests to the server. By keeping the connection open and using it across multiple requests, the application stays responsive and avoids the cost of reconnecting each time.

This makes your gRPC client more efficient and ready for production use.

Implementing load balancing

Use load balancing if multiple instances of the gRPC server are running. You can use a load balancer such as Envoy or a gRPC load balancer.

Here is an example of a client with load balancing:

```
grpc.Dial("dns:///my-grpc-service.default.svc.cluster.local:50051", grpc.
WithInsecure())
```

Using load balancing ensures that traffic is spread across multiple server instances, which helps improve reliability, performance, and scalability. It allows the gRPC client to automatically distribute requests without needing to manage server addresses manually. This setup is useful in production environments where services are running in Kubernetes or other distributed systems.

Proper error handling and retries

Errors can occur due to network failures, server timeouts, or invalid inputs. Implementing error handling ensures that the application can gracefully handle these scenarios.

Basic error handling in the client

When building a gRPC client, it is important to handle errors properly to make the application more reliable and easier to debug. This example shows how the client can safely call the server to fetch the original URL from a shortened one, while also checking for any issues that might happen during the request:

```
func getOriginalURL(shortUrl string) {
    ctx, cancel := context.WithTimeout(context.Background(), time.Second)
    defer cancel()

    res, err := client.GetOriginalURL(
        ctx,
        &pb.GetRequest{ShortUrl: shortUrl}
    )
```

```
    if err != nil {
        log.Printf("Error fetching original URL: %v", err)
        return
    }

    log.Printf("Original URL: %s", res.OriginalUrl)
}
```

Implementing retries with backoff

When connecting to a gRPC server, network issues or server unavailability can sometimes cause temporary failures. Implementing retries with backoff can help the client automatically recover from these failures by attempting to reconnect after short delays, improving the reliability of the application:

```
opts := []grpc.DialOption{
    grpc.WithInsecure(),
    grpc.WithDefaultCallOptions(grpc.MaxCallRecvMsgSize(4 * 1024 * 1024)),
}
conn, err := grpc.Dial("localhost:50051", opts...)
if err != nil {
    log.Fatalf("Could not connect: %v", err)
}
defer conn.Close()
```

This setup prepares the connection with basic options, but for full retry and backoff support, it's possible to add retry policies or use middleware that handles retry logic automatically based on specific error codes or timeouts.

Enabling security with TLS

gRPC supports secure communication using **Transport Layer Security** (**TLS**), ensuring that the data exchanged between clients and servers is encrypted.

Enabling TLS on the server

To protect data exchanged between the client and server, it is important to enable TLS. TLS encrypts the communication channel and ensures that the server is authenticated, which helps prevent eavesdropping and tampering. This section shows how to configure a gRPC server to use TLS by loading a certificate and private key and using them when starting the server:

```go
import (
    "log"
    "net"

    "google.golang.org/grpc"
    "google.golang.org/grpc/credentials"

    pb "url-shortener/proto"
)

type URLShortenerServer struct {
    pb.UnimplementedURLShortenerServer
    urlMap map[string]string
}

func main() {
    certFile := "server.crt"
    keyFile := "server.key"
    creds, err := credentials.NewServerTLSFromFile(certFile, keyFile)
    if err != nil {
        log.Fatalf("Failed to load TLS keys: %v", err)
    }

    server := grpc.NewServer(grpc.Creds(creds))
    pb.RegisterURLShortenerServer(
        server,
        &URLShortenerServer{
            urlMap: make(map[string]string),
        }
    )

    lis, err := net.Listen("tcp", ":50051")
    if err != nil {
        log.Fatalf("Failed to listen: %v", err)
    }

    log.Println("gRPC server with TLS listening on port 50051")
    server.Serve(lis)
}
```

Now, the gRPC server is configured to use TLS, which means all communication with clients will be encrypted and secure. This setup ensures that sensitive information, such as URLs and statistics, is protected during transmission.

Enabling TLS is a critical step toward building reliable and production-ready services that users can trust.

Configuring TLS on the client

To securely connect a gRPC client to a server that uses TLS, the client must be configured to trust the server's certificate. This is done by loading the **Certificate Authority (CA)** certificate and using it to establish a secure connection. The CA certificate helps the client verify that it is communicating with the right server and that the connection is encrypted:

```
func createSecureClient() pb.URLShortenerClient {
    creds, err := credentials.NewClientTLSFromFile("ca.crt", "")
    if err != nil {
        log.Fatalf("Failed to load CA cert: %v", err)
    }

    conn, err := grpc.Dial(
        "localhost:50051",
        grpc.WithTransportCredentials(creds)
    )
    if err != nil {
        log.Fatalf("Failed to connect: %v", err)
    }

    return pb.NewURLShortenerClient(conn)
}
```

Once the secure connection is established, the client can safely send and receive data over the network. This setup improves trust and security in communication and is recommended for production environments.

Using deadlines and timeouts

Deadlines and timeouts prevent long-running requests from consuming system resources indefinitely.

Versioning gRPC services

As gRPC services evolve, you need to introduce changes without breaking existing clients. Versioning allows smooth transitions between different API versions:

```
syntax = "proto3";

package urlshortener.v1;

service URLShortenerV1 {
    rpc ShortenURL(URLRequest) returns (URLResponse);
}

package urlshortener.v2;

service URLShortenerV2 {
    rpc ShortenURL(URLRequestV2) returns (URLResponseV2);
}
```

This setup allows supporting both old and new clients at the same time. It gives the flexibility to roll out updates gradually, while keeping the service stable and reliable for users already using earlier versions.

Monitoring and logging gRPC requests

Monitoring and logging help track performance issues and debug errors in production environments. One way to achieve this is by using a unary interceptor, which lets us add cross-cutting logic around every gRPC request. We can define a logging interceptor like this:

```
import (
    "context"
    "log"
    "net"

    "google.golang.org/grpc"
    "google.golang.org/grpc/credentials"

    pb "url-shortener/proto"
)
```

```
func loggingInterceptor(
    ctx context.Context,
    req interface{},
    info *grpc.UnaryServerInfo,
    handler grpc.UnaryHandler,
) (interface{}, error) {
    log.Printf("Received request for method: %s", info.FullMethod)
    resp, err := handler(ctx, req)
    if err != nil {
        log.Printf("Error handling request: %v", err)
    }
    return resp, err
}
```

Then, we can attach it to the gRPC server during setup:

```
func main() {
    certFile := "server.crt"
    keyFile := "server.key"
    creds, err := credentials.NewServerTLSFromFile(certFile, keyFile)
    if err != nil {
        log.Fatalf("Failed to load TLS keys: %v", err)
    }

    server := grpc.NewServer(
        grpc.Creds(creds),
        grpc.UnaryInterceptor(loggingInterceptor),
    )

    pb.RegisterURLShortenerServer(server, &URLShortenerServer{
        urlMap: make(map[string]string),
    })

    lis, err := net.Listen("tcp", ":50051")
    if err != nil {
        log.Fatalf("Failed to listen: %v", err)
    }
```

```
    log.Println(
        "gRPC server with TLS and logging interceptor listening on
        port 50051"
    )
    server.Serve(lis)
}
```

If Prometheus is used for observability, we can integrate metrics using the `go-grpc-middleware` ecosystem. It provides out-of-the-box middleware for logging, monitoring, authentication, and more. For example, we can add a Prometheus interceptor like this:

```
import (
    grpc_prometheus "github.com/grpc-ecosystem/go-grpc-prometheus"
)

server := grpc.NewServer(
    grpc.Creds(creds),
    grpc.ChainUnaryInterceptor(
        loggingInterceptor,
        grpc_prometheus.UnaryServerInterceptor,
    ),
)
```

Adding logging like this gives better visibility into how the gRPC server is being used. It helps to catch problems early and understand what's happening during each request, making it easier to maintain and improve the service.

Summary

In this chapter, we learned how to define service contracts using Protocol Buffers (Protobuf). Protobuf helps us create a clear and efficient way to describe the data and services that our gRPC server and client will use. By defining message types and service methods in `.proto` files, we ensure that our microservices communicate smoothly and avoid errors caused by mismatched data formats.

We also explored how to implement streaming with gRPC, which allows continuous data exchange between the client and server. We covered the different types of streams (server-side, client-side, and bidirectional) and demonstrated how to implement each in a URL shortener project. Streaming is especially useful for real-time updates or sending large amounts of data efficiently.

Finally, we discussed best practices for using gRPC in microservices, including connection management, error handling, using TLS for secure communication, setting deadlines to prevent timeouts, versioning APIs to maintain backward compatibility, and adding monitoring with tools such as Prometheus. Following these best practices ensures that our gRPC applications remain reliable, secure, and easy to maintain as they scale.

The next chapter introduces how to build Terraform providers using Go. You'll get a hands-on look at how Terraform works behind the scenes and learn how to add support for custom resources by implementing core features such as create, read, update, and delete.

Part 2

Build Custom Terraform Providers with Go

Part 2 focuses on extending Terraform using Go to create, test, and publish custom providers. We begin with building providers from scratch and explain how to implement the core CRUD operations and manage resource state. We then move on to testing, showing how to write unit and integration tests to verify provider behavior and ensure reliability.

After that, we cover documenting and publishing providers, including writing clear resource documentation, maintaining changelogs, and releasing providers to the Terraform Registry. The final chapter demonstrates how to automate testing and validation in CI/CD pipelines, ensuring consistent quality and faster delivery.

Together, these chapters guide you through the complete life cycle of a Terraform provider, from development and testing to documentation, automation, and release.

This part of the book includes the following chapters:

- *Chapter 7, Using Go to Build Custom Terraform Providers*
- *Chapter 8, Writing Unit Tests and Integration Tests for Terraform Providers*
- *Chapter 9, Documenting and Publishing Terraform Providers*
- *Chapter 10, Automating Testing in Pipelines*

7

Using Go to Build Custom Terraform Providers

Using Go to build custom Terraform providers is important because it allows developers to extend Terraform's capabilities beyond its default offerings. Terraform providers act as bridges between Terraform and external APIs or services, enabling users to manage different types of infrastructure. By creating custom providers, developers can automate the provisioning and management of resources that are not supported by default providers. Since Terraform is written in Go, using Go to create providers ensures seamless integration, high performance, and reliability.

Building custom providers with Go also gives teams full control over how their infrastructure resources are managed. Developers can define custom resource types, implement specific lifecycle behaviors, and tailor API interactions to meet their organization's unique needs. This approach enhances automation, reduces manual intervention, and ensures consistency in infrastructure provisioning, ultimately increasing efficiency and minimizing errors in managing complex environments.

In this chapter, we are going to cover the following topics:

- Learn what Terraform providers are and how the provider model works
- Understand how to build your own custom Terraform provider using Go
- Learn how to implement **Create**, **Read**, **Update**, and **Delete** (**CRUD**) operations for resources
- Explore how to manage and maintain resource state in the provider
- See how to connect the provider with external APIs and services

Introduction to Terraform providers and the provider model

Terraform is a powerful **Infrastructure as Code (IaC)** tool that allows developers to manage cloud resources and APIs efficiently. It uses providers to interact with different APIs and services. A **provider** is a plugin that enables Terraform to communicate with cloud platforms, databases, and other APIs.

In this section, we will explore the basics of Terraform providers, the provider model, and how to build a custom provider in Go. We will use the URL shortener as an example to explain each concept clearly.

What is a Terraform provider?

A Terraform provider is a plugin that implements resource management for a particular service or platform. Think of it as a bridge between Terraform and the API.

Providers allow Terraform to manage resources by making API calls and interpreting the results. Each provider defines resources and data sources that users can declare in their Terraform configuration.

Here is a list of popular Terraform providers:

- `aws`: Manages AWS cloud infrastructure
- `azurerm`: Manages Microsoft Azure resources
- `google`: Manages Google Cloud Platform resources
- `http`: Manages HTTP resources and APIs

The Terraform provider model

The key concepts in the provider model are as follows:

- **Provider schema**: Defines the provider's configuration settings
- **Resource schema**: Specifies the attributes of the resources managed by the provider
- **CRUD operations**: Defines CRUD methods for the resources

Setting up the project structure

To start building a custom Terraform provider with Go, the first step is to set up the project with the right folder structure and initialize the environment. This provides a clean foundation to organize the provider code and dependencies.

Official documentation can be found at `https://www.hashicorp.com/en/blog/writing-custom-terraform-providers`.

Here's the basic file structure of the project:

```
/terraform-provider-urlshortener
├── /examples
├── /internal
    ├── provider.go
    ├── client.go
│   └── resource_shorturl.go
├── /main.go
└── /go.mod
```

The `/internal` directory contains the core implementation of the provider logic. This is where we define files such as `provider.go`, which implements the `Provider` definition, and individual resource files such as `resource_shorturl.go`, or any other custom resource or data source.

If the provider supports multiple resources or data sources, it's a good practice to place each in its own file (for example, `redirect.go`, `analytics.go`, and so on) within the `/internal` folder. This keeps the code modular and maintainable. The `provider.go` file typically registers all available resources and data sources with Terraform, serving as the entry point for the provider logic.

Now, let's initialize the project:

```
# Create the project folder:
mkdir terraform-provider-urlshortener
cd terraform-provider-urlshortener
# Initialize the Go module:
go mod init github.com/example/terraform-provider-urlshortener
```

Once the project structure is in place and the Go module is initialized, we can begin writing the provider logic. Instead of installing dependencies manually (`go get <package_name>`), it's recommended to import required packages directly in the `.go` files (for example, `provider.go`). Go modules will automatically track those imports.

After importing the required packages in Go files, run the following:

```
go mod tidy
```

This command automatically adds any missing dependencies to `go.mod` and downloads them. It also cleans up any unused dependencies, helping to keep the project tidy and up to date.

A typical workflow is to import what is needed in the `.go` files, then run `go mod tidy` to ensure that the module has exactly the dependencies it requires, nothing more, nothing less.

Why this design

Provider-level configuration (API key) is defined in the provider schema and mapped to a typed Go model (`types.String`) with `tfsdk` tags.

We configure building the client and store it in `resp.ResourceData` or `resp.DataSourceData` so resources can retrieve it during configuration and CRUD operations.

Resources implement CRUD and use `req.Plan`, `req.State`, and `resp.State.Set` to read plan/state and write state, as the framework expects. Use `resp.State.RemoveResource()` from `Read` if the remote object no longer exists; `Delete()` need not call `RemoveResource()`, a successful `Delete()` operation implicitly removes the state.

Defining the provider

The provider serves as the entry point for Terraform to interact with the custom resources. Providers define the structure and configuration logic that Terraform will use when initializing the provider.

First, create a new file called `provider.go` in the `./provider/` directory. In that file, define a type called `urlShortenerProvider` with a `string` field to hold the API key. Then, add a `Configure()` method to this type. This method will be called by Terraform when ivru&nting ` tfsdk:"api_key"`

```
}
package provider

import (
  "context"
  "os"

  "github.com/hashicorp/terraform-plugin-framework/datasource"
  "github.com/hashicorp/terraform-plugin-framework/path"
  "github.com/hashicorp/terraform-plugin-framework/provider"
  providerschema "github.com/hashicorp/terraform-plugin-framework/
    provider/schema"
  "github.com/hashicorp/terraform-plugin-framework/resource"
  "github.com/hashicorp/terraform-plugin-framework/types"
)
```

```
// Ensure provider implements framework.Provider
var _ provider.Provider = &urlShortenerProvider{}

// New returns a factory for the provider (used by providerserver).
func New(version string) func() provider.Provider {
  return func() provider.Provider {
    return &urlShortenerProvider{
      version: version,
    }
  }
}

type urlShortenerProvider struct {
  version string
  apiKey string
}

// provider-level model mapping (used with tfsdk tags)
type urlShortenerProviderModel struct {
  APIKey types.String `tfsdk:"api_key"`
}
```

The `urlShortenerProvider` type holds the provider's configuration, here, just an API key as a string:

```
// Configure - build a client and make it available to resources/data-
sources
func (p *urlShortenerProvider) Configure(ctx context.
Context, req provider.ConfigureRequest, resp *provider.
ConfigureResponse) {
// Map provider config to the typed model
var config urlShortenerProviderModel
resp.Diagnostics.Append(req.Config.Get(ctx, &config)...)
if resp.Diagnostics.HasError() {
return
}
// If the value is unknown at configure time, produce a useful attribute
// diagnostic.
```

```
if config.APIKey.IsUnknown() {
    resp.Diagnostics.AddAttributeError(
        path.Root("api_key"),
        "Unknown API Key",
        "The provider cannot create a URL Shortener client as the `api_key
        ` value is unknown. "+
            "Set it in the provider block or provide the value via the
            URLSHORTENER_API_KEY environment variable.",
    )
    return
}

// Environment fallback: env var wins unless provider config provided one
apiKey := os.Getenv("URLSHORTENER_API_KEY")
if !config.APIKey.IsNull() {
    apiKey = config.APIKey.ValueString()
}

if apiKey == "" {
    resp.Diagnostics.AddAttributeError(
        path.Root("api_key"),
        "Missing API Key",
        "No API key was provided. Set `api_key` in the provider
        configuration or set the URLSHORTENER_API_KEY environment
        variable.",
    )
    return
}

// Construct the client
client := &urlShortenerClient{
    APIKey:     apiKey,
    HTTPClient: nil,
}

// Make client available to resources and data sources.
resp.ResourceData = client
resp.DataSourceData = client
```

```
p.apiKey = apiKey
}
```

The `Configure()` method reads the API key from the Terraform configuration when Terraform starts. It extracts the value and saves it into the `APIKey` field so the provider can use it later to authenticate requests. This method also reports any errors back to Terraform to help troubleshoot configuration issues. This setup is essential to make sure the provider has what it needs before it manages any resources.

Next, create the `client.go` file in the root directory to serve as the program's entry point. This file uses the recommended pattern for launching Terraform providers with the latest `terraform-plugin-framework` package:

```
package main

import (
  "context"
  "log"

  "github.com/example/terraform-provider-urlshortener/internal/provider"
  "github.com/hashicorp/terraform-plugin-framework/providerserver"
)

var (
  version = "dev"
  debug   = flag.Bool("debug", false, "enable debug mode")
)

func main() {
  flag.Parse()

  err := providerserver.Serve(context.Background(), provider.
New(version),  providerserver.ServeOpts{
    Debug: *debug,
  })

  if err != nil {
    log.Fatal(err)
  }
}
```

The `main()` function is the entry point of the provider. It uses `providerserver.Serve()` from the Terraform plugin framework to start the provider. This function takes a context, a factory function (`provider.New(version)`) that returns an instance of the provider, and optional server configuration via `ServeOpts`. In this case, we optionally enable debug mode based on a command-line flag.

This setup ensures that Terraform can correctly discover, initialize, and interact with the provider when users execute Terraform CLI commands.

Defining resources

A resource defines an entity that can be managed by Terraform. Resources have CRUD operations that define how to create, read, update, and delete that entity:

```
func URLResourceSchema() schema.Schema {
  return schema.Schema{
    Attributes: map[string]schema.Attribute{
      "short_url": schema.StringAttribute{
        Required:    true,
        Description: "The shortened URL.",
      },
      "long_url": schema.StringAttribute{
        Required:    true,
        Description: "The original long URL.",
      },
    },
  }
}
```

This schema defines the structure of the URL shortener resource by specifying the required attributes that users must provide in the Terraform configuration.

The `short_url` and `long_url` fields describe the key pieces of data that Terraform will manage, making it easy for users to understand what information needs to be supplied and what will be returned by the provider after resource creation.

This setup forms the foundation for how Terraform will interact with and track the lifecycle of each URL resource.

Implementing CRUD operations

Here is an example implementation of the `Create` operation for a resource in the custom Terraform provider. It explains how to get input data, call an external API, handle errors, and save the resource state:

```
func CreateShortURL(ctx context.Context, req resource.
CreateRequest, resp *resource.CreateResponse) {
  var data struct {
    ShortURL string `tfsdk:"short_url"`
    LongURL  string `tfsdk:"long_url"`
  }

  resp.Diagnostics.Append(req.Plan.Get(ctx, &data)...)

  // Call external API to create short URL
  shortURL, err := CreateShortURLAPI(data.LongURL)
  if err != nil {
    resp.Diagnostics.AddError(
      "Error creating short URL",
      err.Error(),
    )
    return
  }

  data.ShortURL = shortURL
  resp.State.Set(ctx, &data)
}
```

This function shows how to create a resource by reading input values, interacting with an external system, and saving the result back into Terraform state so that it can be tracked and managed correctly in future operations.

Configuring the provider

This example shows how to configure the URL shortener provider and create a short URL resource using Terraform:

```
provider "urlshortener" {
  api_key = "my-secret-api-key"
```

```
}

resource "urlshortener_short_url" "example" {
  long_url = "https://example.com"
}
```

Writing tests for the provider

This section shows how to write a simple test to check that the provider configuration works correctly in Terraform:

```
func TestProviderConfiguration(t *testing.T) {
  resource.UnitTest(t, resource.TestCase{
    Steps: []resource.TestStep{
      {
        Config: `
          provider "urlshortener" {
            api_key = "test-api-key"
          }
        `,
      },
    },
  })
}
```

This test helps ensure that the provider can be configured correctly using a simple Terraform block, which is an important first step in verifying that the provider is working as expected.

Implementing CRUD operations for resources

To manage the lifecycle of resources in a custom Terraform provider, you need to implement four key operations: `Create`, `Read`, `Update`, and `Delete`. These operations allow Terraform to track and manage resources accurately throughout their lifecycle.

Each operation serves a specific purpose:

- `Create`: Add a new resource
- `Read`: Retrieve the current state of the resource
- `Update`: Modify the resource based on configuration changes
- `Delete`: Remove the resource when it's no longer required

Defining the resource schema

Before implementing the CRUD functions, the resource schema must be defined. This schema tells Terraform what properties the resource accepts and what values it returns after operations such as `Create` or `Update`:

```
package provider

import (
  "context"

  "github.com/hashicorp/terraform-plugin-framework/resource"
  "github.com/hashicorp/terraform-plugin-framework/schema"
  "github.com/hashicorp/terraform-plugin-framework/types"
)

type urlShortenerResource struct{}
```

The `Metadata` function sets the resource type name that Terraform will use in configuration files. When Terraform loads the provider, it calls this `Metadata` function to get the name of the resource. In this case, the name is set to `url_shortener`, which means users will refer to it as `resource "url_shortener" { ... }` in their Terraform files:

```
func (r *urlShortenerResource) Metadata(ctx context.Context, req resource.
MetadataRequest, resp *resource.MetadataResponse) {
resp.TypeName = "url_shortener"
}
```

The `Schema` function defines the structure of the URL shortener resource in Terraform. It specifies that `long_url` is a required input that users must provide, and `short_url` is a computed attribute that Terraform will set automatically after creating the resource. This schema tells Terraform what data to expect and manage for this resource:

```
func (r *URLShortenerResource) Schema(
  ctx context.Context, request resource.SchemaRequest,
  response *resource.SchemaResponse
) {
  response.Schema = schema.Schema {
    Attributes: map[string]schema.Attribute {
      "long_url": schema.StringAttribute{
```

```
        Required: true,
      },
      "short_url": schema.StringAttribute{
        Computed: true,
      },
    },
  }
}
```

This schema acts as the foundation for how Terraform interacts with the resource, clearly defining which fields users must provide and which ones Terraform will compute and return after operations like creation or updates.

Implementing the create operation

The `Create` operation adds a new resource. Here, we will generate a shortened URL and store it.

The `Create` function is responsible for creating a new URL shortener resource. It starts by reading the `long_url` value from the planned configuration using the request data. After that, it prepares the full state containing both the long and short URLs and saves it so Terraform can manage the resource. If there is an error while reading the input or saving the state, the function adds an appropriate error message to help with debugging:

```
func (r *URLShortenerResource) Create(
  ctx context.Context, request resource.CreateRequest,
  response *resource.CreateResponse
) {
  var data URLShortenerResourceModel

  // Read the plan into the data model
  response.Diagnostics.Append(request.Plan.Get(ctx, &data)...)

  if response.Diagnostics.HasError() {
    return
  }

  // Generate a short URL
  shortURL := generateShortURL()
```

```
    // Set the short URL in the state
    data.ShortURL = types.StringValue(shortURL)

    // Save the updated state
    response.Diagnostics.Append(response.State.Set(ctx, &data)...)
}
```

Now, we need to define the `generateShortURL()` function. Here's a simple way to do it:

```
func generateShortURL() string {
    rand.Seed(time.Now().UnixNano())
    return "short.ly/" + strconv.Itoa(rand.Intn(10000))
}
```

This function generates a random short URL by picking a random number and appending it to the domain name prefix.

Implementing the Read operation

The `Read` operation retrieves the current state of the resource. It is responsible for syncing the current state of the URL shortener resource with Terraform. It starts by loading the existing state, which includes both the long and short URLs. If reading the state fails, it adds an error to help with troubleshooting. Finally, it saves the updated state so Terraform can stay up to date. If saving the new state fails, it adds another error message to explain the issue:

```
func (r *URLShortenerResource) Read(
    ctx context.Context, req resource.ReadRequest,
    resp *resource.ReadResponse
) {
    // Read the current state
    var state struct {
        LongURL  types.String `tfsdk:"long_url"`
        ShortURL types.String `tfsdk:"short_url"`
    }

    // Get the current state
    diags := req.State.Get(ctx, &state)
    resp.Diagnostics.Append(diags...)
    if resp.Diagnostics.HasError() {
        return
```

```
    }

    // Save the state

    diags = resp.State.Set(ctx, &state)
    resp.Diagnostics.Append(diags...)}
```

We read and save the state to make sure we have the most up-to-date details about the resource. By saving it without altering it, we preserve the current status for future use or processing, ensuring consistency and accuracy in the system.

Implementing the Update operation

The `Update` operation modifies the resource if `long_url` changes. It handles changes to the URL shortener resource when the configuration is modified in Terraform. It begins by reading the current state, which holds the long and short URLs, and also retrieves the planned changes. If either `Read` operation fails, it adds an error to help identify the issue. The function then checks whether the long URL has changed. Finally, it saves the updated state so Terraform can reflect the changes. If saving the state fails, it logs another error to help with debugging:

```
func (r *urlShortenerResource) Update(
  ctx context.Context, req resource.UpdateRequest,
  resp *resource.UpdateResponse
) {
  // Retrieve the current state and plan
  var state struct {
    LongURL types.String tfsdk:"long_url"
    ShortURL types.String tfsdk:"short_url"
  }
  err := req.State.Get(ctx, &state)
  if err != nil {
    resp.Diagnostics.AddError(
      "Error reading state",
      "Could not read the URL shortener state: "+err.Error(),
    )
    return
  }
  var plan struct {
    LongURL types.String `tfsdk:"long_url"`
```

```
    }

    err = req.Plan.Get(ctx, &plan)
    if err != nil {
      resp.Diagnostics.AddError(
        "Error reading plan",
        "Could not read the plan for the URL shortener resource:
        "+err.Error(),
      )
      return
    }

    // If the long URL changed, we'll update the short URL
    if plan.LongURL.ValueString() != state.LongURL.ValueString() {
      state.LongURL = plan.LongURL
      state.ShortURL = generateShortURL()
    }

    // Save the updated state
    err = resp.State.Set(ctx, &state)
    if err != nil {
      resp.Diagnostics.AddError(
        "Error setting state",
        "Could not save the updated URL shortener state: "+err.Error(),
      )
    }
}
```

This completes the implementation of the `Update` operation, which ensures that changes made to the long URL in the Terraform configuration are correctly handled.

By reading the current and planned state, checking for differences, and updating the short URL if needed, this function helps keep the resource data accurate and consistent.

It also includes error handling to make sure any problems during the update process are clearly reported, making it easier to troubleshoot issues during the application.

Implementing the Delete operation

The `Delete` operation removes the resource from the system. It handles removing the URL shortener resource when Terraform destroys it. The function simply removes the resource from Terraform's state to complete the deletion process:

```
func (r *urlShortenerResource) Delete(ctx context.Context, req resource.
DeleteRequest, resp *resource.DeleteResponse) {
// Logic to delete the URL shortener
(if necessary)
resp.State.RemoveResource(ctx)
}
```

This completes the `Delete` operation by ensuring that once a resource is no longer needed, it is cleanly removed from Terraform's state.

Even if no actual deletion logic is required beyond updating the state, this step is important for keeping Terraform's view of the infrastructure accurate.

Including this function helps prevent errors in future plans and applications by making sure obsolete resources are not tracked anymore.

Testing CRUD operations

To make sure our provider works correctly, it is important to test each part of the CRUD process. This includes checking that we can create a new short URL, read its current state, update it when needed, and confirm that the results are as expected. The following are sample configurations to test the `Create`, `Read`, and `Update` operations.

This is the `Create` and `Read` test:

```
resource "url_shortener" "example" {
  long_url = "https://example.com"
}
```

This is the `Update` test:

```
resource "url_shortener" "example" {
  long_url = "https://example2.com"
}
```

Managing resource state and handling the lifecycle

In this section, we will explore how to manage the state and handle the lifecycle of resources when building a custom Terraform provider using Go.

The resource state is essential for keeping track of the current and desired state of infrastructure resources.

Managing the lifecycle ensures that operations such as creating, reading, updating, and deleting resources happen correctly.

Understanding Terraform resource state

The state in Terraform stores metadata about the managed resources. This includes the resource's current attributes, which Terraform uses to determine whether a resource needs to be updated, recreated, or deleted.

In a custom provider, managing resource state means ensuring that the correct data is preserved and updated between operations:

```
func resourceURLShortenerSchema() map[string]*schema.Schema {
  return map[string]*schema.Schema{
    "short_url": {
      Type:     schema.TypeString,
      Required: true,
      ForceNew: true,
    },
    "long_url": {
      Type:     schema.TypeString,
      Required: true,
    },
    "clicks": {
      Type:     schema.TypeInt,
      Computed: true,
    },
  }
}
```

By managing the resource state properly, we help Terraform understand what has changed and what needs to happen next. This makes resource updates safer, more predictable, and easier to debug. With a well-defined schema and clear state handling, the provider can support a reliable and consistent lifecycle for each resource.

Create operation with state management

To create a resource in a custom Terraform provider, we define a function that performs the creation logic, manages state, and returns any errors that might occur. This example shows how to create a shortened URL by simulating an external service and saving the result in Terraform's state:

```
func resourceURLShortenerCreate(
  ctx context.Context, d *schema.ResourceData, m interface{}
) diag.Diagnostics {
  shortURL := d.Get("short_url").(string)
  longURL := d.Get("long_url").(string)

  // Simulate URL creation
  createdShortURL, err := createShortURL(shortURL, longURL)
  if err != nil {
    return diag.FromErr(err)
  }

  d.SetId(createdShortURL)
  d.Set("clicks", 0)

  return resourceURLShortenerRead(ctx, d, m)
}

func createShortURL(shortURL, longURL string) (string, error) {
  // Simulated storage for shortened URLs
  urlStore[shortURL] = longURL
  return shortURL, nil
}
```

By setting the resource ID and updating the state with initial values, the `resourceURLShortenerCreate` function ensures that Terraform can track the resource accurately in future operations. This setup makes it easier for Terraform to perform `Read`, `Update`, or `Delete` actions later. Managing the state during creation is a key part of ensuring the resource lifecycle is handled correctly.

Read operation to maintain state

To keep the Terraform state up to date, the provider must be able to read the latest data from the system and update the resource's state accordingly. The `resourceURLShortenerRead` function performs this task by checking whether the short URL exists and setting the appropriate fields:

```
func resourceURLShortenerRead(
  ctx context.Context, d *schema.ResourceData, m interface{}
) diag.Diagnostics {
  shortURL := d.Id()
  longURL, exists := urlStore[shortURL]

  if !exists {
    d.SetId("") // Mark resource as deleted
    return nil
  }

  d.Set("long_url", longURL)
  d.Set("clicks", getClickCount(shortURL))

  return nil
}
```

If the short URL is not found, the function clears the resource ID to indicate that it has been deleted. If it exists, it updates `long_url` and clicks fields to match the current values. This helps Terraform maintain an accurate view of the resource over time.

Update operation with state tracking

When a resource is updated in Terraform, the provider needs to detect what has changed and apply the necessary updates while keeping the state accurate. This function shows how to check whether `long_url` has changed and, if so, update the stored value to reflect the new URL:

```
func resourceURLShortenerUpdate(
  ctx context.Context, d *schema.ResourceData, m interface{}
) diag.Diagnostics {
  if d.HasChange("long_url") {
    shortURL := d.Id()
    longURL := d.Get("long_url").(string)
```

```
        // Update the long URL
        urlStore[shortURL] = longURL
    }

    return resourceURLShortenerRead(ctx, d, m)
}
```

The `resourceURLShortenerUpdate` function ensures that any changes to `long_url` are captured and saved correctly. After updating the value, it refreshes the state by calling the `Read` function. This helps Terraform stay in sync with the actual data and ensures that future operations behave as expected.

Delete operation and state cleanup

When a resource is no longer needed, Terraform expects the provider to remove it from the system and clean up any related state information. The `resourceURLShortenerDelete` function handles this step by deleting the short URL from the store and clearing the resource's ID to mark it as removed:

```
func resourceURLShortenerDelete(
    ctx context.Context, d *schema.ResourceData, m interface{}
) diag.Diagnostics {
    shortURL := d.Id()

    // Remove the URL from the store
    delete(urlStore, shortURL)

    // Remove resource ID
    d.SetId("")

    return nil
}
```

By deleting the short URL from the internal map and resetting the resource ID, the provider ensures that Terraform will no longer track this resource. This cleanup step is important to prevent stale data and keep the Terraform state accurate for future operations.

Handling lifecycle hooks

Terraform allows lifecycle hooks to control how resources behave during creation, updates, and deletion.

Preventing resource destruction

To protect important infrastructure from being accidentally deleted, Terraform provides a `prevent_destroy` lifecycle setting. This setting tells Terraform to stop and show an error if a resource is about to be destroyed during a `plan` or `apply` operation:

```
resource "url_shortener" "example" {
  short_url = "my-url"
  long_url  = "https://example.com"

  lifecycle {
    prevent_destroy = true
  }
}
```

Ignoring changes to specific attributes

Sometimes, certain fields of a resource may change outside of Terraform or may not need to trigger a change when updated. Terraform provides the `ignore_changes` lifecycle setting to help you skip updates to selected attributes during the `apply` phase:

```
resource "url_shortener" "example" {
  short_url = "my-url"
  long_url  = "https://example.com"

  lifecycle {
    ignore_changes = [
      long_url
    ]
  }
}
```

Implementing resource import

Terraform can manage resources that were created outside of it by importing them into its state. The `import` function lets the provider fetch the resource's current data and make it part of Terraform's managed resources so that you can continue managing it using Terraform configuration:

```
func resourceURLShortenerImporter() *schema.ResourceImporter {
  return &schema.ResourceImporter{
    State: func(
```

```
        d *schema.ResourceData,
        m interface{}
    ) ([]*schema.ResourceData, error) {
        shortURL := d.Id()
        longURL, exists := urlStore[shortURL]

        if !exists {
          return nil, fmt.Errorf("URL not found")
        }


        d.Set("long_url", longURL)

        d.Set("clicks", getClickCount(shortURL))


        return []*schema.ResourceData{d}, nil
    },
  }
}
```

Using lifecycle settings and `import` functions provides better control over how Terraform manages the resources. These features give more flexibility and safety when working with real infrastructure. They also help to manage resources that already exist, without needing to recreate them.

Summary

In this chapter, we explored how to create custom Terraform providers using Go. We started by understanding the Terraform provider model and how it acts as a bridge between Terraform and external APIs. We learned how providers interact with resources and data sources, making it possible to extend Terraform's functionality.

Next, we focused on implementing CRUD operations (`Create`, `Read`, `Update`, and `Delete`) for resources. We covered how to define resource schemas, map API calls to CRUD operations, and manage user-defined inputs efficiently. By using real-world examples, such as building a URL shortener provider, we demonstrated how to handle API requests and manage state transitions between operations.

Finally, we discussed managing resource state and handling lifecycle operations to ensure data consistency. This allows us to use state to track resource changes and prevent drift. We also explored lifecycle management techniques, such as the `import` functionality, to handle existing resources. By mastering these concepts, we can confidently build and manage Terraform providers that interact seamlessly with external services.

In the next chapter, we will focus on testing the Terraform provider code to make sure it works correctly. You'll learn how to write unit tests for resource operations and how to mock API calls so the tests don't rely on real services. This helps catch bugs early and build reliable providers.

8

Writing Unit Tests and Integration Tests for Terraform Providers

Testing is an essential part of building reliable and robust Terraform providers. Unit tests ensure that individual **CRUD** operations (**Create, Read, Update, Delete**) behave as expected, helping to identify potential issues early in the development process. By testing each function independently, developers can verify that API requests, state management, and data transformations are correctly handled. This reduces the risk of introducing bugs when extending provider functionality or modifying resource behavior. Unit tests also give developers confidence that their provider logic remains intact as changes are made over time.

Integration tests go a step further by validating how the entire provider interacts with Terraform and external APIs. These tests ensure that resources are created, updated, and destroyed correctly while maintaining a consistent state. By simulating real-world use cases, integration tests help uncover issues that may not be visible in unit tests, such as network errors, rate limits, or unexpected API responses. Writing thorough unit and integration tests ensures that Terraform providers remain reliable, maintainable, and resilient, reducing the risk of misconfigurations and ensuring that infrastructure changes are applied safely.

In this chapter, we are going to cover the following topics:

- Learn how to write unit tests for CRUD operations of a Terraform resource
- Understand how to mock API calls in tests to avoid relying on real external systems

- Explore how to verify that the resource state is managed correctly during tests
- Use the Terraform SDK's testing tools to write and run tests for custom providers
- Learn how to automate tests to catch issues early and keep the provider reliable

Writing unit tests for resource CRUD operations

Unit testing helps catch mistakes early by checking that each part of the code works the way it should. It gives developers confidence that changes will not break existing functionality and makes it easier to maintain the provider over time. Writing focused tests for each operation also makes it simpler to understand and debug problems when they happen.

In this section, we will explore how to write unit tests for CRUD operations using Go and the Terraform SDK.

Setting up the environment

Before we begin writing tests, we need to set up the Go testing environment:

```
mkdir -p tests

# Install Terraform SDK
go get github.com/hashicorp/terraform-plugin-sdk/v2/helper/schema

# Install the testing framework
go get github.com/stretchr/testify/assert
```

Once the required packages are installed and the test folder is ready, you will have everything set up to start writing and running the unit tests. This setup creates a good foundation for testing the provider code and making sure each part works correctly. With the environment ready, we can now move on to writing actual test cases.

Writing unit tests for CRUD operations

To make sure the provider behaves the way we want, it is important to test each operation one by one. This section includes tests for the `Create`, `Read`, `Update`, and `Delete` functions using Go's `testing` package along with the Terraform SDK and the `testify/assert` library.

Testing the Create operation

We will begin by testing the `Create` operation to ensure that a URL is shortened correctly. This helps to confirm that the resource behaves as expected when it is first created.

Create a new test file, `resource_url_test.go`, inside the `urlshortener/tests` direc_te}"))

```
}
package urlshortener_test

import (
  "context"
  "testing"

  "github.com/stretchr/testify/assert"
  "github.com/hashicorp/terraform-plugin-sdk/v2/helper/schema"
  "github.com/example/terraform-provider-urlshortener/urlshortener"
)

func TestResourceURLCreate(t *testing.T) {
  resource := urlshortener.ResourceURL()
  d := schema.TestResourceDataRaw(
    t,
    resource.Schema,
    map[string]interface{}{
      "original_url": "https://example.com",
    }
  )

  diags := urlshortener.ResourceURLCreate(context.Background(), d, nil)
  assert.Nil(t, diags)
  assert.Equal(t, "https://short.ly/abc123", d.Get("short_url"))
}
```

Once this basic test for the `Create` operation is in place, we can build on it with more test cases that cover edge conditions and errors. Writing focused unit tests like this helps catch bugs early and gives confidence that the resource logic works correctly.

In this test, we simulate a user providing an original URL and check that the `Create` function returns the expected short URL. We use Terraform's `TestResourceDataRaw` helper to create a mock resource, run the `create` function, and use assertions to verify the outcome. This ensures that the resource initializes correctly with the right values.

Testing the Read operation

The Read operation should retrieve and validate the stored data.

```
func TestResourceURLRead(t *testing.T) {
  resource := urlshortener.ResourceURL()
  d := schema.TestResourceDataRaw(
    t,
    resource.Schema,
    map[string]interface{}{
      "original_url": "https://example.com",
      "short_url":    "https://short.ly/abc123",
    }
  )

  diags := urlshortener.ResourceURLRead(context.Background(), d, nil)
  assert.Nil(t, diags)
  assert.Equal(t, "https://short.ly/abc123", d.Get("short_url"))
}
```

In this test, we assume that the short and original URLs are already set. The goal is to check whether the Read function can confirm that the data is still valid and available. We also assert that no errors are returned and that the values match what we expect. This helps confirm that state tracking works as intended.

Testing the Update operation

Updating a URL involves modifying the original URL or regenerating a new short URL.

```
func TestResourceURLUpdate(t *testing.T) {
  resource := urlshortener.ResourceURL()
  d := schema.TestResourceDataRaw(
    t,
    resource.Schema,
    map[string]interface{}{
      "original_url": "https://new-example.com",
    }
  )

  diags := urlshortener.ResourceURLUpdate(context.Background(), d, nil)
```

```
    assert.Nil(t, diags)
    assert.Equal(t, "https://new-example.com", d.Get("original_url"))
}
```

This test checks whether modifying the original URL triggers the correct update behavior. We provide a new URL, call the `Update` function, and verify that the new value is stored correctly in the resource state. This helps ensure the resource reacts properly to configuration changes.

Testing the Delete operation

Deleting a URL should clear its state.

```
func TestResourceURLDelete(t *testing.T) {
    resource := urlshortener.ResourceURL()
    d := schema.TestResourceDataRaw(
        t,
        resource.Schema,
        map[string]interface{}{
            "original_url": "https://example.com",
            "short_url":    "https://short.ly/abc123",
        }
    )

    diags := urlshortener.ResourceURLDelete(context.Background(), d, nil)
    assert.Nil(t, diags)
    assert.Empty(t, d.Id())
}
```

This test confirms that calling the `Delete` function results in the resource ID being removed from the Terraform state. We verify that the ID is empty after deletion, which tells Terraform that the resource no longer exists.

Running the unit tests

To run the tests, use the following command:

```
# Run all tests
go test ./...
```

You should see an output similar to the following:

```
ok     github.com/example/terraform-provider-urlshortener/urlshortener/
tests  0.005s
```

You can now use this output to confirm that the tests are working correctly and that the provider code is behaving as expected.

The `go test ./...` command runs all test files recursively in the current module, so it will pick up any test functions defined using the standard testing package. This command compiles and runs the tests, reports any errors or failed assertions, and shows how long the test suite took to execute. If everything is set up properly, you should see an `ok` message followed by the path to the package and the time it took, indicating all tests passed. Running tests regularly like this helps catch issues early and makes sure changes do not break existing behavior.

Mocking API calls for effective testing

When building a Terraform provider, it's essential to test API interactions without depending on the actual external service. Mocking API calls ensures that tests remain reliable, fast, and isolated. In this section, we'll explore how to mock API calls effectively in Go, focusing on a URL shortener example to demonstrate best practices.

Why mock API calls?

When developing a Terraform provider, you often need to interact with external APIs to create, read, update, or delete resources. However, relying on real API calls during testing introduces several challenges:

- **Slower tests**: Real API calls increase test execution time.
- **Unpredictability**: Network failures or API rate limits can cause tests to fail.
- **Cost**: Using real APIs during testing may incur unnecessary costs.
- **Isolation**: Tests should focus on the provider's logic, not the external service's behavior.

By mocking API calls, we can simulate API responses and focus on testing our provider's functionality.

Setting up a mock HTTP server

Go provides the `httptest` package, which allows us to create a mock HTTP server to handle API requests and return predefined responses.

This test demonstrates how to set up a mock HTTP server in Go using the `httptest` package. It allows us to simulate how an external API behaves without making real HTTP requests.

```
package main
```

```
import (
  "net/http"
  "net/http/httptest"
  "testing"
)

func TestGetShortenedURL(t *testing.T) {
```

Inside the test, we create a mock HTTP server using `httptest.NewServer`. This server will handle incoming requests and send back fake but predictable responses, which helps in testing without depending on real APIs.

```
  // Create a mock server
  mockServer := httptest.NewServer(
    http.HandlerFunc(
      func(w http.ResponseWriter, r *http.Request) {
```

We define what the mock server should do when it receives a request to `/shorten` using the `POST` method. It responds with a `200 OK` status and a JSON payload containing the shortened URL.

```
        if r.URL.Path == "/shorten" && r.Method == http.MethodPost {
          w.WriteHeader(http.StatusOK)
          w.Write([]byte(`{"short_url": "https://short.ly/abc123"}`))
          return
        }
        w.WriteHeader(http.StatusNotFound)
      }
    )
  )
```

We defer closing the mock server so it shuts down when the test completes. This is important to free up resources and avoid conflicts in future tests.

```
  defer mockServer.Close()

  // Use the mock server URL
  apiURL := mockServer.URL
```

Now we call the function under test, `shortenURL`, passing in the mock server's URL and the long URL we want to shorten. We then check if it returns the expected result.

```
    shortURL, err := shortenURL(apiURL, "https://example.com")
    if err != nil {
      t.Fatalf("Error shortening URL: %v", err)
    }
```

Finally, we verify the response from the function. If the shortened URL does not match what we expect, we report an error.

```
    if shortURL != "https://short.ly/abc123" {
      t.Errorf("Expected short URL, got %s", shortURL)
    }
  }
```

This kind of test is useful for verifying how your code interacts with external HTTP services without depending on the real services being available or reliable.

Mocking HTTP requests with http.Client

In some cases, you may want to replace `http.Client` with a custom client that uses mock responses.

Replacing `http.Client` with a custom client is useful, especially when writing tests or when needing more control over how HTTP requests are handled. By default, `http.Client` sends actual requests over the network, but this behavior can be problematic in unit tests. We may not want tests to depend on an external API or internet connectivity, as that makes them slow, unreliable, and hard to reproduce. Using a custom client allows us to simulate API responses without making actual network calls, making the tests faster and more stable.

Another reason could be when you may want to inject special behavior into the HTTP calls. For example, you might want to automatically retry failed requests, log all outgoing traffic, or set specific headers or timeouts. A custom client allows us to control all of this in one place, rather than duplicating that logic throughout the code base.

Using a custom `http.Client` also encourages good software design by making the code more flexible and easier to test. If the function accepts `http.Client` as a parameter rather than creating it internally, it becomes easier to test in isolation. This is a common practice in dependency injection, where the function receives everything it needs from the outside, making it easier to reuse and verify.

The following function uses the built-in `http.Post` method to send the request, `json.Marshal` to convert the request body into JSON format, and `json.NewDecoder` to read the JSON response. These are standard tools in Go for working with APIs and JSON.

```
package main

import (
  "bytes"
  "encoding/json"
  "errors"
  "net/http"
)

// shortenURL sends a request to shorten a URL
func shortenURL(apiURL, longURL string) (string, error) {
  payload, _ := json.Marshal(map[string]string{"url": longURL})
  resp, err := http.Post(
    apiURL+"/shorten", "application/json", bytes.NewBuffer(payload)
  )
  if err != nil {
    return "", err
  }
  defer resp.Body.Close()

  if resp.StatusCode != http.StatusOK {
    return "", errors.New("failed to shorten URL")
  }

  var result map[string]string
  json.NewDecoder(resp.Body).Decode(&result)
  return result["short_url"], nil
}
```

This function makes it easy to connect to a URL shortening service, send a request with the original long URL, and get back a short URL as the response. By structuring the logic this way, it becomes much easier to replace `http.Client` later with a *mock* for testing, and the function stays clean and reusable.

Using httptest to mock API responses

When testing a provider, it's important to simulate different API responses to cover edge cases.

We are going to use Go's `httptest` package to mock API responses for testing how the Terraform provider handles error cases. Instead of calling a real API, we set up a fake HTTP server that behaves like the real one and returns specific responses we want to test.

This allows us to simulate situations such as internal server errors or unexpected paths, and verify that the provider logic handles them correctly.

The `httptest.NewServer` function creates a local HTTP server that we control, and `http.HandlerFunc` defines the custom behavior for incoming requests.

In this case, when the request path is `/shorten`, the mock server responds with an `HTTP 500` status and an error message. The test then calls the real `shortenURL` function using the mock server's URL, and checks that an error is returned, as expected.

This approach helps ensure that the code behaves correctly even when the backend service fails.

```
func TestAPIErrorHandling(t *testing.T) {
  mockServer := httptest.NewServer(
    http.HandlerFunc(func(w http.ResponseWriter, r *http.Request
  ) {
    if r.URL.Path == "/shorten" {
      w.WriteHeader(http.StatusInternalServerError)
      w.Write([]byte(`{"error": "Internal Server Error"}`))
      return
    }
    w.WriteHeader(http.StatusNotFound)
  }))
  defer mockServer.Close()

  // API URL points to mock server
  apiURL := mockServer.URL

  _, err := shortenURL(apiURL, "https://example.com")
  if err == nil {
    t.Error("Expected an error, but got none")
  }
}
```

By simulating errors like this in a controlled environment, you can confirm that the provider code does not break or behave unexpectedly in real-world situations. It also ensures that error handling is not just present but actually works as intended under different conditions.

Mocking API calls with interfaces

To decouple API logic, you can define an interface and mock it during tests.

In this section, we focus on mocking API calls using interfaces in Go. This technique helps separate the actual implementation of the API from the rest of the code so we can test components independently.

We start by defining an interface called `URLShortener` with a `Shorten` method, which represents any service that can shorten a URL.

Then we create a mock implementation of this interface called `MockURLShortener`, which simulates behavior for known inputs. If the URL matches a specific string, it returns a fake shortened URL; otherwise, it returns an error.

In our test function, `TestMockShorten`, we use this mock implementation instead of a real API. This allows us to check that the code behaves correctly when interacting with the `Shorten` method, without depending on any actual network calls. It also makes the tests faster and more reliable, since they don't rely on external systems.

```
type URLShortener interface {
  Shorten(url string) (string, error)
}

// Mock implementation
type MockURLShortener struct {}

func (m *MockURLShortener) Shorten(url string) (string, error) {
  if url == "https://example.com" {
    return "https://short.ly/abc123", nil
  }
  return "", errors.New("invalid URL")
}
```

It's usage in tests:

```
func TestMockShorten(t *testing.T) {
  mockShortener := &MockURLShortener{}

  shortURL, err := mockShortener.Shorten("https://example.com")
  if err != nil {
    t.Fatalf("Unexpected error: %v", err)
  }

  if shortURL != "https://short.ly/abc123" {
    t.Errorf("Expected shortened URL, got %s", shortURL)
  }
}
```

Using interfaces in this way gives more flexibility and makes the tests easier to manage and extend. It's a common pattern in Go for improving testability and maintaining clean separation between logic and dependencies.

Using gomock for advanced mocking

`gomock` is a powerful package that generates mock interfaces and enhances test coverage.

In this section, we use `gomock`, a popular mocking framework for Go that helps generate mock implementations of interfaces automatically.

This makes the tests more maintainable and expressive, especially when you are working with complex logic or want to enforce strict expectations about how the mocks are used.

To get started, we first install `mockgen`, a tool that generates mock code based on the interfaces, and also import the `gomock` package for use in tests.

We then use the `mockgen` command to generate a mock version of the `URLShortener` interface and save it under the `mocks` package.

```
$ go install github.com/golang/mock/mockgen@latest
$ go get github.com/golang/mock/gomock
mockgen -source=url_shortener.go -destination=mocks/mock_url_shortener.go
-package=mocks
```

Once you have installed the tools and generated the mock code, you are ready to use the mock interface in the tests to simulate different behaviors and validate how the provider code interacts with external systems. This setup helps to write more reliable and isolated tests and gives better control over the flow of data during testing.

Using mocks in tests

In this test example, we create `gomock.Controller` to manage the lifecycle of the mock and then use the generated `NewMockURLShortener` constructor to create a mock instance.

We define an expectation that the `Shorten` method will be called with a specific input and return a predefined result.

Then, we invoke the method and verify the result, making sure the output matches what we expect.

```
func TestShortenWithMock(t *testing.T) {
  ctrl := gomock.NewController(t)
  defer ctrl.Finish()

  mockShortener := mocks.NewMockURLShortener(ctrl)
  mockShortener.EXPECT().Shorten("https://example.com").Return(
    "https://short.ly/abc123", nil
  )

  shortURL, err := mockShortener.Shorten("https://example.com")
  if err != nil {
    t.Fatalf("Error: %v", err)
  }

  if shortURL != "https://short.ly/abc123" {
    t.Errorf("Expected shortened URL, got %s", shortURL)
  }
}
```

By running this test, you can confirm that the mock behaves as expected and that the code correctly calls the `Shorten` method with the right input. This gives confidence that the logic integrates well with the interface and helps catch issues early in development without needing to call the real external service.

Summary

In this chapter, we explored the importance of writing unit tests for resource CRUD operations in Terraform providers. We covered how to create tests for the `Create`, `Read`, `Update`, and `Delete` functions, ensuring that each function behaves as expected. Through detailed examples, we demonstrated how to validate provider behavior and maintain stability during infrastructure changes. Writing these tests helps prevent unexpected bugs and keeps the provider's functionality reliable.

We then dived into the process of mocking API calls for effective testing. By simulating API responses, we learned how to test provider logic without depending on external services. This approach makes it easier to isolate the provider's functionality and verify that it handles different scenarios correctly. Mocking API calls is essential for maintaining test reliability and reducing external dependencies.

By combining unit testing with API mocking, we ensure that Terraform providers function accurately under various conditions. These techniques help identify errors early, streamline development, and improve overall provider quality. As a result, developers can confidently manage their infrastructure using custom Terraform providers with strong test coverage.

In the next chapter, we will look at how to document and publish Terraform providers so that others can use it. We'll also learn how to publish the provider to the public Terraform Registry where anyone can discover and use it, or how to set up a private registry for internal use within an organization.

9

Documenting and Publishing Terraform Providers

Documenting and publishing a Terraform provider is the final and arguably most critical step in the provider development lifecycle. Even the most well-designed provider is only as useful as its documentation allows it to be. Clear, accurate, and user-friendly documentation ensures that the provider is accessible, not only to the team but to all users, too. It serves as the primary source of truth for how users interact with the resources and data sources, helping them understand required arguments, expected behaviors, and best practices. Without it, users are left to guess at configuration, which can lead to misuse, frustration, or abandonment. Good documentation transforms the provider from a personal tool into a reliable building block that others can confidently adopt and build upon.

Beyond documentation, publishing the provider significantly increases its value and impact. By making the provider discoverable, versioned, and easy to integrate, we enable reusability, collaboration, and standardization. Publishing also introduces the need for semantic versioning and changelogs, which are key to maintaining trust and stability over time. Consumers of the provider need to know what's changed, what to expect from each version, and how to upgrade safely. Whether we're supporting a closed team or the global Terraform community, publishing the provider with proper documentation and a clear release process makes the work truly production-grade and empowers others to confidently use, extend, and contribute to it.

In this chapter, we are going to cover the following topics:

- Generating documentation for your Terraform provider using `tfplugindocs`
- Structuring your provider documentation for clarity and usability

- Writing high-quality documentation for individual resources and data sources
- Incorporating usage examples and argument references effectively
- Implementing semantic versioning for your provider releases
- Maintaining a changelog that communicates changes and deprecations
- Tagging releases using Git and managing version lifecycle
- Preparing your provider for distribution and meeting registry requirements
- Publishing your provider to the public Terraform Registry
- Managing private registry publishing for internal consumption

Generating provider documentation

Good documentation is one of the most important parts of building a Terraform provider. It helps users understand what the provider does, what resources and data sources it offers, and how to use them correctly. Instead of writing everything manually, the Terraform ecosystem offers tools to make this easier. One of the most powerful tools for this purpose is `tfplugindocs`, which can automatically generate documentation files based on the project code.

The `tfplugindocs` tool looks at the schema definitions, descriptions, and examples in the source code, and then creates Markdown files that match the layout expected by the Terraform Registry. This ensures consistency and helps avoid missing or outdated documentation.

Let's say we've finished building the Terraform provider for a URL shortener service. The provider includes a `short_url` resource that takes a long URL and creates a short version. We've written the schema and some helpful descriptions directly in the source code. Now, we want to generate the documentation so we can publish it.

To get started with `tfplugindocs`, first, we have to install it by adding it to the development environment. Once available, running the tool against the provider's code base creates a set of `.md` files under a `docs/` folder. These files include sections such as `Example Usage`, `Argument Reference`, and `Attributes Reference`, all filled in based on the schema information in the resource definition.

Setting up the environment for tfplugindocs

Before generating documentation for the Terraform provider, we need to set up the development environment to support the `tfplugindocs` tool.

The first thing is to install the latest version of `tfplugindocs`. You can do this by running the following command:

```
go install github.com/hashicorp/terraform-plugin-docs/cmd/tfplugindocs@
latest
```

This command builds and installs the `tfplugindocs` binary into the Go `bin` path (typically `$HOME/go/bin`).

Let's check whether the tool is installed and works as expected:

```
tfplugindocs --version
```

This command should print the installed version number, confirming that the `tfplugindocs` tool is ready.

Customizing the documentation

Although not required, you can customize how `tfplugindocs` works using a configuration file named `.terraform-docs.yml`.

For example, the following YAML file customizes the generated documentat.0.0

```
provider:
  name: urlshortener
  description: Yet another URL shortener service.
  source: registry.terraform.io/<name>/urlshortener
  version: 1.0.0
```

This metadata helps ensure the documentation is generated accurately. However, most of the provider info will be inferred from the actual code and provider registration.

With this environment ready, we're now able to run `tfplugindocs` and begin generating high-quality documentation for the provider. In the next section, we'll use this setup to create documentation files and customize them for resources such as `shorten`.

Generating documentation for a resource

When writing documentation for a Terraform provider, it is important to clearly describe each resource the provider offers so users know how to use it correctly.

This section explains how documentation is generated for a typical resource by showing how the descriptions written in the schema translate into user-friendly documentation. We'll see how the resource definition in code becomes part of the final generated Markdown file, and how we can enhance this documentation further with custom usage examples. We will begin documenting an example resource.

Here's a simplified schema for the `shorten` resource:

```
func resourceShortURL() *schema.Resource {
  return &schema.Resource{
    Create: resourceShortURLCreate,
    Read:   resourceShortURLRead,
    Delete: resourceShortURLDelete,

    Schema: map[string]*schema.Schema{
      "long_url": {
        Type:        schema.TypeString,
        Required:    true,
        Description: "The original, long URL to be shortened.",
      },
      "short_code": {
        Type:        schema.TypeString,
        Computed:    true,
        Description: "The generated short code for the URL.",
      },
    },
  }
}
```

Notice the `Description` fields. These are the strings that `tfplugindocs` uses to populate the documentation. For example, the generated Markdown file for the `shorten` resource would include the following:

````
## shorten

### Example Usage

```hcl
resource "urlshortener_shorten" "example" {
 long_url = "https://www.example.com/some/long/path"
 }
```

### Argument Reference
````

```
long_url - (Required) The original, long URL to be shortened.

Attribute Reference

short_code - The generated short code for the URL.
```

We can also add custom examples by placing them in a file named after the resource, for example, `docs/resources/shorten.md`, and using special comment markers to preserve them, as in this example:

````
```markdown
<!-- example-start -->
resource "urlshortener_shorten" "with_tag" {
  long_url = "https://www.example.com/about"
}
<!-- example-end -->
````

These sections stay in place even after regenerating the docs, as long as they're marked correctly.

If we also define data sources in the provider, `tfplugindocs` works the same way.

For example, the following function defines a data source:

```
func dataSourceOriginalURL() *schema.Resource {
  return &schema.Resource{
    Read: dataSourceOriginalURLRead,
    Schema: map[string]*schema.Schema{
      "short_code": {
        Type:        schema.TypeString,
        Required:    true,
        Description: "The short code to look up.",
      },
      "long_url": {
        Type:        schema.TypeString,
        Computed:    true,
        Description: "The original long URL.",
      },
    },
  }
}
```
```

This would generate the following documentation:

````
## original_url

### Example Usage

```hcl
data "urlshortener_original_url" "lookup" {
  short_code = "abc123"
}
````

Having documentation automatically generated ensures accuracy, especially as the schemas evolve. We can regenerate documentation whenever the schema definitions change, so users always get the latest information. This saves time and eliminates the risk of forgetting to update documentation manually.

The output of `tfplugindocs` is structured to align with Terraform Registry requirements, making it easy to publish. If the provider is private, we can still generate docs the same way and host them wherever we want.

To get the best results from `tfplugindocs`, we should be thorough in the schema descriptions. Instead of vague descriptions such as `some value`, we should write clear and helpful sentences such as `The original, long URL to be shortened`. This extra clarity greatly improves the user experience.

Now that we know how to use tools to automatically create the documentation, it's time to focus on making it actually good. While a tool can build the basic files from the code, it's up to us to write clear descriptions and create helpful examples. The next section will show the best ways to write documentation that is easy for anyone to understand and use.

Best practices for writing provider documentation

Writing good documentation is just as important as writing good code, especially when the project is a Terraform provider. When users interact with the provider, they often start with the documentation. It should be clear, complete, and helpful.

In this section, we'll walk through best practices for documenting resources and data sources.
````

Organizing documentation effectively

Resource documentation in Terraform is organized around sections such as `Example Usage`, `Argument Reference`, `Attributes Reference`, `Import`, `Timeouts`, and so on. Users rely on these sections to quickly understand what a resource does, how to configure it, and what values they can expect in return.

Here's a minimal structure for the `urlshortener_shorten` resource:

```
resource "urlshortener_shorten" "example" {
  destination_url = "https://example.com/long-url"
  expiration_days = 15
}
```

In the documentation, this usage block belongs under the `Example Usage` section.

By following a clear and familiar structure, we can help users quickly find the information they need and reduce confusion when using the resource, making documentation more useful and much easier to navigate.

Writing a helpful example usage

The `Example Usage` section should reflect a real-world use case, ideally something immediately usable by someone copying and pasting. Avoid overly complex setups unless absolutely necessary. Clarity is the key:

````
## Example Usage
```hcl
resource "urlshortener_shorten" "default" {
  destination_url = "https://example.com/blog/post-1"
  expiration_days = 15
}
````

The preceding example shows how to create a short URL. Users can immediately understand the purpose and try it themselves.

Explaining arguments clearly

Every configurable field in the schema should be documented under `Argument Reference`. Users need to know the expected data type, if it's required, and a short description:

```
## Argument Reference
```
```

```
The following arguments are supported:

- `long_url` (Required) - The original URL that will be shortened. Must be
a valid HTTP or HTTPS URL.
- `expiration_days` (Optional) - Number of days until the short URL
expires. Defaults to 30.
- `custom_alias` (Optional) - A custom path segment for the short URL.
Must be unique if specified.
```

Avoid vague descriptions. Instead of saying `Specifies a URL`, say `The original URL that will be shortened`.

Documenting computed attributes

If the resource generates values such as IDs or timestamps, those should be listed in `Attributes Reference`. This helps users to understand what output to expect and how they can use it in other Terraform configurations:

```
## Attributes Reference

The following attributes are exported:

- `id` - The unique identifier of the short URL.
- `short_url` - The complete shortened URL (e.g., https://short.ly/
abc123).
- `created_at` - Timestamp of when the short URL was created.
```

These attributes are often used in outputs or passed into other modules.

Providing multiple examples

Sometimes one example isn't enough. If the resource supports advanced features such as authentication, custom headers, or different regions, consider offering multiple usage blocks:

````
### Example with Custom Alias

```hcl
resource "urlshortener_shorten" "custom" {
  destination_url = "https://example.com/faq"
  custom_alias    = "help"
}
````
````

This creates a short URL at `https://short.ly/help`, pointing to the FAQ.

Be explicit about defaults and optional behavior

Whenever a provider has optional fields, be clear about their defaults. Also, note whether there's any mutual exclusivity or dependency between fields:

```
- `expiration_days` (Optional) - Number of days until the short URL
expires. Defaults to 30. Set to 0 for no expiration.
```

Being clear about default values and optional behavior ensures that users do not make incorrect assumptions and can confidently configure the resource based on their needs, leading to fewer surprises during deployment.

Clarifying import behavior

If the resource supports importing, include an `Import` section:

````
## Import

Short URLs can be imported using the resource ID:

```sh
terraform import urlshortener_shorten.example short_alias
```
````

Including a clear and simple import example helps users understand how to bring existing infrastructure under Terraform management, making the resource more accessible and easier to adopt in real-world projects.

Keeping changelogs relevant to docs

While changelogs are typically a separate concern, it's helpful to link changes in behavior to the documentation. For example, if a new field was added in version 1.2.0, consider adding a note:

```
> Note: The `custom_alias` field was added in provider version 1.2.0.
```

Adding relevant changelog notes directly in the documentation helps users understand when features became available and encourages them to upgrade or adjust their configurations based on the provider version they are using.

Using consistent terminology

Be consistent across all resources and data sources. If you call something a "short URL" in one place, avoid switching to "alias" or "link" elsewhere unless they refer to different concepts.

Providing complete context in data sources

Data sources often return useful details about existing resources. The documentation should include input parameters and all exported attributes:

```
Example:

data "urlshortener_shorten" "by_alias" {
  custom_alias = "docs"
}
```

This allows users to fetch an existing short URL with a known alias.

Using comments in code samples when helpful

Comments in examples can help users understand why certain choices are made:

```
resource "urlshortener_shorten" "expiring" {
  destination_url = "https://example.com/limited-offer"
  expiration_days = 3 # Offer ends soon
}
```

Adding comments to code samples makes the documentation easier to follow, especially for new users, and can reduce confusion by explaining the purpose or reasoning behind specific values or configuration choices.

Avoiding redundancy across resources

If multiple resources share common behavior, for example, authentication, consider referring to a shared documentation section instead of repeating the same text.

Keeping documentation concise and avoiding repetition not only makes it easier to maintain but also helps users focus on the differences between resources without being distracted by repeated information.

Validating with real users

Once documentation is written, test it. Ask someone unfamiliar with the provider to follow the examples. Their confusion is the clue for improvement.

By following these best practices, we can ensure that the Terraform provider's documentation is clear, helpful, and usable for both new users and seasoned engineers. Writing great documentation takes time, but it pays off by making the provider easier to adopt and integrate into real-world infrastructure.

Next, we'll dive into how to version the provider correctly and maintain a clear changelog so users always know what's changed and when.

Implementing provider versioning and changelogs

Versioning and changelog management help users understand what has changed between versions, manage upgrade risks, and stay informed about new features, improvements, and fixes. In this section, we'll explore how to implement proper versioning using Git tags, follow semantic versioning practices, and maintain a changelog that is clear, complete, and consistent.

Understanding semantic versioning

Terraform providers follow semantic versioning (`semver`), which uses a three-part format:

```
MAJOR.MINOR.PATCH
```

Let's see what these do:

- `MAJOR` changes break backward compatibility
- `MINOR` changes introduce new features in a backward-compatible way
- `PATCH` changes are for backward-compatible bug fixes

Here are some examples:

- `v1.0.0` might be the first stable release
- `v1.1.0` could add a new feature
- `v1.1.1` would fix a bug

Understanding how semantic versioning works helps both provider developers and users know what to expect from each release, making upgrades safer and communication clearer.

Using Git tags to version the provider

Git tags represent versions of the code. When it's ready to release a new version of the provider, just create a new Git tag. This tag will be used by the Terraform Registry to track the release.

Let's say we're developing `terraform-provider-urlshortener`. After finishing development for the first version, we commit the latest code and create a tag:

```
git tag v1.0.0
git push origin v1.0.0
```

This marks the v1.0.0 release. When the tag is pushed, the Terraform Registry will detect it and trigger a build.

If we later fix a bug in the provider's logic for resolving short URLs, we can tag a patch release:

```
git tag v1.0.1
git push origin v1.0.1
```

Here are some example version changes and what justifies them:

- **Major version change**:

  ```
  schema.Resource{
    Schema: map[string]*schema.Schema{
      "short_url": {
        Type:     schema.TypeString,
        Required: true,
      },
      "destination_url": {
        Type:     schema.TypeString,
        Required: true,
      },
    },
  }
  ```

  If we rename `destination_url` to `long_url`, it breaks backward compatibility. We would need to bump the version to `v2.0.0`.

- **Minor version change**: Let's introduce a new optional field called `description`:

  ```
  "description": {
    Type:     schema.TypeString,
  ```

```
    Optional: true,
  },
```

That's a non-breaking feature, so it would be `v1.1.0`.

- **Patch version change**: If the existing `short_url` logic has a bug, and we fix the regular expression used to validate it, that's a patch:

```
  "short_url": {
    ValidateFunc: validation.StringMatch(regexp.MustCompile(
      `^[a-zA-Z0-9]{6}$`), "must be 6 alphanumeric characters"
    ),
  },
```

Fixing the regex without changing the input format would be `v1.0.1`.

Now that we've seen how to version the provider using Git tags and follow semantic versioning principles to communicate the nature of each release, the next important step is keeping a clear record of what has changed between versions. Version numbers alone don't tell the full story; users and contributors need an easy way to understand what's new, what's fixed, and what might affect existing usage.

This is where a well-maintained changelog becomes important. By writing clear and consistent changelog entries for every release, we not only help users stay informed but also make the provider feel more professional and trustworthy.

Writing a changelog

The changelog should document what was changed in each version. It's better to use a format such as *Keep a Changelog* (`https://keepachangelog.com/`), which encourages readability and consistency.

Place the changelog in a `CHANGELOG.md` file at the root of the project.

Here is an example changelog:

```
# Changelog

All notable changes to this project will be documented in this file.

## [1.1.0] - 2025-06-01
### Added
```

```
- Support for `description` field in the `url_mapping` resource

## [1.0.1] - 2025-05-15
### Fixed
- Validation logic for `short_url` regex pattern

## [1.0.0] - 2025-05-01
### Added
- Initial release of `url_mapping` resource with `short_url` and `long_
url` fields
```

This changelog format clearly separates different releases and categorizes changes as `Added`, `Changed`, `Deprecated`, `Removed`, `Fixed`, or `Security`.

It is also a good idea to include an `[Unreleased]` section at the top of the file. This section collects all new changes as the work progresses, making it easier to review and finalize them before creating a new release.

To add it, simply include a heading such as `## [Unreleased]` above the latest release in the changelog and list any ongoing updates there until a new version is published.

Automating changelog creation

While changelogs can be written manually, it's helpful to automate generating them from Git history using tools. Popular options include `git-chglog` (`https://github.com/git-chglog/git-chglog`), `conventional-changelog` (`https://github.com/conventional-changelog/conventional-changelog`), `release-please` (`https://github.com/googleapis/release-please`), and `goreleaser` (`https://github.com/goreleaser/goreleaser`).

Recently, AI-based tools have started to gain popularity as well, where a changelog can be generated from Git diffs using large language models to summarize the main changes in natural language.

For best results, follow conventional commit messages such as the following:

```
feat: add description field to url_mapping
fix: correct regex for short_url validation
```

These can then be automatically parsed into changelog entries.

Versioning and Terraform Registry

When publishing the provider to the Terraform Registry, it expects tags to follow semantic versioning and begin with `v` (for example, `v1.0.0`). The registry uses the GitHub release tags to track versions and display changelogs to users.

Include release notes in GitHub releases to help users decide whether to upgrade and how.

An example of GitHub release is the following:

```
Release v1.1.0

What's New:
- You can now add a `description` to your shortened URLs.
```

This message becomes the release description shown on the Terraform Registry.

Keeping the changelog up to date

It's best to update the changelog with each pull request that introduces a version-worthy change. This ensures that the changelog stays accurate and prevents delays during release time.

Versioning and changelog practices form the foundation of a trustworthy and user-friendly Terraform provider. With semantic versioning, users know exactly when a change might impact them. With well-written changelogs, they know exactly what changed and why it matters. Tagging releases properly and maintaining documentation of changes not only improves the development workflow but also makes life easier for the community that depends on the provider.

Publishing to the public Terraform Registry

Publishing a provider to the public Terraform Registry is the final step in making it accessible to the world. This process involves understanding the registry requirements, preparing the GitHub repository properly, and ensuring that the provider is versioned and tagged correctly.

In this section, we will walk through the complete lifecycle of publishing the provider, focusing on the tools, formats, and practices required to meet the public registry standards.

Understanding the registry requirements

The Terraform Registry requires all public providers to follow specific conventions. Providers must be hosted on GitHub under a repository name that follows the `terraform-provider-<NAME>` pattern. For the URL shortener, the repository name would be `terraform-provider-urlshortener`.

The main Go module must be rooted at the repository's root, and the repository must contain a `main.go` file that initializes and serves the provider using the `plugin.Serve` function from `terraform-plugin-sdk`.

Each release must use a Git tag that starts with `v` (for example, `v1.0.0`) and include the compiled binaries in `.zip` files named by platform, such as `terraform-provider-urlshortener_1.0.0_linux_amd64.zip`.

Each release also needs a manifest file, a SHA256 `sums` file, and a **GNU Privacy Guard (GPG)** signature of that `sums` file. The manifest tells the Registry which Terraform protocol version the provider supports, and the GPG signature allows HashiCorp to verify that the release was created by a trusted publisher. Before the first release, the provider's public GPG key must be uploaded to the Terraform Registry account.

After the first publish, new releases are discovered automatically by the Registry when tagged and released on GitHub. Tools such as `GoReleaser` can automate building, packaging, and signing releases. This setup ensures that every version follows Terraform's validation rules and can be safely consumed by users.

Registering the provider

Terraform uses a GitHub topic to discover public providers. Add the `terraform-provider` topic to the GitHub repository.

Also, ensure that the repository is public and follows the naming convention. After a few minutes, the Terraform Registry will pick it up automatically.

No manual publishing is needed. The registry fetches metadata from the GitHub repo, reads the versions, and builds the documentation site based on your docs and examples.

Validating the provider manifest

The registry will expect a proper provider manifest in the provider binary. This includes the required version, name, and provider definition. If the provider fails to load or crashes, the registry won't be able to index it.

Build the provider with the correct Go environment to produce the proper binary:

```
GOOS=linux GOARCH=amd64 go build -o terraform-provider-urlshortener
```

Zip the binary and upload it as part of the GitHub release.

Registry UI and metadata

Once the release is live, the Registry UI will show the provider. Users will be able to see tabs such as `Overview`, `Inputs`, `Outputs`, `Resources`, and `Examples`. These are automatically generated from the `docs/` directory.

For instance, the `docs/resources/shorten.md` file will be rendered under the `Resources` section for the `urlshortener_shorten` resource.

Managing multiple versions

Once the first release is published, it's possible to create new versions by repeating the tagging and releasing steps. The registry will show available versions on the UI and allow users to select the version they want to use.

Always test releases with the following:

```
terraform init
```

Use a sample config with the `required_providers` block:

```
terraform {
  required_providers {
    urlshortener = {
      source  = "enginpolat/urlshortener"
      version = "~> 1.0"
    }
  }
}
```

Publishing to the Terraform Registry is the gateway to sharing the provider with everyone. By following the expected structure, using semantic versioning, tagging releases properly, and writing solid documentation, the provider becomes discoverable and maintainable.

The URL shortener example shows how a simple but useful provider can be structured, versioned, and released. This pattern can be repeated for any other provider you build, helping you contribute to the Terraform ecosystem in a sustainable and developer-friendly way.

Publishing to a private Terraform registry for internal consumption

In this section, the focus is on how organizations can publish their Terraform providers privately instead of sharing them publicly. Some providers are designed for internal systems or private APIs, and publishing them to the public Terraform Registry is not always appropriate.

Many organizations build internal providers for private APIs or infrastructure, and prefer to publish them in a private registry instead of the public Terraform Registry.

A private registry allows teams to control access, enforce internal standards, and keep sensitive logic or credentials out of public view.

Private provider publishing works much like public publishing but requires hosting the registry within the organization's infrastructure or using a supported service such as Terraform Cloud or Terraform Enterprise. These platforms include built-in support for private registries.

For example, when using Terraform Cloud, a provider can be uploaded under the organization's private registry with versioned releases. Users within that organization can then reference the provider as follows:

```
terraform {
  required_providers {
    urlshortener = {
      source  = "app.terraform.io/<my-org>/<namespace>/urlshortener"
      version = "1.0.0"
    }
  }
}
```

Terraform will automatically authenticate with Terraform Cloud and download the provider binary securely.

For organizations that manage their own private registry, Terraform supports a self-hosted registry structure following the **Terraform Registry Protocol** (`https://developer.hashicorp.com/terraform/internals/module-registry-protocol`). This typically involves serving version metadata and provider binaries from internal storage, such as an Azure blob, Amazon S3 bucket, or internal web service.

Using a private registry provides the same versioning, documentation, and discovery experience as the public one, but scoped to trusted users. This approach helps large teams safely distribute providers across environments while maintaining full control over who can access and update them.

Summary

Publishing a Terraform provider to the public Registry is the final and most important step in making it available to others. To do this, we need to make sure the provider is hosted on GitHub with the right naming format, uses semantic versioning, and includes a main entry point that registers the provider properly. The Registry discovers the provider automatically if the GitHub repository is public and tagged correctly, meaning there's no need to upload anything manually.

To make the provider usable and trustworthy, it should have proper documentation, version tags, and a clear changelog. Users rely on version numbers to know when something has changed, and changelogs help them understand what was added, fixed, or removed. Using Git tags for each release, writing meaningful release notes, and including detailed documentation files all help ensure the provider works well with the Terraform Registry's UI and backend systems.

In the URL shortener example, we walked through how to document a provider, prepare it for release, tag it with versions, and publish it. This process not only helps others discover and use the provider but also builds trust and consistency in how it evolves. Once published, users can easily integrate your provider with Terraform by referencing it by name and version, making it a reusable and reliable part of their infrastructure code.

In the next chapter, we will look at how to automate testing by adding it to CI/CD pipelines. You'll see how tools such as GitHub Actions can run the tests automatically whenever new code is pushed to the repo, helping to catch issues early and keep the infrastructure reliable.

10

Automating Testing in Pipelines

Automating testing in **continuous integration and continuous deployment** (**CI/CD**) pipelines is crucial for ensuring the reliability of the Terraform provider. By integrating unit and integration tests into the pipeline, developers can verify that their provider correctly implements Terraform's expected behavior, preventing regressions and bugs before deployment. Automated testing eliminates the need for manual verification, reducing human error and allowing for faster iterations. Without automation, testing provider code would be inconsistent and time-consuming, making it harder to maintain stable and predictable behavior across different releases.

Furthermore, running tests in a CI/CD pipeline ensures that every change to the provider code is validated across multiple environments and use cases. By leveraging tools such as GitHub Actions, teams can automatically execute tests, generate reports, and detect failures early in the development cycle. This helps maintain high-quality provider functionality while accelerating the release process. Automated testing also improves collaboration by providing immediate feedback on code changes, allowing teams to fix issues proactively and ship more reliable Terraform providers.

This chapter focuses on testing the Terraform provider itself, rather than testing general Terraform configurations. Provider tests verify the behavior of the custom provider code, while configuration tests check user-written Terraform files.

In this chapter, we will cover the following topics:

- Setting up GitHub Actions to run tests automatically for Terraform code
- Adding unit tests and integration tests to the CI/CD pipeline
- Making sure tests run reliably across different environments
- Generating test reports to understand results clearly
- Handling test failures to fix problems quickly and keep the pipeline healthy

Setting up GitHub Actions for Terraform testing

In this section, we will explore how to automate the testing of Terraform provider code using GitHub Actions. By integrating unit and integration tests into a CI/CD pipeline, we ensure that our Terraform provider remains stable, reliable, and free from regressions. We will cover setting up workflows, running tests, handling failures, and ensuring smooth automation.

Understanding GitHub Actions

GitHub Actions is a powerful automation tool that allows us to create workflows for CI and continuous deployment. For Terraform providers, GitHub Actions can do the following:

- Automatically run unit tests when code changes
- Perform integration tests against a test Terraform configuration
- Generate test reports and handle failures
- Ensure Terraform provider code remains stable across releases

Here is an example of a simple GitHub Actions workflow that runs tests whenever code is pushed to the repository:

```
name: Terraform Provider Tests

on:
  push:
    branches:
      - main
  pull_request:
    branches:
      - main

jobs:
  test:
    runs-on: ubuntu-latest

    steps:
      - name: Checkout code
        uses: actions/checkout@v4

      - name: Set up Go
```

```
        uses: actions/setup-go@v5
        with:
          go-version: 1.24

      - name: Install dependencies
        run: go mod tidy

      - name: Run unit tests
        run: go test ./...
```

This workflow does the following:

- Triggers on push and pull requests to the main branch
- Runs on an `ubuntu-latest` machine
- Checks out the code
- Sets up Go
- Installs dependencies
- Runs all Go tests

Running tests in GitHub Actions with a build matrix

CI helps ensure that a Terraform provider works reliably across different Go versions and environments. GitHub Actions makes this easy by using a build matrix, which lets the same workflow run tests on multiple Go versions at the same time. This approach gives early warnings if a change breaks compatibility.

The following example shows a simple GitHub Actions workflow that uses a matrix with two Go versions. We can expand this pattern later for more operating systems or additional versions:

```
name: Provider Tests

on:
  push:
    branches: [ main ]
  pull_request:

jobs:
  test:
    runs-on: ubuntu-latest
```

```
    strategy:
      matrix:
        go-version: [ '1.21', '1.22' ]

    steps:
      - uses: actions/checkout@v4

      - name: Set up Go
        uses: actions/setup-go@v5
        with:
          go-version: ${{ matrix.go-version }}

      - name: Install dependencies
        run: go mod download

      - name: Run tests
        run: go test ./... -v
```

This workflow checks out the repository, installs the correct Go version from the matrix, downloads dependencies, and runs the full test suite. Each Go version in the matrix runs in parallel, which helps catch compatibility issues early and keeps the provider stable across upgrades.

Setting up a Terraform provider for GitHub Actions

To automate testing, we must ensure our Terraform provider is structured correctly. A common folder structure for a provider may look like this:

```
terraform-provider-urlshortener/
|— .github/workflows/    # GitHub Actions workflows
|— internal/             # Internal provider logic
|— provider.go           # Provider definition
|— resources.go          # Resource implementations
|— main_test.go          # Test entry point
|— go.mod                # Go module dependencies
|— go.sum                # Dependency checksums
```

By having a correctly structured folder layout, we can do the following:

- Easily integrate with CI/CD tools such as GitHub Actions
- Keep provider logic and tests well separated and maintainable
- Ensure that Go tooling (such as `go test`) and dependency management (`go mod`) work smoothly
- Set a foundation for the testing automation steps that follow, making the project easier to test, scale, and collaborate on

Including code coverage in custom Terraform provider projects is very important because it helps us understand how much of the provider logic is being tested through automated tests.

When we build a provider, we want to make sure that every function, edge case, and error condition works as expected. Code coverage tools tell us which parts of the code are being tested and which are not, so we can identify and fix gaps in our test suite.

This is especially valuable in infrastructure code, where undetected bugs can lead to unexpected resource changes or failed deployments. By generating and reporting coverage in CI/CD pipelines, we ensure that test quality is continuously monitored and visible to everyone.

Over time, this helps us build confidence in the provider and avoid regressions. Including a test coverage report also makes it easier to track improvements and helps reviewers quickly assess the quality of changes.

Let's update the workflow to include test reports:

```
    - name: Run unit tests with coverage
        run: go test ./... -coverprofile=coverage.out

      - name: Upload coverage report
        uses: actions/upload-artifact@v3
        with:
          name: coverage-report
          path: coverage.out
```

Generating and publishing a test coverage report in the CI/CD pipeline not only helps ensure that the Terraform provider is well tested but also gives the team clear visibility into how much of the code is covered by tests, making it easier to catch issues early, maintain code quality, and confidently release new updates.

Running unit and integration tests in CI/CD pipelines

To make sure the Terraform provider works correctly in real-world scenarios, it is important to run both **unit tests** and **integration tests** automatically in the CI/CD pipeline. Unit tests help check individual functions and small parts of the code in isolation, while integration tests verify that the provider works as expected when used with actual Terraform configurations and possibly real APIs.

In this section, we will walk through how to handle integration tests by setting up Terraform commands such as `init`, `validate`, and `apply` in GitHub Actions. We will also show how to manage test failures by printing logs when something goes wrong, which helps with quick debugging.

You will learn how to use the official Terraform plugin test framework to write proper integration tests, and how to run them using Go's testing tags. Finally, we will explain how to skip flaky tests in certain conditions and how to tag tests so that only relevant ones run in the pipeline.

Validating Terraform configuration in CI/CD

In CI/CD pipelines, it is important to automatically check and apply the Terraform configurations to make sure everything works correctly. The following steps show how to initialize the Terraform environment, validate the configuration files to catch any errors, and then apply the configuration to create or update resources without needing manual approval:

```
- name: Initialize Terraform
  run: terraform init

- name: Validate Terraform Configuration
  run: terraform validate

- name: Apply Terraform Configuration
  run: terraform apply -auto-approve
```

This workflow does the following:

- **Initializes Terraform**: It sets up everything Terraform needs to start working on your project
- **Validates the configuration**: It checks the Terraform files to make sure they are written correctly and that there are no mistakes
- **Applies the configuration**: It runs the Terraform command to create or update the cloud resources based on the configuration, doing this automatically without asking for confirmation

Running these steps in an automated pipeline helps catch problems early and ensures that the infrastructure changes are applied consistently and reliably. This process makes it easier to maintain and deploy Terraform configurations as part of the development workflow.

Managing test failures in GitHub Actions

When running tests in GitHub Actions, it is important to handle test failures properly so we can quickly find out what went wrong and fix issues efficiently. This section shows how to manage test failures and get useful information from logs during the CI/CD process:

```
- name: Fail on test failure
  run: |
    go test ./... || exit 1

- name: Print logs on failure
  if: failure()
  run: cat terraform.log
```

This workflow does the following:

- Runs all the Go tests, and if any test fails, it stops the workflow immediately with an error
- If the tests fail, it automatically prints the contents of the `terraform.log` file, so it'll be possible to see what caused the failure
- This setup helps quickly identify problems by showing detailed logs when something goes wrong during testing

By setting up these steps, we make sure that any test failures are clearly reported and that helpful logs are available to speed up troubleshooting and improve overall test reliability.

Implementing integration tests

To make sure the Terraform provider works correctly in real-world scenarios, we need to write integration tests that simulate how users would actually use the provider with real or mock infrastructure. This section explains how to write such tests using the Terraform framework SDK.

```
func TestAccURLShortenerResource_basic(t *testing.T) {
    t := schema.TestCase{
        PreCheck: func() { testAccPreCheck(t) },
        Providers: testAccProviders,
        Steps: []schema.TestStep{
            {
```

```
                Config: testAccURLShortenerResourceConfig(
                    https://example.com
                ),
                Check: schema.ComposeTestCheckFunc(
                    schema.TestCheckResourceAttr(
                        "urlshortener_link.test",
                        "original_url",
                        "https://example.com"
                    ),
                ),
            },
        },
    }
    schema.Test(t, &t)
}
```

This workflow does the following:

- Defines a test function that checks whether the Terraform provider can create a resource correctly
- Uses the `testAccPreCheck` function to make sure any required setup is done before the test runs
- Sets up the test with the provider and a Terraform configuration that creates a URL shortener resource pointing to `https://example.com`
- Checks that the `original_url` attribute in the created resource matches `https://example.com`
- Runs the test using the Terraform framework SDK's testing tools

To run integration tests for the Terraform provider, we use the Go testing tool with a specific build tag that tells it to include only the integration tests. These tests often interact with real APIs or mock services, so they are separated from unit tests for better control.

To run only the integration tests, we can use the `go test -tags=integration ./...` command in the terminal. This tells Go to look through all directories (`./...`) and execute any tests that are marked with the `//go:build integration` tag.

This approach makes it easy to run just the integration tests without triggering every single test in the project. This is especially helpful in CI/CD pipelines where we may want to run unit tests quickly on every commit but only run slower integration tests during merge or release stages.

We've already seen how to write integration tests using the Terraform framework SDK and how to run them locally with the `` `go test -tags=integration ./...` `` command.

Now we want to make sure these tests run every time code is pushed to the repository, so we can catch any problems before they affect users. By adding integration tests to the GitHub Actions workflow, we create an automated safety net that verifies the provider works correctly with real or mock infrastructure on every code change.

This is especially helpful for integration tests because they can catch issues that unit tests might miss, like authentication problems, API changes, or incorrect resource configurations.

Let's add the integration test step to the CI/CD pipeline:

```
- name: Run integration tests
  run: go test -tags=integration ./...
```

Including this step in the CI/CD pipeline helps automate the testing of real-world scenarios, so any issues with the provider's functionality are caught early. It also ensures consistency by running the same test logic in both local and automated environments.

Marking tests as skipped

Sometimes, certain tests may be flaky, unreliable, or take a long time to run. For example, they might fail intermittently due to network issues, API rate limits, or other factors that are not caused by bugs in the code itself. Running these tests in every CI/CD run can slow down feedback loops or cause confusion when builds fail for reasons unrelated to actual code problems.

To manage this, we can conditionally skip such tests using Go's testing tools.

In the example shown, the `TestFlakyFeature` function is an integration test that we might not want to run during a quick test cycle. Inside the function, we use `testing.Short()` to check whether the test suite is running in **short mode**. This is a built-in method in Go's testing framework that returns `true` when tests are executed with the `-short` flag, as follows: `go test -short`.

This flag signals to the Go runtime that the developer or CI/CD pipeline wants to run a quicker subset of tests, usually only the most critical unit tests:

```
func TestFlakyFeature(t *testing.T) {
    if testing.Short() {
        t.Skip("Skipping flaky test in short mode")
    }
    // Test logic here
}
```

When `testing.Short()` returns `true`, the code calls `t.Skip()` to skip the test. The `t.Skip()` function stops the current test immediately and marks it as **skipped**. It also prints a message explaining why the test was skipped, which helps maintain transparency in test reports.

This approach is helpful for large projects that include a mix of fast and slow tests, and it allows teams to maintain a balance between speed and test coverage during different stages of development or automation.

Tagging and running tests based on tags

Tagging in Go is a way to give special instructions to the Go tools, usually by adding extra information to the code without changing how it runs. Some tags are used to tell other tools how to handle data, and some are used to tell the Go compiler how to build the program.

One important kind of tag is the `//go:build` tag, which goes at the very top of a Go file. This tag tells Go when it should include that file while building the program.

For example, if you write `//go:build windows`, it means "only use this file if the program is being built for *Windows*." If you write `//go:build linux || darwin`, it means "use this file if the program is being built for *Linux or macOS*."

This is very useful when you need different code for different systems, such as when certain features only work on Windows or behave differently on Linux.

Instead of writing a lot of `if` statements in the code, we can put system-specific code in separate files and use the `//go:build` tag to tell Go which file to use. Even though it looks like a comment, it's actually a special instruction that Go understands and uses during the build process. This helps keep the code clean, organized, and easier to maintain, especially when building programs that run on many different systems.

Tagging tests allows us to selectively run specific types of tests, such as unit tests, integration tests, or performance tests. This is useful in CI/CD pipelines to ensure faster feedback loops.

Platform-specific tagging

We can use build tags to write tests (or any Go code) that only run on specific operating systems such as Linux, Windows, or macOS. This is useful when the provider or integration behaves differently depending on the platform:

```
//go:build linux

package provider_test
```

```
import "testing"

func TestLinuxOnlyFeature(t *testing.T) {
    t.Log("Running on Linux only")
}
```

Architecture-specific tagging

We can also target tests to specific CPU architectures such as **amd64** or **arm64**. This is especially helpful when writing low-level integration tests or provider code that interacts with architecture-sensitive binaries or containers.

```
//go:build arm64

package provider_test

import "testing"

func TestARM64SpecificLogic(t *testing.T) {
    t.Log("This test runs only on ARM64 architecture")
}
```

This test will only execute when running on an ARM64 processor. If the test suite runs on an Intel or AMD processor (amd64), Go will skip this test entirely because the build tag doesn't match the system architecture. This is useful in CI/CD pipelines where different runners may use different architectures, or when team members use different types of computers.

For instance, if a developer with an Apple Silicon Mac writes code that uses ARM64-specific features, they can write a test like this to verify it works correctly on their machine, while the same test suite can still run successfully on teammates' Intel-based computers without causing failures.

Custom tagging for unit and integration tests

Custom tags let us label the tests by purpose, such as **unit**, **integration**, or **perf**. These tags give us fine control over which tests run in different CI/CD stages.

```
//go:build integration

package provider_test

import "testing"
```

```
func TestAccCustomIntegration(t *testing.T) {
    t.Log("This is an integration test")
}
```

This test will only run when the `` `go test -tags=integration` `` command is executed. Without the `` `-tags=integration` `` flag, Go will skip this test entirely, treating it as if it doesn't exist. This separation is important because integration tests typically take longer to run and may require external services or cloud resources, while unit tests are fast and self-contained.

By using custom tags, development teams can run quick unit tests on every code change for immediate feedback, and reserve slower integration tests for important stages like pull request reviews or production deployments.

Combining multiple tags

We can combine multiple tags using logical `AND` and `OR` operations to refine test conditions even further.

Here is an example of an `AND` operation:

```
//go:build linux && integration

package provider_test

import "testing"

func TestLinuxIntegration(t *testing.T) {
    t.Log("Runs only on Linux during integration tests")
}
```

Here is an example of an `OR` operation:

```
//go:build linux || windows

package provider_test

import "testing"

func TestLinuxOrWindows(t *testing.T) {
    t.Log("Runs on either Linux or Windows")
}
```

Negative tagging

We can exclude a test from being compiled for specific tags using negation:

```
//go:build !windows
package provider_test
import "testing"
func TestNotOnWindows(t *testing.T) {
    t.Log("This test does not run on Windows")
}
```

Go allows us to run tests that are conditionally compiled based on `//go:build` tags using the `-tags` flag in the go `test` command.

Here is how to run only integration tests:

```
go test -tags=integration ./...
```

Here is how to run only unit tests:

```
go test -tags=unit ./...
```

Here is how to run multiple tagged tests combined:

```
go test -tags="integration linux" ./...
```

Here is how to run all tests:

```
go test ./...
```

By structuring tests with appropriate tags, you can optimize CI/CD workflows and ensure relevant tests run based on the context of the changes.

Generating reports and managing test failures

Effective testing involves not only running tests but also capturing meaningful test reports and handling failures efficiently. Reports help developers analyze test results, identify patterns, and debug issues quickly.

Go's built-in `testing` package provides output in a human-readable format, but it lacks structured reporting. To generate detailed test reports, we can use `gotestsum`, which formats test output and supports JUnit XML reports:

```
go install gotest.tools/gotestsum@latest
```

Run the tests and generate a JUnit XML report:

```
gotestsum --junitfile report.xml --format short-verbose
```

Modify the GitHub Actions workflow to generate and store test reports:

```
jobs:
  test:
    runs-on: ubuntu-latest
    steps:
      - name: Checkout Code
        uses: actions/checkout@v4

      - name: Setup Go
        uses: actions/setup-go@v5
        with:
          go-version: 1.24

      - name: Install gotestsum
        run: go install gotest.tools/gotestsum@latest

      - name: Run Tests and Generate Reports
        run: gotestsum --junitfile report.xml --format short-verbose

      - name: Upload Test Report
        uses: actions/upload-artifact@v3
        with:
          name: test-report
          path: report.xml
```

Generating structured test reports and managing failures properly not only improves developer productivity but also helps teams catch issues earlier and build more reliable Terraform providers over time.

Notifying developers of failures

Test failures should be immediately visible to developers so they can take prompt action. In this section, we will explore different ways to notify developers when a Terraform provider test fails, including the following:

- GitHub Actions' built-in notifications (commenting on pull requests, setting commit statuses)
- Sending email notifications using GitHub Actions

Commenting on a pull request when tests fail

We can post a comment on the associated pull request to alert developers about test failures:

```
    - name: Comment on PR if Tests Fail
      if: failure() && github.event_name == 'pull_request'
      run: |
        curl -s -X POST -H "Authorization: token ${{ \
        secrets.GITHUB_TOKEN }}" \
        -H "Accept: application/vnd.github.v3+json" \
        https://api.github.com/repos/${{ github.repository }}/issues/ \
        ${{ github.event.pull_request.number }}/comments \
        -d '{"body": "**Test Failure Detected!** Please check the \
        CI/CD logs for details."}'
```

This step runs only if a test fails (`if: failure()`). It uses the GitHub API to post a comment on the pull request, informing developers about the failure.

This workflow does the following:

- It uses `curl` to send a `POST` request to the GitHub API
- The `-s` flag makes the command run in silent mode, so it won't output progress or errors
- The `Authorization` header uses the GitHub-provided `GITHUB_TOKEN` secret to authenticate the request
- The `Accept` header specifies that we are using version 3 of the GitHub API
- The request is sent to the pull request's comment endpoint, targeting the current pull request based on its number
- The `-d` option sends a JSON payload with a comment body saying: `"**Test Failure Detected!** Please check the CI/CD logs for details."`
- The result is that GitHub posts a comment on the pull request to notify the developer of a test failure in the CI/CD pipeline

Adding a comment to the pull request when tests fail makes it easier to notice problems quickly, stay informed, and take action without having to dig into the logs or check the workflow manually. This is especially helpful in larger teams where multiple people may be working on the same repository and might not immediately notice failed checks in the **GitHub Actions** tab. Posting a visible comment on the pull request brings attention to the issue directly where the code changes are being reviewed.

Setting the commit status to failed

If the test fails, we can explicitly set a commit status to indicate failure:

```
    - name: Mark Commit as Failed
      if: failure()
      run: |
        curl -s -X POST -H "Authorization: \
        token ${{ secrets.GITHUB_TOKEN }}" \
        -H "Accept: application/vnd.github.v3+json" \
        https://api.github.com/repos/${{ github.repository }} \
        /statuses/${{ github.sha }} \
        -d '{"state": "failure", "context": "CI/CD Pipeline", \
        "description": "Tests failed. Check logs."}'
```

This ensures that in the GitHub UI, the commit is marked with a ✖ (`failure`) status, making it obvious that tests did not pass.

Marking the commit status as failed makes it visually clear in the GitHub interface that something went wrong with the build or the test process. This helps reviewers, maintainers, and contributors quickly spot issues without needing to open logs or dig into the **Actions** tab. It also prevents merging code that has known problems, especially when required status checks are enforced in the repository settings.

Sending email notifications via GitHub Actions

GitHub Actions allows sending emails using GitHub secrets and SMTP. Here's how you can send an email notification when tests fail.

Add your email provider's SMTP credentials as GitHub secrets:

- `SMTP_SERVER` (for example, `smtp.gmail.com`)
- `SMTP_USERNAME` (your email)
- `SMTP_PASSWORD` (use an app password if using Gmail/Outlook)

The following is an example of a GitHub Actions step that sends an email notification on failure:

```
- name: Send Email on Failure
  if: failure()
  run: |
    echo "Subject: Terraform Provider Test Failure" > email.txt
    echo "From: ${{ secrets.SMTP_USERNAME }}" >> email.txt
    echo "To: dev-team@example.com" >> email.txt
    echo "" >> email.txt
    echo "The CI/CD pipeline has failed. Please check the logs in
    GitHub Actions." >> email.txt
    sendmail -S ${{ secrets.SMTP_SERVER }} -au
    ${{ secrets.SMTP_USERNAME }} -ap
    ${{ secrets.SMTP_PASSWORD }} dev-team@example.com < email.txt
```

This script does the following:

- Composes an email with the subject `Terraform Provider Test Failure`
- Sends it to `dev-team@example.com` using the configured SMTP server

Sending email notifications makes sure that the right people know immediately when something goes wrong in the pipeline. It reduces the risk of unnoticed failures and allows the team to respond quickly without needing to constantly check GitHub.

Summary

In this chapter, we explored how to automate testing for Terraform provider code using GitHub Actions. We started by setting up a CI/CD pipeline to run tests automatically whenever code changes are pushed. This ensures that every change is validated before merging, reducing the risk of introducing errors. We also configured our workflow to run both unit and integration tests, allowing us to verify that individual components and real-world interactions with APIs work as expected.

Unit tests help confirm that individual functions in the provider behave correctly, while integration tests validate how the provider interacts with external services. By tagging and organizing tests, we made it possible to run different sets of tests based on the scenario, ensuring efficient and targeted test execution. This structured approach helps catch issues early and maintain high-quality provider code.

Finally, we covered generating reports and managing test failures. We learned how to capture test results in structured reports, notify developers about failures using GitHub's built-in features, and send alerts through emails. These notification mechanisms ensure that teams can quickly respond to failures and keep their Terraform provider reliable. By automating testing and failure management, we improve code quality and streamline the development workflow.

The next chapter will show how to connect Go applications with AWS services using the AWS SDK. You'll learn how to upload files to S3, manage EC2 instances, and interact with cloud resources directly from the code.

Part 3

Go for Cloud Services

Part 3 focuses on using Go to build applications that run natively in the cloud. It begins by showing how to integrate Go applications with major cloud platforms such as Azure and AWS, covering authentication, working with SDKs, and managing cloud resources such as storage and virtual machines.

It then moves into serverless computing, demonstrating how to build, deploy, and manage event-driven functions using Azure Functions and AWS Lambda. It shows how Go can simplify cloud automation, improve scalability, and reduce operational overhead.

Together, the following chapters help you understand how to apply Go in real-world cloud environments, from SDK-based integrations to fully serverless applications.

This part of the book includes the following chapters:

- *Chapter 11, Integrating Go Applications with the AWS SDK*
- *Chapter 12, Integrating Go Applications with the Azure SDK*
- *Chapter 13, Serverless Computing Using AWS Lambda*
- *Chapter 14, Serverless Computing Using Azure Functions*

11

Integrating Go Applications with the AWS SDK

Integrating Go applications with the AWS SDK is a powerful way to build cloud-native software that can programmatically manage infrastructure and services at scale. Instead of relying on manual configurations or external tooling, Go developers can directly interact with AWS services such as S3, EC2, DynamoDB, and more – right from the application. This tight integration enables better automation, faster deployment cycles, and fine-grained control over cloud resources, making it easier to build highly responsive and efficient systems that react in real time to business needs.

Beyond just automation, using the AWS SDK for Go allows developers to optimize performance and scalability. Go's concurrency model and low memory footprint make it ideal for cloud workloads, and when combined with the AWS SDK, teams can write robust backend systems that dynamically manage resources based on usage. Whether you're building a microservice that spins up EC2 instances based on traffic or an application that archives user uploads to S3, mastering the AWS SDK unlocks the full potential of cloud computing from within your Go code.

In this chapter, we will cover the following topics:

- Introduction to how to use the AWS SDK
- How to connect Go applications to AWS services
- How to upload and manage files in S3
- How to create and manage EC2 instances from Go code
- Automate common AWS tasks using Go

Introduction to the AWS SDK for Go

The AWS SDK for Go is a collection of Go packages that makes it easier to interact with AWS services such as S3, EC2, DynamoDB, and more. Instead of writing raw HTTP requests or dealing with low-level authentication, you can use this SDK to simplify your code. It's especially useful for building cloud-native applications that need to scale, automate, and integrate deeply with AWS.

Why use the AWS SDK in Go applications?

Go is a fast, concurrent, and efficient language, ideal for backend services. When combined with the AWS SDK, it becomes a powerful tool for building cloud-native software. Here are a few reasons to use it:

- **Simplicity**: High-level abstractions for common AWS tasks
- **Performance**: Efficient networking and concurrency with Go routines
- **Automation**: Programmatically manage infrastructure
- **Security**: Automatic signing of AWS requests and support for IAM roles

Setting up the AWS SDK for Go

Before we can start using AWS services in the Go application, we need to set up the project with the AWS SDK so that the code can communicate with services such as S3 and EC2.

```
go mod init github.com/yourname/urlshortener
go get github.com/aws/aws-sdk-go-v2
```

For S3 or EC2, you'll also need these service-specific packages:

```
go get github.com/aws/aws-sdk-go-v2/service/s3
go get github.com/aws/aws-sdk-go-v2/service/ec2
```

Once the project is initialized and the required packages are added, the Go application is ready to start interacting with AWS services using the SDK.

Setting up AWS credentials

You can set up AWS credentials in a few different ways depending on the environment, security needs, and how you're running the Go application.

Using ~/.aws/credentials and ~/.aws/config files

Using `~/.aws/credentials` and `~/.aws/config` files is the most common approach for local development.

- These files are automatically read by the AWS SDK when the application runs locally
- Use this when developing on your own machine
- You can store multiple profiles (such as default, dev, prod) and switch between them easily using the `AWS_PROFILE` environment variable
- This method is secure because the credentials are stored in the home directory and not exposed directly in the code or shell environment

Here's an example file:

```
[default]
aws_access_key_id = {key}
aws_secret_access_key = {secret}
region = us-west-2
```

Using environment variables

You can also set credentials in the shell or CI/CD system using environment variables:

```
export AWS_ACCESS_KEY_ID={key}
export AWS_SECRET_ACCESS_KEY={secret}
export AWS_REGION=us-west-2
```

Use this approach when deploying using CI/CD pipelines (such as **GitHub Actions**, **GitLab CI**, or **Azure DevOps**), Docker containers, or Kubernetes Pods.

- It's quick and easy to configure temporarily for a session or container
- Environment variables take precedence over credentials files
- Be cautious not to hardcode secrets in scripts or source code

Other options

In addition to credentials files and environment variables, there are other ways to provide AWS credentials, depending on where the application runs. These options are especially useful for production environments or larger teams. These options help improve security by avoiding hard-coded credentials and make it easier to manage access across multiple users or systems.

- **IAM roles (in EC2, ECS, or Lambda)**: Use this in production environments where the compute service is granted permissions through roles, avoiding hardcoded keys
- **AWS SSO or Identity Center**: Useful for enterprise setups where users log in through single sign-on

Each of these methods has its use case. For local development, the credentials file is recommended. For automation or deployment pipelines, environment variables are common. In production environments on AWS infrastructure, using IAM roles is the most secure and maintainable approach.

Creating an AWS Session (SDK V2)

When working with AWS services, the very first thing the application needs is a configuration object. This object, called `cfg`, is created by loading the default configuration using `config.LoadDefaultConfig(context.TODO())`.

Think of it as setting up the application's connection settings to AWS. It contains essential information such as **credentials**, **region**, and **retry logic**.

This configuration is not just a convenience; it is required. Every AWS service client (such as S3, EC2, DynamoDB, and so on) depends on this config object to authenticate the requests and determine how they should be sent.

This configuration should be created at the beginning of the application and reused whenever you create a new service client.

This is especially important in long-running services, command-line tools, and infrastructure automation tools.

When to use it:

- Anytime you need to make calls to AWS services from the application
- In command-line tools that automate cloud infrastructure tasks (for example, provisioning EC2 instances or uploading files to S3)
- In microservices or APIs that interact with cloud resources dynamically
- In background jobs or batch scripts that process data using AWS services

Why it's needed:

- It securely loads the AWS credentials and preferred region
- It handles built-in retry policies and service-specific settings
- It abstracts away the details of how the app connects to AWS, so you don't need to configure clients manually

```
package main

import (
```

```
    "context"
    "fmt"
    "github.com/aws/aws-sdk-go-v2/aws"
    "github.com/aws/aws-sdk-go-v2/config"
)

func main() {
    cfg, err := config.LoadDefaultConfig(context.TODO())
    if err != nil {
        panic("Unable to load SDK config, " + err.Error())
    }

    fmt.Println("AWS config loaded for region:", cfg.Region)
}
```

In summary, the AWS config object is like a passport for the application to talk to AWS. It ensures the app is authenticated, knows where to send requests, and how to behave if something goes wrong (such as a temporary failure).

You only need to create it once and then pass it to each AWS client you use.

Creating an S3 client

After setting up the AWS configuration, the next step to interact with Amazon S3 is to create an S3 client.

The S3 client is a special object provided by the AWS SDK that knows how to talk to the S3 service.

You create it by passing your configuration object to the `s3.NewFromConfig(cfg)` function.

You can use `s3Client` to perform operations such as uploading files, listing buckets, and downloading data.

```
import "github.com/aws/aws-sdk-go-v2/service/s3"
s3Client := s3.NewFromConfig(cfg)
```

You should create the S3 client and reuse it throughout the application whenever you need to perform any operation involving S3. It acts like the application's official channel to communicate with S3.

Using the SDK in the URL shortener example

Let's assume you're building a URL shortener and want to store logs (such as access logs or shortened link usage) in an Amazon S3 bucket. Here's an example of how to store logs using code:

```
import (
    "bytes"
    "context"
    "github.com/aws/aws-sdk-go-v2/aws"
    "github.com/aws/aws-sdk-go-v2/service/s3"
    "github.com/aws/aws-sdk-go-v2/service/s3/types"
)

func uploadLogFile(
    s3Client *s3.Client, bucketName, key string, content []byte
) error {
    _, err := s3Client.PutObject(context.TODO(), &s3.PutObjectInput{
        Bucket: &bucketName,
        Key:    &key,
        Body:   bytes.NewReader(content),
        ContentType: aws.String("text/plain"),
        ACL:    types.ObjectCannedACLPrivate,
    })
    return err
}
```

This code does the following:

- Imports necessary packages, including the S3 service client and S3-related types
- Implements the `uploadLogFile` function, which takes four parameters:
    - `s3Client`: An already created S3 client, which is used to send requests to Amazon S3
    - `bucketName`: The name of the S3 bucket where the log file should be uploaded
    - `key`: The object key (such as a file name or path) that determines where the log file will be stored inside the bucket
    - `content`: The actual content of the log file, as a byte slice

The function does the following:

- Calls `PutObject`, which is the method used to upload a file (object) to S3

- Wraps the log content in `bytes.NewReader`, which converts the byte slice into a format that the SDK can stream to S3
- The `Bucket` and `Key` fields tell S3 where to store the file
- `ContentType` is set to "`text/plain`" to indicate the file type
- The **Access Control List** (**ACL**) is set to private, which means the file will not be publicly accessible

If the upload is successful, the function returns `nil`. If something goes wrong (for example, the bucket doesn't exist, or credentials are missing), the error is returned so the caller can handle it (logging or retrying).

Understanding error handling

When you use the AWS SDK in Go, most operations return two things: the result of the operation and an error. This is the standard pattern in Go. You should always check the error value to make sure the operation was successful before using the result.

```
result, err := s3Client.SomeOperation()
if err != nil {
    log.Fatalf("Operation failed: %v", err)
}
```

The error can often be cast into AWS-specific types for more detail:

```
var ae smithy.APIError
if errors.As(err, &ae) {
    fmt.Printf("API error: %s - %s\n", ae.ErrorCode(), ae.ErrorMessage())
}
```

Here is how the preceding code works, step by step:

- When we call an AWS SDK function such as `s3Client.SomeOperation()`, it gives back `result` and `err`.
- If something goes wrong, `err` will not be `nil`. We must check it.
- If `err` is not `nil`, we should handle the failure. In this example, we use `log.Fatalf(...)` to print an error message and stop the program immediately.

To get more detailed information about the error, the SDK provides structured error types. One of those is `smithy.APIError`, which includes AWS-specific information such as the error code and message returned by the service.

To extract more details, we can use `errors.As()` to check if the error is of type `smithy.APIError`.

If it is, we can access the following:

- `ae.ErrorCode()`: A short code such as **AccessDenied** or **NoSuchBucket** that describes the type of error
- `ae.ErrorMessage()`: A human-readable message with more detail about what went wrong

This pattern is useful when we want to handle different errors in different ways, such as retrying on throttling errors or showing a custom message if a bucket is missing.

Paginating results

When we call AWS operations such as `ListObjectsV2` (to list objects in an S3 bucket) or `DescribeInstances` (to list EC2 instances), the response may not include all results in a single call. This is because many AWS operations, such as listing objects or instances, return paginated results, meaning only a portion of the full list is returned per request. We must fetch the next page of results until you've seen them all.

The AWS SDK provides paginators to help you handle this easily.

```
paginator := s3.NewListObjectsV2Paginator(s3Client, &s3.
ListObjectsV2Input{
    Bucket: aws.String("bucket-name"),
})

for paginator.HasMorePages() {
    page, err := paginator.NextPage(context.TODO())
    if err != nil {
        log.Fatalf("Error fetching page: %v", err)
    }

    for _, obj := range page.Contents {
        fmt.Println("Found object:", *obj.Key)
    }
}
```

Here's what the preceding code is doing:

- `s3.NewListObjectsV2Paginator(...)` creates a `paginator` object that knows how to request and walk through each page of S3 object listings from the specified bucket (`bucket-name`)

- The `paginator.HasMorePages()` loop continues as long as there are more pages to fetch
- `paginator.NextPage(...)` makes the actual API call to retrieve the next batch of results
- If there's an error while fetching a page, it logs and exits the program
- Inside the loop, it processes each object in `page.Contents` by printing the object's key (its name in the bucket)

This approach is important when dealing with services that contain a large number of items.

Instead of writing custom logic to track pagination tokens or handle limits, the SDK's `paginator` simplifies everything so you can just loop through all items safely and efficiently.

Now that we've learned how to set up the AWS SDK and connect to AWS services securely, let's put that knowledge into action. In the next section, we'll dive into a common real-world task: uploading files to Amazon S3. We'll see how to create a client, upload files, manage permissions, and so on, programmatically.

Common AWS tasks: Uploading files to S3

In this section, we'll focus on one of the most commonly used services in AWS: **Amazon S3 (Simple Storage Service)**. S3 lets you store files (called **objects**) in a highly available and durable way. In Go applications, especially cloud-native ones such as a URL shortener, you may want to upload logs, exports, or static content such as thumbnails and analytics data to S3. We'll walk through how to upload files, manage metadata, set permissions, and make your integration production-ready.

Setting up the AWS SDK and S3 client

To begin, we need to import the AWS SDK for Go and create an S3 client. We'll use the official AWS SDK v2.

```
go get github.com/aws/aws-sdk-go-v2
go get github.com/aws/aws-sdk-go-v2/service/s3
```

Initializing the S3 client

Before performing any operations on S3, we need to initialize a client that has credentials, region, and other necessary settings. This setup pattern is common for all AWS services when using the AWS SDK.

```
package main

import (
```

```
    "context"
    "fmt"
    "log"
    "github.com/aws/aws-sdk-go-v2/aws"
    "github.com/aws/aws-sdk-go-v2/config"
    "github.com/aws/aws-sdk-go-v2/service/s3"
)

func main() {
    cfg, err := config.LoadDefaultConfig(context.TODO())
    if err != nil {
        log.Fatalf("unable to load SDK config, %v", err)
    }

    client := s3.NewFromConfig(cfg)
    fmt.Println("S3 client initialized")
}
```

Here's what the preceding code does:

- To load the default AWS configuration from the environment, the `config.LoadDefaultConfig(context.TODO())` function is called. This function looks for credentials in common locations such as `~/.aws/credentials`, environment variables (`AWS_ACCESS_KEY_ID`, `AWS_SECRET_ACCESS_KEY`), or IAM roles if running on AWS infrastructure such as EC2 or Lambda. The context is used for cancellation or timeouts.
- If loading the configuration fails, the program logs the error and exits using `log.Fatalf(...)`.
- The `s3.NewFromConfig(cfg)` function call creates a new S3 client using the configuration object that was just loaded. This client is what we'll use to call S3 API methods, such as `PutObject` (to upload a file) or `ListBuckets`.
- Once the client is successfully created, `fmt.Println("S3 client initialized")` confirms with a message to the console.

Uploading a file to S3

It's a common and essential operation to upload files from the local environment to an Amazon S3 bucket when building applications that handle logs, media files, user uploads, or backups. Let's upload a basic file from the local disk to a bucket named `urlshortener-assets`.

```
import (
    "os"
    "github.com/aws/aws-sdk-go-v2/feature/s3/manager"
)

func uploadFile(client *s3.Client, bucket, key, filename string) error {
    file, err := os.Open(filename)
    if err != nil {
        return fmt.Errorf("failed to open file %q, %v", filename, err)
    }
    defer file.Close()

    uploader := manager.NewUploader(client)

    _, err = uploader.Upload(context.TODO(), &s3.PutObjectInput{
        Bucket: aws.String(bucket),
        Key:    aws.String(key),
        Body:   file,
    })

    if err != nil {
        return fmt.Errorf("failed to upload file, %v", err)
    }

    fmt.Printf("Successfully uploaded %q to %q\n", filename, bucket)
    return nil
}
```

Let's call the function:

```
err = uploadFile(
    client, "urlshortener-assets", "logs/log1.txt", "./log1.txt"
)
if err != nil {
    log.Fatalf("Upload failed: %v", err)
}
```

Here's what this code does:

- `file, err := os.Open(filename)` opens the specified file from the local disk. This is the file we want to upload to S3. If the file can't be opened (e.g., it doesn't exist or you lack permissions), the function immediately returns an error.
- `defer file.Close()` ensures that when the function is done (successfully or with an error), the file is closed properly to free up system resources.
- `uploader := manager.NewUploader(client)` creates a new instance of a simple uploader. The AWS SDK provides a high-level uploader (`manager.Uploader`) that automatically handles large files, multipart uploads, and retries. It wraps around the standard S3 client to make uploading simpler.
- `_, err = uploader.Upload(context.TODO(), &s3.PutObjectInput{ ... })` actually initiates the upload. We provide the `Bucket` name, `Key` (path in the bucket), and `Body` (file to be uploaded). If the upload fails (for example, due to a network error or invalid permissions), the function returns an error explaining what went wrong.

We use best practices such as error checking, deferred cleanup, and high-level upload management to handle various edge cases – for example, large files and intermittent failures. Once these patterns are understood, we can adapt them to upload images, logs, backups, or any other data to S3.

Adding metadata to files

Attaching metadata to S3 objects gives a flexible way to tag and organize files without needing an external database or modifying the file itself.

For example, we can do the following:

- Identify who uploaded the file (`UserId`)
- Track when files were uploaded (`UploadedAt`)
- Filter or search files later using these attributes

Let's apply conditional logic in Lambda functions or other AWS services based on metadata.

```
_, err = uploader.Upload(context.TODO(), &s3.PutObjectInput{
    Bucket: aws.String(bucket),
    Key:    aws.String(key),
    Body:   file,
    Metadata: map[string]string{
        "UserId": "12345",
        "UploadedAt": time.Now().Format(time.RFC3339),
```

```
    },
})
```

Here's what this code does:

- We call the `uploader.Upload` method and provide a `PutObjectInput` object
- We attach a couple of custom metadata key-value pairs
- `UserId` might represent the ID of the user who uploaded the file
- `UploadedAt` stores the exact upload time in ISO 8601 format (RFC3339), which is both human-readable and easily machine-parsed

These metadata values are stored with the file in S3 but are not part of the file content itself. We can later retrieve them when listing or downloading objects, and use them for auditing, filtering, access control, and other use cases.

Making files public

Making files public is ideal when we want to serve content directly from S3 without requiring signed URLs or special permissions. It's especially good when doing the following:

- Hosting static website assets (images, JavaScript, CSS)
- Sharing downloadable logs or reports
- Delivering public documents or media

However, we have to be careful with public access. We should avoid uploading sensitive or private data this way and ensure that the bucket's settings and policies do not accidentally expose more than intended.

For long-term or secure public delivery, we may also consider using **Amazon CloudFront** with signed URLs or bucket policies.

Here's how to programmatically make an uploaded object publicly accessible:

```
_, err = uploader.Upload(context.TODO(), &s3.PutObjectInput{
    Bucket: aws.String(bucket),
    Key:    aws.String(key),
    Body:   file,
    ACL:    s3.ObjectCannedACLPublicRead,
})
```

Then we can access it:

```
https://<bucket-name>.s3.amazonaws.com/<key>
```

This code uses the `uploader.Upload` function to send a file (`Body: file`) to the specified S3 bucket under the given key (file path/name in the bucket).

It then makes the file public (`ACL: s3.ObjectCannedACLPublicRead`).

- This applies a predefined Amazon S3 permission setting, known as a *canned* ACL, called `public-read`
- When applied, it means anyone can read (download or view) the object; no authentication is needed
- Only the object itself is public, not the entire bucket

Once uploaded with `public-read`, anyone can access the file using this URL pattern: https://<bucket-name>.s3.amazonaws.com/<key>

Using S3 for the URL shortener

By storing thumbnails of the URLs using predictable keys such as `thumbnails/{shortID}.png`, we'll have a structured way to associate assets with specific shortened URLs. This allows us to do the following:

- Easily retrieve thumbnails based on the short ID
- Maintain clean and organized bucket contents
- Overwrite existing thumbnails by uploading to the same key
- Reduce the chances of filename collisions, since each key is tied to a unique short ID

This pattern is very common in content-addressable solutions, where resources (such as images, logs, or metadata) are grouped and managed based on identifiers.

Suppose we want to store thumbnails of shortened URLs in S3. We can do so by doing the following:

```go
func uploadThumbnail(
    client *s3.Client, shortID string, filepath string
) error {
    key := fmt.Sprintf("thumbnails/%s.png", shortID)
    return uploadFile(client, "urlshortener-assets", key, filepath)
}
```

The `uploadThumbnail` function is a wrapper around a more generic `uploadFile` function. It accepts an S3 client (`client`), `shortID` representing the shortened URL (for example, "`abc123`", ...), and the local file path of the thumbnail (`filepath`).

It constructs a meaningful S3 object key using `fmt.Sprintf("thumbnails/%s.png", shortID)`. This results in object keys such as `thumbnails/abc123.png`, which makes it easier to retrieve thumbnails later.

Finally, it uploads the file to an S3 bucket named `urlshortener-assets` using that key.

Listing files in a bucket

Listing objects in a bucket could be required in many real-world scenarios, such as the following:

- In a user-facing application, it allows users to view or manage the files they've uploaded
- In admin tools, developers can use it to audit or analyze bucket contents
- For automations or backups, we can filter or process files programmatically

This approach uses the simple `ListObjectsV2` method, which works well for buckets with a moderate number of files.

For large datasets, or if we need to filter by prefix (for example, listing only thumbnails or logs), we can enhance the function by passing additional options, such as `Prefix`, or using pagination with `paginator`.

```
func listObjects(client *s3.Client, bucket string) {
    resp, err := client.ListObjectsV2(
        context.TODO(), &s3.ListObjectsV2Input{
            Bucket: aws.String(bucket),
        }
    )
    if err != nil {
        log.Fatalf("Failed to list objects: %v", err)
    }

    for _, item := range resp.Contents {
        fmt.Println("Name:", *item.Key, "\tSize:", item.Size)
    }
}
```

This code defines a `listObjects` function that accepts an S3 client and a bucket name. It calls `ListObjectsV2`, a standard S3 API operation used to fetch a list of all objects (files) in the specified bucket. If the request fails, the error is logged, and the program stops using `log.Fatalf`. If the request is successful, it loops over each file (`item`) in the response and prints out the name of the file and its size in bytes.

Deleting files from S3

To keep the buckets organized and to maintain data hygiene, it's important to delete files from S3. Over time, unused or outdated files such as expired thumbnails, logs, or temporary data can accumulate and consume unnecessary space. Removing them helps avoid clutter, reduces the chance of exposing stale data, and ensures your application stores only what's actively needed. It also aligns with data retention policies and improves overall efficiency.

This function demonstrates how to delete a specific file from an S3 bucket:

```
func deleteFile(client *s3.Client, bucket, key string) error {
    _, err := client.DeleteObject(context.TODO(), &s3.DeleteObjectInput{
        Bucket: aws.String(bucket),
        Key:    aws.String(key),
    })
    return err
}
```

The `deleteFile` function accepts three arguments:

- `client`: An initialized `s3.Client` used to communicate with AWS S3
- `bucket`: The name of the S3 bucket where the file is stored
- `key`: The full path or name of the file to be deleted (also known as the **object key**)

The function calls `DeleteObject`, which is the AWS S3 operation to permanently remove a file. The `context.TODO()` function is used to provide context for the request, and it can be replaced with a proper context that supports timeouts or cancellation if needed.

If the deletion fails, the function returns an error, allowing the calling code to handle it appropriately.

Now that we have learned how to work with S3 for storing and managing files, let's shift gears and explore another powerful AWS service: EC2. In the next section, we'll see how to launch, manage, and automate virtual servers programmatically using the AWS SDK.

Managing EC2 instances programmatically

In this section, you will learn how to manage Amazon EC2 instances using the AWS SDK for Go. Managing EC2 programmatically lets you build automation into your cloud infrastructure. We'll use a URL shortener service as an example to demonstrate launching new instances, listing running instances, stopping and starting them, and eventually terminating instances.

Before starting, ensure the following:

- You have an AWS account with appropriate permissions
- AWS credentials are configured on the machine (`~/.aws/credentials`)

The AWS SDK for Go is included in the project by using the following commands:

```
go get github.com/aws/aws-sdk-go-v2/aws
go get github.com/aws/aws-sdk-go-v2/config
go get github.com/aws/aws-sdk-go-v2/service/ec2
```

Launching a new EC2 instance

To automate infrastructure provisioning, scale applications dynamically, or integrate deployment into CI/CD pipelines, instead of manually logging into the AWS console and configuring everything by hand, we do it programmatically.

Creating instances programmatically allows us to quickly spin up servers on demand based on application needs, traffic patterns, or deployment events.

In this example, we will launch a `t2.micro` EC2 instance running Amazon Linux 2. Later, we will simulate deploying the URL shortener application to it.

```
input := &ec2.RunInstancesInput{
    ImageId:      aws.String(
        "ami-0abcdef1234567890"
    ), // Update to valid AMI ID
    InstanceType: ec2.InstanceTypeT2Micro,
    MinCount:     aws.Int32(1),
    MaxCount:     aws.Int32(1),
    KeyName:      aws.String("my-key-pair"), // Replace with your key pair
    SecurityGroupIds: []string{
        "sg-0123456789abcdef0"
    }, // Replace with your security group ID
```

```
}

result, err := ec2Client.RunInstances(context.TODO(), input)
if err != nil {
    log.Fatalf("could not launch instance: %v", err)
}

for _, inst := range result.Instances {
    fmt.Printf("Launched instance with ID: %s\n", *inst.InstanceId)
}
```

This code creates an `&ec2.RunInstancesInput` instance with the following parameters:

- `ImageId`: This specifies the operating system and base image.
- `InstanceType`: This defines the size and resources of the virtual machine. `t2.micro` is available in the AWS Free Tier.
- `MinCount` and `MaxCount`: These define how many instances to launch.
- `KeyName`: The name of an existing EC2 key pair in the account, used to SSH into the instance.
- `SecurityGroupIds`: Controls what traffic is allowed in and out of the instance.

After calling `RunInstances`, the code checks for errors and then prints the ID of the newly launched instance.

Describing running instances

When we need to see which EC2 instances are currently running, stopped, or terminated, for managing and monitoring purposes, we can use the `DescribeInstances` API.

This API provides useful metadata such as instance IDs, IP addresses, states, and tags. It is especially helpful in environments with many instances, where manual tracking becomes difficult. Automating this visibility allows you to make informed decisions about scaling, debugging, or cleaning up unused resources.

```
input := &ec2.DescribeInstancesInput{}

output, err := ec2Client.DescribeInstances(context.TODO(), input)
if err != nil {
    log.Fatalf("failed to describe instances: %v", err)
}
```

```
for _, reservation := range output.Reservations {
    for _, inst := range reservation.Instances {
        fmt.Printf(
            "Instance ID: %s,
            State: %s\n",
            *inst.InstanceId,
            inst.State.Name
        )
    }
}
```

This code uses the `DescribeInstances` API from the AWS SDK to retrieve information about EC2 instances in the account.

- `input := &ec2.DescribeInstancesInput{}` creates an empty input struct, which means it will fetch details about all instances unless filters are added
- The `ec2Client.DescribeInstances(...)` call sends the request to AWS
- If the call fails, the program logs the error and stops
- The response contains a list of reservations, each of which may contain one or more instances
- The nested `for` loops go through each reservation and its instances, printing out the instance ID and its current state (such as running, stopped, and so on)

Stopping an instance

When we no longer need an EC2 instance to be running but want to preserve its configuration, data, and volume attachments, we can stop it.

Stopping the instance helps reduce costs as AWS does not charge for stopped compute resources.

Programmatically stopping instances allows you to automate these savings and controls as part of a larger infrastructure management strategy.

```
input := &ec2.StopInstancesInput{
    InstanceIds: []string{"i-0123456789abcdef0"},
}

_, err := ec2Client.StopInstances(context.TODO(), input)
if err != nil {
    log.Fatalf("failed to stop instance: %v", err)
```

```
} else {
    fmt.Println("Instance stopped")
}
```

This code stops a running EC2 instance.

- The `StopInstancesInput` struct is created with the `InstanceIds` field, which takes a list of instance IDs to stop
- The `ec2Client.StopInstances(...)` call sends a stop request to AWS for the specified instance
- If the request fails, the program logs the error and exits
- If successful, it prints a success message confirming the instance has been stopped

Starting an instance

When we want to bring a previously stopped virtual machine back online, we can start it programmatically. This is useful for scaling operations, scheduled workloads, or resuming development and testing environments that were paused to save costs.

Automating this process through code allows you to integrate instance management into scripts, CI/CD pipelines, or cloud automation tools, ensuring systems are available exactly when needed without requiring manual intervention.

```
input := &ec2.StartInstancesInput{
    InstanceIds: []string{"i-0123456789abcdef0"},
}

_, err := ec2Client.StartInstances(context.TODO(), input)
if err != nil {
    log.Fatalf("failed to start instance: %v", err)
} else {
    fmt.Println("Instance started")
}
```

This code starts a previously stopped EC2 instance.

- It creates a `StartInstancesInput` object that specifies the instance ID(s) to be started
- The `ec2Client.StartInstances(...)` call sends the request to AWS to start the instance
- If there's an error, the code logs it and exits
- If the request is successful, it prints a confirmation message

Terminating an instance

Terminating an EC2 instance means permanently deleting the virtual machine and stopping all charges associated with it.

This is useful when an instance is no longer needed, such as after completing a temporary job, cleaning up development resources, or replacing outdated infrastructure.

Doing this programmatically allows you to clean up resources automatically, avoid unnecessary costs, and keep the cloud environment organized and efficient.

```
input := &ec2.TerminateInstancesInput{
    InstanceIds: []string{"i-0123456789abcdef0"},
}

_, err := ec2Client.TerminateInstances(context.TODO(), input)
if err != nil {
    log.Fatalf("failed to terminate instance: %v", err)
} else {
    fmt.Println("Instance terminated")
}
```

This code creates a `TerminateInstancesInput` object and specifies the instance ID to be terminated.

The `ec2Client.TerminateInstances` method sends a termination request to AWS.

If the call fails, it logs a fatal error and exits. If successful, it prints a confirmation message saying the instance was terminated.

Tagging instances

Tagging EC2 instances helps organize and manage cloud resources by assigning descriptive metadata. Tags are **key-value** pairs that allow you to identify instances by purpose, owner, environment, application, cost center, and so on.

This makes it easier to filter instances in the AWS console, automate actions based on tags, and generate usage or billing reports.

For example, tagging an instance with `App: url-shortener` clearly indicates its role in your infrastructure, which improves clarity, governance, and automation.

In this example, we will add tags to identify instances:

```
_, err := ec2Client.CreateTags(context.TODO(), &ec2.CreateTagsInput{
    Resources: []string{"i-0123456789abcdef0"},
    Tags: []ec2types.Tag{
        {
            Key:   aws.String("App"),
            Value: aws.String("url-shortener"),
        },
    },
})

if err != nil {
    log.Fatalf("failed to tag instance: %v", err)
}
```

This code uses the `CreateTags` API and passes the ID of the instance to be tagged.

The `Tags` field is a list of key-value pairs. In this case, it tags the instance with `App: url-shortener`.

If tagging fails, the program logs a fatal error.

Deploying a URL shortener to EC2 (simplified)

Using **user data** to deploy an application automates the initial setup of the server, reducing the need for manual SSH access and configuration.

This approach is especially useful in scalable cloud environments where instances are created and terminated frequently.

With a user data script, we can ensure that every instance is consistently configured and ready to serve traffic with minimal human intervention.

```
userData := "#!/bin/bash\n" +
    "yum update -y\n" +
    "yum install -y git golang\n" +
    "git clone https://github.com/your/repo.git\n" +
    "cd repo && go build -o app && ./app &"

encoded := base64.StdEncoding.EncodeToString([]byte(userData))

input := &ec2.RunInstancesInput{
```

```
        ImageId:      aws.String("ami-0abcdef1234567890"),
        InstanceType: ec2.InstanceTypeT2Micro,
        MinCount:     aws.Int32(1),
        MaxCount:     aws.Int32(1),
        UserData:     aws.String(encoded),
        KeyName:      aws.String("my-key"),
        SecurityGroupIds: []string{"sg-0123456789abcdef0"},
    }
```

This code demonstrates how to automatically deploy the URL shortener application to an EC2 instance using user data and a script that runs at startup.

- The `userData` string is a shell script that updates the system, installs Git and Go, clones the application repository, builds the app, and runs it in the background
- The script is base64-encoded, which is required by AWS for `UserData` input
- The `RunInstancesInput` struct is used to launch the EC2 instance with `UserData` attached, so the script runs automatically when the instance boots.

We've now seen how to programmatically launch, stop, start, and terminate EC2 instances using the AWS SDK. These skills allow us to manage compute resources dynamically, scaling up when demand grows and shutting down when they're no longer needed. This kind of automation not only saves time but also helps reduce costs and improve operational efficiency.

Summary

In this chapter, we began by learning about the AWS SDK for Go. You now understand how this SDK allows Go applications to talk to AWS services such as S3 and EC2. We covered how to set up your Go project, configure AWS credentials, and use the SDK to make secure and reliable API calls to the cloud.

Next, we explored how to work with Amazon S3, a popular cloud storage service. You learned how to upload files, set file permissions, add metadata, and handle errors. These tasks are essential when building applications such as a URL shortener that might need to store or serve files, such as QR codes or logs, from the cloud.

Finally, we looked at managing EC2 instances programmatically. We covered how to launch new instances, check their status, and terminate them when they're no longer needed. This gives you the ability to build applications that can scale up or down automatically, saving costs and improving performance in real-world cloud environments.

In the next chapter, we'll dive into how to connect Go applications with Azure cloud services using the Azure SDK for Go. You'll learn how to set up secure authentication, work with Azure Storage to manage files, and control virtual machines directly from the code. This will help to build and manage cloud-powered apps on Azure more effectively.

Join the CloudPro Newsletter with 44000+ Subscribers

12

Integrating Go Applications with the Azure SDK

Integrating Go applications with the Azure SDK enables developers to manage cloud infrastructure programmatically with precision and speed. Instead of relying on manual steps or using multiple scripts, developers can use Go code to provision resources such as storage accounts, virtual machines, and network interfaces directly from their applications. This level of automation simplifies workflows, reduces human error, and makes applications more cloud-native and scalable. For example, a Go-based microservice can automatically spin up temporary VMs for load testing or archive files to Azure Blob Storage as part of its processing logic.

Another key reason to integrate Go with the Azure SDK is to build secure, cost-efficient, and resilient systems. By embedding cloud operations directly into your Go applications, you can dynamically react to changes – such as scaling resources when usage spikes or deallocating unused VMs to save cost. Using the SDK also makes it easier to enforce security practices by handling credentials via Azure Active Directory or environment configurations, and by setting resource access policies in code. As a result, developers can ensure consistent infrastructure standards while rapidly delivering new features.

In this chapter, we will cover the following topics:

- Setting up the Azure SDK and authentication: We'll learn how to configure the SDK, authenticate using a service principal, and manage credentials securely
- Working with Azure Storage: We'll learn how to upload, download, and manage blob data in Azure Storage, including handling containers, metadata, and access controls

- Managing Azure Virtual Machines (VMs): We'll explore how to programmatically create, update, and delete VMs using the Azure SDK

Setting up the Azure SDK for Go and authentication

This section focuses on configuring the Azure SDK for Go and setting up secure authentication for accessing Azure resources. You will learn how to authenticate using service principals, manage credentials safely, and make sure your Go applications can interact securely with Azure services.

Installing the Azure SDK for Go

Before we begin coding, we need to install the required Azure SDK packages. Microsoft maintains Azure SDKs for Go as part of the `github.com/Azure/azure-sdk-for-go` repository.

```
go get github.com/Azure/azure-sdk-for-go/sdk/azidentity
```

We can also install SDKs for specific services:

```
go get github.com/Azure/azure-sdk-for-go/sdk/storage/azblob
```

We'll use `azidentity` for authentication and other service SDKs for working with Azure.

Authenticating with Azure using service principals

To interact with Azure securely, we need to authenticate first. One of the most common and secure ways is to use a **service principal** with a client secret.

As a prerequisite, you should have the Azure CLI installed and be logged in.

Let's create a service principal:

```
az ad sp create-for-rbac --name "urlshortener-app" --role contributor
--scopes /subscriptions/<your-subscription-id> --sdk-auth
```

Copy the JSON output. This contains the client ID, secret, tenant ID, and subscription ID.

Storing and accessing credentials securely

To securely connect to Azure services, we need a way to provide authentication credentials without hardcoding them in the source code. Two common approaches are using environment variables and `.env` files.

Environment variables are ideal for production and CI/CD pipelines because they keep sensitive information outside of the code base and are managed by the operating system or deployment platform.

On the other hand, .env files are better suited for local development, allowing you to store credentials in a file that is loaded at runtime, typically using a package such as godotenv.

Option 1: Environment variables

Export the service principal credentials as environment variables:

```
export AZURE_CLIENT_ID="<appId>"
export AZURE_CLIENT_SECRET="<password>"
export AZURE_TENANT_ID="<tenant>"
```

Option 2: .env file (for local dev only)

Create an .env file:

```
AZURE_CLIENT_ID=xxxx
AZURE_CLIENT_SECRET=xxxx
AZURE_TENANT_ID=xxxx
```

Load it in Go using the godotenv package:

```
import (
    "github.com/joho/godotenv"
    "log"
)

func init() {
    err := godotenv.Load()
    if err != nil {
        log.Fatal("Error loading .env file")
    }
}
```

Using environment variables or a .env file helps us keep Azure credentials secure and separate from the source code, making the application safer and easier to manage, especially across different environments such as development, testing, and production.

Using the Azure Identity SDK for authentication

The `azidentity` package offers several credential types. For service principal authentication, we will use `NewClientSecretCredential`.

```
import (
    "context"
    "log"
    "github.com/Azure/azure-sdk-for-go/sdk/azidentity"
)

func getCredential() *azidentity.ClientSecretCredential {
    cred, err := azidentity.NewClientSecretCredential(
        os.Getenv("AZURE_TENANT_ID"),
        os.Getenv("AZURE_CLIENT_ID"),
        os.Getenv("AZURE_CLIENT_SECRET"),
        nil,
    )
    if err != nil {
        log.Fatalf("Failed to create credential: %v", err)
    }
    return cred
}
```

This code defines a function called `getCredential` that uses the Azure SDK to create a secure credential object. It reads the **tenant ID**, **client ID**, and **client secret** from environment variables, then uses them to create a `ClientSecretCredential` using the `azidentity` package.

If the credential creation fails, the application logs a fatal error and stops. If successful, the credential object is returned and can be used to interact with Azure resources securely.

Now the credential object is ready and can be passed on to any Azure SDK client.

Authenticating in a project

Imagine we're building the URL shortener service that stores links in Azure Blob Storage. First, we need to authenticate and get a client to interact with the storage service.

```
import (
    "github.com/Azure/azure-sdk-for-go/sdk/storage/azblob"
    "github.com/Azure/azure-sdk-for-go/sdk/azidentity"
```

```
)

func getBlobClient() *azblob.Client {
    cred := getCredential()

    client, err := azblob.NewClient(
        "https://<your-storage-account>.blob.core.windows.net/",
        cred,
        nil
    )
    if err != nil {
        log.Fatalf("failed to create blob client: %v", err)
    }
    return client
}
```

This code defines the `getBlobClient` function to create and return an **Azure Blob Storage** client. It first retrieves a credential object (we defined the `getCredential()` function earlier). Then it creates a new `azblob.Client` by providing the Blob Storage endpoint URL and the credential. If the client creation fails, it logs a fatal error and stops the program.

Now, the application is securely connected to Azure Storage.

Using other credential types

The Azure SDK supports multiple credential types:

- `DefaultAzureCredential`: This tries several auth methods, including environment, managed identity, and more
- `EnvironmentCredential`: This reads credentials from environment variables
- `ManagedIdentityCredential`: This is used for VMs and services with managed identity

Using DefaultAzureCredential

`ClientSecretCredential` is very good for local development and CI/CD pipelines, but Azure also provides a more flexible and convenient option, `DefaultAzureCredential`. This credential type automatically tries several authentication methods in a predefined order, making it ideal for applications that run in different environments without changing the authentication code. Let's see how to use it:

```
cred, err := azidentity.NewDefaultAzureCredential(nil)
```

This is useful in production, where managed identity is preferred.

Best practices for managing credentials

When working with cloud applications, it's very important to manage credentials carefully to keep the application secure and prevent accidental leaks of sensitive information. Here are some common and recommended practices to handle authentication details in a safe and reliable way:

- Avoid hardcoding credentials
- Use Azure Key Vault for sensitive data
- Use environment variables and managed identities in production
- Store credentials securely in GitHub Action secrets during CI/CD

Following these best practices will help to avoid security risks, keep secrets safe, and make the application more secure and easier to manage.

Interacting with Azure Storage: Uploading and managing blobs

In this section, we'll learn how to use the Azure SDK to work with Azure Storage – specifically, how to upload, download, and manage blobs inside containers. We'll build this with a practical example based on a URL shortener service that stores its link metadata as blobs in Azure Storage.

Install the `azblob` package:

```
go get github.com/Azure/azure-sdk-for-go/sdk/storage/azblob
```

Authenticating with Azure Blob Storage

We'll connect to Azure Blob Storage using a shared key or connection string. You can retrieve this from the Azure portal, under your **Storage Account** settings.

```
package main

import (
    "context"
    "fmt"
    "log"
    "github.com/Azure/azure-sdk-for-go/sdk/storage/azblob"
)
```

```
func main() {
    connectionString := "<your-connection-string>"
    serviceClient, err := azblob.NewServiceClientFromConnectionString(
        connectionString, nil
    )
    if err != nil {
        log.Fatalf("Failed to create service client: %v", err)
    }
    fmt.Println("Connected to Azure Blob Storage")
}
```

This code connects to Azure Blob Storage using a connection string. In the `main` function, it calls `azblob.NewServiceClientFromConnectionString`, passing in the connection string to create a `serviceClient`. If the connection is successful, it prints a confirmation message: **Connected to Azure Blob Storage**. If there's an error (for example, an invalid connection string), it logs the failure and stops the program.

Creating a container

Think of containers as folders in the cloud that help organize blobs. For example, our URL shortener could have a container named `links` where all shortened URLs are stored.

```
containerClient := serviceClient.NewContainerClient("links")
_, err = containerClient.Create(context.Background(), nil)
if err != nil {
    log.Fatalf("Failed to create container: %v", err)
}
fmt.Println("Container 'links' created")
```

This code creates a new container named `links` in Azure Blob Storage using the previously initialized `serviceClient`. First, it creates a `containerClient` for the `links` container. Then, it attempts to create the container with `containerClient.Create()`.

If the operation fails (for example, if the container already exists), it logs the error and exits. If successful, it prints a message confirming that the container was created.

Uploading a blob

We may upload data to Azure Blob Storage when we need a reliable and scalable way to store application data in the cloud. In the case of the URL shortener, this means saving information about each shortened URL – for example, the original link and its short code.

By uploading blobs, we ensure that the service can retrieve, manage, and serve this data efficiently whenever needed.

It also allows you to add metadata, set access permissions, and organize files within containers, making it easier to maintain and extend the application over time.

We will upload a file containing metadata of a shortened URL:

```
blobClient := containerClient.NewBlockBlobClient("ms.json")

uploadData := `{"short":"ms", "original":"https://www.microsoft.com"}`
_, err = blobClient.UploadBuffer(
    context.Background(),
    []byte(uploadData),
    &azblob.UploadBufferOptions{},
)
if err != nil {
    log.Fatalf("Upload failed: %v", err)
}
fmt.Println("Uploaded ms.json' blob")
```

This code uploads a small JSON file named (`ms.json`) to an Azure Blob Storage container. It first creates a `blobClient` for the blob using the container client. Then, it defines the content to upload as a JSON string and converts it to a byte slice.

The `UploadBuffer` method uploads the data to Azure. If the upload fails, it logs the error and exits. If successful, it prints a confirmation that the blob was uploaded.

Setting metadata and access permissions

When we need to attach custom information to files so that we can use this data for searching, filtering, or applying specific business logic without changing the file content itself, we set custom metadata for each blob as follows:

```
metadata := map[string]*string{
    "owner": to.Ptr("admin"),
    "category": to.Ptr("search"),
}
_, err = blobClient.SetMetadata(context.Background(), metadata, nil)
if err != nil {
    log.Fatalf("Setting metadata failed: %v", err)
```

```
}
fmt.Println("Metadata set for 'ms.json'")
```

This code sets custom metadata for a blob. It creates a metadata map with key-value pairs, using pointers as required by the SDK. The `SetMetadata` method is then called on `blobClient` to apply this metadata.

If there's an error during the operation, it's logged, and the program exits. Otherwise, it confirms that the metadata was successfully set for the `ms.json` blob.

Listing blobs in a container

Listing blobs is important when we want to see which files are stored, manage them, or provide users with a view of available data. This helps in organizing, searching, and performing actions such as downloads or deletions on specific blobs.

```
pager := containerClient.ListBlobsFlat(nil)
for pager.NextPage(context.Background()) {
    for _, blob := range pager.PageResponse().Segment.BlobItems {
        fmt.Printf("Blob: %s\n", *blob.Name)
    }
}
if err := pager.Err(); err != nil {
    log.Fatalf("Error listing blobs: %v", err)
}
```

This code uses a pager to iterate through all blobs stored in an Azure Blob Storage container. It calls `ListBlobsFlat` to get a paginated list of blobs. For each page, it loops over the blob items and prints their names. After the loop, it checks for any errors that may have happened during paging and logs a fatal error if any are found.

Downloading a Blob

Downloading blobs is also important, especially when we need to retrieve and use the actual content of the files. This allows the application to process, display, or transform the data stored remotely.

```
getResp, err := blobClient.DownloadStream(context.Background(), nil)
if err != nil {
    log.Fatalf("Download failed: %v", err)
}
```

```
body := &bytes.Buffer{}
_, err = body.ReadFrom(getResp.Body)
if err != nil {
    log.Fatalf("Reading blob failed: %v", err)
}
fmt.Printf("Blob content: %s\n", body.String())
```

This code downloads the content of a blob using the `DownloadStream` method from the Azure SDK. It first requests the blob data stream and checks for any errors during the download. Then it reads the data from the response body into a buffer.

If reading the data fails, it logs a fatal error. If not, it prints the content of the blob as a string.

Deleting a blob

Deleting blobs helps us keep Azure Blob Storage organized by removing files that are no longer needed. It also helps maintain data hygiene and ensures that outdated or irrelevant data does not clutter the storage.

```
_, err = blobClient.Delete(context.Background(), nil)
if err != nil {
    log.Fatalf("Failed to delete blob: %v", err)
}
fmt.Println("Blob 'ms.json' deleted")
```

This code deletes a specific blob using the `Delete` method. It calls the method on `blobClient` to remove the blob, checks for any errors during the deletion process, and logs a fatal error if it fails. If successful, it prints a confirmation message indicating that the blob named `ms.json` has been deleted.

Using a blob client in a project

In many applications, we need to save and retrieve data efficiently and reliably. For example, a URL shortener service may want to store the mapping between short URLs and their original long URLs.

Here's a simple function to store shortened URL data as a blob:

```
func saveShortURL(blobName string, short string, original string) error {
    data := fmt.Sprintf(
        `{"short":"%s", "original":"%s"}`, short, original
    )
```

```
    blobClient := containerClient.NewBlockBlobClient(blobName)
    _, err := blobClient.UploadBuffer(
        context.Background(),
        []byte(data),
        azblob.UploadOption{}
    )
    return err
}
```

Here's a corresponding function to read it back:

```
func getShortURL(blobName string) (string, error) {
    blobClient := containerClient.NewBlockBlobClient(blobName)
    resp, err := blobClient.DownloadStream(context.Background(), nil)
    if err != nil {
        return "", err
    }
    buf := &bytes.Buffer{}
    _, err = buf.ReadFrom(resp.Body)
    return buf.String(), err
}
```

This code shows two functions: one to save and one to retrieve shortened URL data. The `saveShortURL` function creates a JSON string with the short and original URLs, then uploads it as a blob with the given name. The `getShortURL` function downloads the blob content by its name and returns it as a string.

Now that we've covered working with Azure Storage, let's turn our attention to another critical area of cloud infrastructure, virtual machines. In the next section, we'll dive into how to manage Azure Virtual Machines programmatically. We'll learn how to create, start, stop, and delete VMs, to give the application the ability to automate compute resource provisioning and lifecycle management in Azure.

Managing virtual machines programmatically

In this section, we will learn how to programmatically manage Azure **Virtual Machines (VMs)** using the Azure SDK. This is useful when an application – such as our URL shortener service – needs to programmatically create, update, or remove VMs based on demand. You'll see how to provision a VM, update it, and delete it.

Before getting started, let's export the following credentials as environment variables:

```
export AZURE_CLIENT_ID="<your-client-id>"
export AZURE_CLIENT_SECRET="<your-client-secret>"
export AZURE_TENANT_ID="<your-tenant-id>"
export AZURE_SUBSCRIPTION_ID="<your-subscription-id>"
```

Installing required Azure SDK packages

Before we start managing Azure resources programmatically, we need to install the necessary Azure SDK packages. These packages provide the tools and APIs required to interact with Azure services such as virtual machines, subscriptions, and authentication. Use the following `go get` commands to install them:

```
go get github.com/Azure/azure-sdk-for-go/sdk/resourcemanager/compute/
armcompute@latest
go get github.com/Azure/azure-sdk-for-go/sdk/resourcemanager/resources/
armsubscriptions@latest
go get github.com/Azure/azure-sdk-for-go/sdk/azidentity@latest
```

Authenticating to Azure

To interact securely with Azure services, an application needs to authenticate itself and prove its identity. We can use the recommended `DefaultAzureCredential`, which supports multiple authentication methods and works well in different environments.

```
package main

import (
    "context"
    "fmt"
    "log"

    "github.com/Azure/azure-sdk-for-go/sdk/azidentity"
)

func getAzureCredential() *azidentity.DefaultAzureCredential {
    cred, err := azidentity.NewDefaultAzureCredential(nil)
    if err != nil {
        log.Fatalf("Failed to get credential: %v", err)
```

```
    }
    return cred
}
```

The `getAzureCredential` function creates and returns a credential object by calling `NewDefaultAzureCredential`. If the process fails, it logs a fatal error.

This credential will then be used to authorize requests to Azure services securely.

Creating a virtual machine

To run workloads on Azure programmatically, we often need to create VMs using code instead of manual steps.

Automating VM creation allows you to scale easily, reproduce environments, and streamline infrastructure setup for applications such as a URL shortener backend.

```
package main

import (
    "context"
    "log"
    "github.com/Azure/azure-sdk-for-go/sdk/azidentity"
    "github.com/Azure/azure-sdk-for-go/sdk/
        resourcemanager/compute/armcompute"
    "github.com/Azure/azure-sdk-for-go/sdk/to"
)

func createVM() {
    cred, err := azidentity.NewDefaultAzureCredential(nil)
    if err != nil {
        log.Fatal(err)
    }

    client, err := armcompute.NewVirtualMachinesClient(
        "<subscription-id>", cred, nil
    )
    if err != nil {
        log.Fatal(err)
    }
```

```
ctx := context.Background()
vmName := "shortener-vm"

vmParams := armcompute.VirtualMachine{
    Location: to.Ptr("eastus"),
    Properties: &armcompute.VirtualMachineProperties{
        HardwareProfile: &armcompute.HardwareProfile{
            VMSize: armcompute.VirtualMachineSizeTypesStandardB1s,
        },
        StorageProfile: &armcompute.StorageProfile{
            ImageReference: &armcompute.ImageReference{
                Publisher: to.Ptr("Canonical"),
                Offer:     to.Ptr("UbuntuServer"),
                SKU:       to.Ptr("18.04-LTS"),
                Version:   to.Ptr("latest"),
            },
        },
        OSProfile: &armcompute.OSProfile{
            ComputerName:  to.Ptr(vmName),
            AdminUsername: to.Ptr("azureuser"),
            AdminPassword: to.Ptr("P@ssw0rd1234"),
        },
    },
}

pollerResp, err := client.BeginCreateOrUpdate(
    ctx, "urlshortener-rg", vmName, vmParams, nil
)
if err != nil {
    log.Fatal(err)
}

_, err = pollerResp.PollUntilDone(ctx, nil)
if err != nil {
    log.Fatal(err)
}
```

```
    log.Println("VM created successfully")
}
```

This code demonstrates how to create a new virtual machine in Azure. It starts by authenticating with `DefaultAzureCredential`, then creates a `VirtualMachinesClient` for the specified subscription.

The `vmParams` object defines configuration details such as location, VM size, OS image, admin credentials, and so on. The `BeginCreateOrUpdate` method initiates the VM creation in the `urlshortener-rg` resource group, and `PollUntilDone` waits for the deployment to complete. Once successful, it logs that the VM has been created.

Starting VMs

To use a VM in Azure after it's been created or stopped, first we have to start it. Automating the startup process through code is helpful for managing environments dynamically, such as turning on resources only when needed to save costs or prepare for tasks.

```
func startVM(
    client *armcompute.VirtualMachinesClient,
    ctx context.Context,
    rgName,
    vmName string
) {
    poller, err := client.BeginStart(ctx, rgName, vmName, nil)
    if err != nil {
        log.Fatal(err)
    }
    _, err = poller.PollUntilDone(ctx, nil)
    if err != nil {
        log.Fatal(err)
    }
    log.Println("VM started")
}
```

This code defines a `startVM` function that starts an existing Azure virtual machine. It takes `VirtualMachinesClient`, context, resource group name, and VM name as parameters. The `BeginStart` method initiates the VM start operation, which returns a `poller` object. `PollUntilDone` waits for the operation to complete.

If successful, it logs that the VM has started; otherwise, it logs the error and stops execution.

Stopping VMs

To save costs or manage compute resources efficiently, we may want to stop Azure VMs when they are not in use. Doing this programmatically allows you to automate resource control in applications or maintenance workflows.

```
func stopVM(
    client *armcompute.VirtualMachinesClient,
    ctx context.Context,
    rgName,
    vmName string
) {
    poller, err := client.BeginPowerOff(ctx, rgName, vmName, nil)
    if err != nil {
        log.Fatal(err)
    }
    _, err = poller.PollUntilDone(ctx, nil)
    if err != nil {
        log.Fatal(err)
    }
    log.Println("VM stopped")
}
```

This function takes `VirtualMachinesClient`, context, resource group name, and VM name as input. The function calls `BeginPowerOff` to initiate the shutdown process and uses `PollUntilDone` to wait until the operation completes.

If successful, it logs that the VM was stopped; otherwise, it logs the encountered error and halts execution.

Deleting VMs

When a VM is no longer needed, deleting it helps free up resources and avoid unnecessary costs. Automating VM deletion ensures the clean-up is consistent and integrated into application lifecycle or resource management routines.

```
func deleteVM(
    client *armcompute.VirtualMachinesClient,
    ctx context.Context,
```

```
    rgName, vmName string
) {
    poller, err := client.BeginDelete(ctx, rgName, vmName, nil)
    if err != nil {
        log.Fatal(err)
    }
    _, err = poller.PollUntilDone(ctx, nil)
    if err != nil {
        log.Fatal(err)
    }
    log.Println("VM deleted")
}
```

This function calls `BeginDelete` to start the deletion process, and `PollUntilDone` waits for the operation to finish.

If the deletion is successful, it logs a confirmation message; otherwise, it logs the error and exits the program.

Building a complete URL shortener with Azure integration

Now that we have covered the individual Azure services, let's bring everything together by building a complete URL shortener application that uses multiple Azure services working in harmony. This project will demonstrate how Azure Blob Storage, VMs, and the Azure SDK can be combined to create a real-world application.

We will have the following features:

- Store shortened URL mappings in Azure Blob Storage
- Track usage statistics for each shortened URL
- Automatically provision Azure VMs when traffic exceeds a threshold
- Clean up resources when they're no longer needed

This integration shows how different Azure services can work together to build scalable and cost-effective applications.

First, let's define the data structures we'll use throughout the application:

```
package main

import (
    "context"
    "encoding/json"
    "fmt"
    "log"
    "os"
    "time"

    "github.com/Azure/azure-sdk-for-go/sdk/azidentity"
    "github.com/Azure/azure-sdk-for-go/sdk/
        resourcemanager/compute/armcompute"
    "github.com/Azure/azure-sdk-for-go/sdk/storage/azblob"
    "github.com/Azure/azure-sdk-for-go/sdk/to"
)

type URLMapping struct {
    Short       string    `json:"short"`
    Original    string    `json:"original"`
    AccessCount int       `json:"access_count"`
    CreatedAt   time.Time `json:"created_at"`
}

type URLShortenerService struct {
    storageClient  *azblob.Client
    vmClient       *armcompute.VirtualMachinesClient
    containerName  string
    resourceGroup  string
    subscriptionID string
    ctx            context.Context
}
```

The `URLMapping` struct holds all the information about a shortened URL. It includes the short code, the original URL, how many times it's been accessed, and when it was created. The JSON tags tell Go how to convert this struct to and from JSON format when storing it in Azure Blob Storage.

The `URLShortenerService` struct is the main coordinator for the application. It holds clients for both Azure Blob Storage and VMs, allowing interaction with both services. We also store configuration such as the container name and resource group, so we don't have to pass them around everywhere.

Now let's create a function to initialize the service with all the necessary Azure clients:

```
func NewURLShortenerService() (*URLShortenerService, error) {
  ctx := context.Background()
  cred, err := azidentity.NewDefaultAzureCredential(nil)
  if err != nil {
    return nil, fmt.Errorf("failed to create credential: %w", err)
  }
  // Create storage client
  storageAccount := os.Getenv("AZURE_STORAGE_ACCOUNT")
  storageURL := fmt.Sprintf(
    "https://%s.blob.core.windows.net/", storageAccount
  )
  storageClient, err := azblob.NewClient(storageURL, cred, nil)
  if err != nil {
    return nil, fmt.Errorf("failed to create storage client: %w", err)
  }
  // Create VM client
  subscriptionID := os.Getenv("AZURE_SUBSCRIPTION_ID")
  vmClient, err := armcompute.NewVirtualMachinesClient(
    subscriptionID, cred, nil
  )
  if err != nil {
    return nil, fmt.Errorf("failed to create VM client: %w", err)
  }
  return &URLShortenerService{
    storageClient:  storageClient,
    vmClient:       vmClient,
    containerName:  "url-mappings",
    resourceGroup:  "urlshortener-rg",
    subscriptionID: subscriptionID,
    ctx:            ctx,
  }, nil
}
```

This function sets up everything we need to work with Azure. First, it authenticates using `DefaultAzureCredential`, which automatically tries multiple authentication methods. Then it creates a storage client by reading the storage account name from an environment variable and building the URL. Finally, it creates a VM client for managing virtual machines. By doing all this setup once, we avoid repeating authentication steps throughout our code.

Before we can store any URLs, we need to make sure our storage container exists:

```
func (s *URLShortenerService) Initialize() error {
    containerClient := s.storageClient.NewContainerClient(s.containerName)
    _, err := containerClient.Create(s.ctx, nil)
    if err != nil {
        log.Printf("Container may already exist: %v", err)
    }
    return nil
}
```

This function tries to create the container where we'll store URL mappings. If the container already exists, Azure will return an error, but that's fine; we just log it and continue. This makes the code safe to run multiple times without breaking.

Now let's implement the core functionality, creating shortened URLs:

```
func (s *URLShortenerService) CreateShortURL(short, original string) error {
    mapping := URLMapping{
        Short:       short,
        Original:    original,
        AccessCount: 0,
        CreatedAt:   time.Now(),
    }

    data, err := json.Marshal(mapping)
    if err != nil {
        return fmt.Errorf("failed to marshal URL mapping: %w", err)
    }

    blobName := fmt.Sprintf("%s.json", short)
    containerClient := s.storageClient.NewContainerClient(s.containerName)
    blobClient := containerClient.NewBlockBlobClient(blobName)
```

```
    _, err = blobClient.UploadBuffer(
        s.ctx, data, &azblob.UploadBufferOptions{}
    )
    if err != nil {
        return fmt.Errorf("failed to upload blob: %w", err)
    }

    log.Printf("Created short URL: %s -> %s", short, original)
    return nil
}
```

This function creates a new shortened URL and stores it in Azure Blob Storage. It first creates a `URLMapping` object with all the details, including setting the access count to zero since no one has used it yet. Then it converts this object to JSON format and uploads it as a blob. Each shortened URL gets its own file named after the short code, such as `gh.json` or `ms.json`.

When someone uses a shortened URL, we need to retrieve the original URL and track the access:

```
func (s *URLShortenerService) GetOriginalURL(short string) (string, error)
{
    blobName := fmt.Sprintf("%s.json", short)
    containerClient := s.storageClient.NewContainerClient(s.containerName)
    blobClient := containerClient.NewBlockBlobClient(blobName)

    // Download current data
    resp, err := blobClient.DownloadStream(s.ctx, nil)
    if err != nil {
        return "", fmt.Errorf("URL not found: %w", err)
    }

    var mapping URLMapping
    if err := json.NewDecoder(resp.Body).Decode(&mapping); err != nil {
        return "", fmt.Errorf("failed to decode mapping: %w", err)
    }

    // Update access count
    mapping.AccessCount++
    data, _ := json.Marshal(mapping)
```

```
    _, err = blobClient.UploadBuffer(
        s.ctx, data, &azblob.UploadBufferOptions{}
    )
    if err != nil {
        log.Printf("Failed to update access count: %v", err)
    }

    return mapping.Original, nil
}
```

This function demonstrates a common pattern when working with blob storage: download, modify, and re-upload. It first downloads the blob containing the URL mapping, decodes the JSON into a struct, increments the access counter, and uploads the updated data back to storage. This way, we can track how popular each shortened URL is. If updating the counter fails, we still return the original URL; it's better to serve the user than to fail because of a tracking issue.

To make scaling decisions, we need to know how much traffic our service is handling:

`GetTotalTraffic` calculates total traffic across all URLs:

```
func (s *URLShortenerService) GetTotalTraffic() (int, error) {
    containerClient := s.storageClient.NewContainerClient(s.containerName)
    pager := containerClient.NewListBlobsFlatPager(nil)

    totalAccess := 0
    for pager.More() {
        page, err := pager.NextPage(s.ctx)
        if err != nil {
            return 0, fmt.Errorf("failed to list blobs: %w", err)
        }

        for _, blob := range page.Segment.BlobItems {
            blobClient := containerClient.NewBlockBlobClient(*blob.Name)
            resp, err := blobClient.DownloadStream(s.ctx, nil)
            if err != nil {
                continue
            }

            var mapping URLMapping
```

```
            if err :=
            json.NewDecoder(resp.Body).Decode(&mapping); err !=
            nil {
                continue
            }
            totalAccess += mapping.AccessCount
        }
    }

    return totalAccess, nil
}
```

This function iterates through all the blobs in our container and adds up the access counts. Azure returns blobs in pages, so we use a pager to loop through them efficiently. For each blob, we download it, decode the JSON, and add its access count to our total. If any individual blob fails to download or decode, we just skip it and continue; one corrupted file shouldn't break our entire traffic calculation.

One of the powerful features of our service is automatic scaling when traffic gets high:

```
func (s *URLShortenerService) ScaleResources(trafficThreshold int) error {
    traffic, err := s.GetTotalTraffic()
    if err != nil {
        return fmt.Errorf("failed to get traffic: %w", err)
    }

    log.Printf("Current traffic: %d requests", traffic)

    if traffic > trafficThreshold {
        log.Println(
            "Traffic threshold exceeded, provisioning additional VM..."
        )
        return s.provisionVM()
    }

    log.Println("Traffic within normal range")
    return nil
}
```

This function checks if the traffic has exceeded a threshold and automatically provisions a new VM if needed. This is a simplified example of auto-scaling. In a production environment, we would use more sophisticated metrics such as requests per second or CPU usage, and we would probably use Azure's built-in auto-scaling features. But this demonstrates the concept of making infrastructure decisions based on application data.

When we need more capacity, we create a new VM programmatically:

```
func (s *URLShortenerService) provisionVM() error {
    vmName := fmt.Sprintf("shortener-vm-%d", time.Now().Unix())

    vmParams := armcompute.VirtualMachine{
        Location: to.Ptr("eastus"),
        Properties: &armcompute.VirtualMachineProperties{
            HardwareProfile: &armcompute.HardwareProfile{
                VMSize: to.Ptr(
                    armcompute.VirtualMachineSizeTypesStandardB1S
                ),
            },
            StorageProfile: &armcompute.StorageProfile{
                ImageReference: &armcompute.ImageReference{
                    Publisher: to.Ptr("Canonical"),
                    Offer:     to.Ptr("0001-com-ubuntu-server-jammy"),
                    SKU:       to.Ptr("22_04-lts"),
                    Version:   to.Ptr("latest"),
                },
            },
            OSProfile: &armcompute.OSProfile{
                ComputerName:  to.Ptr(vmName),
                AdminUsername: to.Ptr("azureuser"),
                AdminPassword: to.Ptr("P@ssw0rd1234!"),
            },
        },
    }

    poller, err := s.vmClient.BeginCreateOrUpdate(
        s.ctx,
        s.resourceGroup,
```

```
        vmName,
        vmParams,
        nil,
    )
    if err != nil {
        return fmt.Errorf("failed to begin VM creation: %w", err)
    }

    _, err = poller.PollUntilDone(s.ctx, nil)
    if err != nil {
        return fmt.Errorf("failed to create VM: %w", err)
    }

    log.Printf("Successfully provisioned VM: %s", vmName)
    return nil
}
```

This function creates a new Azure VM with a specific configuration. We use a timestamp in the VM name to ensure uniqueness; each VM gets a name such as `shortener-vm-1699564800`. The VM is configured with a small size (`Standard_B1s`) running Ubuntu 22.04. Creating a VM is a long-running operation, so we use a `poller` to wait until it's complete. In a real application, we would also configure networking, install the application on the VM, and add it to a load balancer.

This complete example shows the power of integrating multiple Azure services in a single application. By combining Blob Storage for data persistence, virtual machines for compute resources, and the Azure SDK for automation, we have built a scalable URL shortener that can adapt to changing demand.

The key takeaway is that Azure services work better together than in isolation. Storage provides the persistence layer, VMs provide the processing power, and the SDK gives us the tools to orchestrate everything programmatically. This architecture is similar to what you'd use for many real-world applications, whether we're building a web service, a data processing pipeline, or a monitoring system.

As our applications grow, we can extend this pattern by adding more Azure services. For example, we could add Azure Functions for serverless processing, Azure SQL Database for relational data, or Azure Monitor for observability. The Azure SDK provides a consistent way to interact with all these services from Go code.

Summary

In the first section, we learned how to set up the Azure SDK for Go and configure authentication using service principals. This included creating credentials in Azure Active Directory, assigning the right permissions, and securely storing them in environment variables or configuration files. With this setup, Go applications can safely connect to Azure and perform actions without manual sign-in.

Next, the focus was on working with Azure Storage, specifically managing blob files. You discovered how to upload and download files programmatically, organize them into containers, and apply permissions or metadata as needed. These skills are particularly helpful for applications such as a URL shortener that might need to store assets such as logs or images in the cloud.

Finally, the last section covered managing Azure virtual machines using Go. You explored how to provision new VMs, start and stop them, and clean up resources when they're no longer needed. By learning how to control VMs from code, developers can build applications that automatically adjust compute resources based on real-time demand or deployment scenarios.

In the next chapter, we'll shift gears to serverless computing with AWS Lambda. You'll get a hands-on look at how to build and run code without managing servers, set up triggers to respond to events, and connect Lambda functions with other AWS services to create powerful and scalable applications.

13

Serverless Computing Using AWS Lambda

Serverless computing with AWS Lambda lets developers build and run code without having to manage or provision servers. This means we can focus entirely on writing applications' logic, while AWS takes care of the rest, such as scaling, maintenance, and availability. This is especially helpful for applications that have unpredictable or fluctuating workloads, such as a URL shortener service where traffic can spike at random times. With AWS Lambda, applications can automatically scale up during high traffic and scale down to zero when idle, helping reduce costs and operational complexity.

Another key benefit of AWS Lambda is how easily it integrates with other AWS services, such as S3, DynamoDB, and API Gateway. This enables developers to build powerful event-driven systems where actions are triggered by real-time events, for example, a file upload or an HTTP request. For example, we can create a Lambda function that automatically logs shortened URLs to a database whenever a new link is created via API Gateway. This kind of seamless integration makes AWS Lambda an ideal foundation for modern, cloud-native applications that prioritize agility, scalability, and low overhead.

In this chapter, we will cover the following topics:

- What serverless computing is and how AWS Lambda fits into it
- How to create, deploy, and manage Lambda functions using the AWS SDK
- How to set up triggers so Lambda functions run in response to events from services such as S3 or API Gateway

- How to connect Lambda functions to other AWS services, such as SNS or DynamoDB, to build complete serverless applications
- Best practices for building, testing, and managing scalable, event-driven systems with Lambda

Creating and deploying Lambda functions

Lambda functions only run when needed, which saves money and resources. They scale automatically, so the system can handle just one request or thousands at once.

They are also quick to set up and connect easily with other AWS services. This makes them ideal for building flexible and cost-efficient applications.

Before deploying a Lambda function, the local development environment must be prepared. This involves configuring the Go toolchain, setting up dependencies, and ensuring that the function code can be compiled for AWS's runtime environment.

The following section explains how to set up the environment step by step to get ready for Lambda development.

Setting up the Go environment

To get started, let's first initialize the Go module to set up the project environment:

```
mkdir url-shortener-lambda
cd url-shortener-lambda
go mod init github.com/<yourusername>/url-shortener-lambda
```

Let's install the required packages:

```
go get github.com/aws/aws-lambda-go/lambda
```

To build a serverless backend with AWS Lambda, we write small functions that run in the cloud. These functions are called **handlers**. They run automatically when something triggers them, such as a web request or a file being uploaded. We don't need to set up or manage any servers; AWS takes care of that for us.

Let's create a simple Lambda function in `main.go`:

```
package main

import (
    "context"
```

```
    "fmt"
    "github.com/aws/aws-lambda-go/lambda"
)

type Request struct {
    URL string `json:"url"`
}

type Response struct {
    ShortURL string `json:"short_url"`
}

func handler(ctx context.Context, req Request) (Response, error) {
    // Placeholder logic for URL shortening
    shortURL := fmt.Sprintf("https://short.ly/%x", len(req.URL))
    return Response{ShortURL: shortURL}, nil
}

func main() {
    lambda.Start(handler)
}
```

This code defines a simple AWS Lambda function that receives a URL and returns a shortened version of it. The `Request` and `Response` structs define the expected input and output formats. The `handler` function takes a request, calculates the shortened URL, and returns it.

Finally, the `main` function calls `lambda.Start(handler)`, which registers the handler with AWS Lambda to start processing events.

You may have noticed that the handler function takes `context.Context` as its first parameter. This is a special object that Go uses to manage the life cycle of a function call. In Lambda functions, `context` is especially important because it carries information about the execution environment and helps manage timeouts.

The `context` object provides several useful features:

- **Timeout management**: Lambda functions have a maximum execution time (configured when the function is created). `context` helps the code know when time is running out. We can check whether `context` is about to expire and handle it gracefully:

```
func handler(ctx context.Context, req Request) (Response, error) {
    // Check if running out of time
    select {
    case <-ctx.Done():
        return Response{}, fmt.Errorf("function timed out")
    default:
        // Continue processing
    }

    // Normal logic here
    shortURL := fmt.Sprintf("https://short.ly/%x", len(req.URL))
    return Response{ShortURL: shortURL}, nil
}
```

- **Passing context to other AWS services**: When the Lambda function calls other AWS services, such as **DynamoDB** or **S3**, it should pass the context along. This ensures that if Lambda is about to timeout, those service calls will also be canceled:

```
func handler(ctx context.Context, req Request) (Response, error) {
    // When calling AWS SDK, always pass the context
    result, err := dynamoClient.PutItem(ctx, input)
    if err != nil {
        return Response{}, err
    }

    return Response{ShortURL: "https://short.ly/abc"}, nil
}
```

- **Request information**: `context` also carries metadata about the Lambda invocation, such as the request ID, which can be useful for logging and debugging:

```
func handler(ctx context.Context, req Request) (Response, error) {
    lambdaContext, _ := lambdacontext.FromContext(ctx)
    fmt.Printf("Request ID: %s\n", lambdaContext.AwsRequestID)
```

```
    // Logic goes here
    return Response{ShortURL: "https://short.ly/abc"}, nil
}
```

For simple Lambda functions, you might not use `context` actively in code, but it's still important to include it as a parameter. As functions become more complex and interact with other services, `context` becomes essential for proper timeout handling and request tracking.

Building the executable

AWS Lambda runs functions in a Linux-based environment with a specific architecture (usually `x86_64` or `amd64`).

There are two main ways to build and deploy a Go Lambda function, and which one we choose depends on the runtime we are using.

Option 1: Using a custom runtime with bootstrap

If we are using a custom runtime (such as `provided.al2`), AWS Lambda looks for an executable file named exactly `bootstrap`. This is a special name that tells Lambda where to find the function code.

```
GOOS=linux GOARCH=amd64 go build -o bootstrap main.go
zip function.zip bootstrap
```

When we deploy this, we will use `provided.al2` as the runtime in the Lambda configuration:

```
aws lambda create-function \
  --runtime provided.al2 \
  --handler bootstrap \
  ...
```

Option 2: Using the official Go runtime with a named handler

If we are using the official AWS Lambda Go runtime (such as `go1.x`), we can name the binary anything we want. We just need to tell Lambda what that name is in the handler configuration:

```
GOOS=linux GOARCH=amd64 go build -o url-shortener-handler main.go
zip handler.zip url-shortener-handler
```

Then, when we deploy, we specify the handler name to match the binary:

```
aws lambda create-function \
  --runtime go1.x \
```

```
    --handler url-shortener-handler \
    ...
```

Which option should we use?

For most cases, using the custom runtime with `bootstrap` (*Option 1*) is simpler and more flexible. It works with *any* Go version and gives more control.

The official Go runtime (*Option 2*) is easier if we want AWS to manage the Go runtime version for us, but it may lag behind the latest Go releases.

In the rest of this chapter, we'll use *Option 1* with the custom runtime and `bootstrap` naming convention.

Creating a deployment package

Before a Lambda function can run in AWS, it needs permission to access other AWS services and resources. This is done by assigning an IAM role to the function. IAM roles define what the function is allowed to do.

Think of an IAM role like a badge that gives specific permissions. When a Lambda function "assumes" a role, it's like picking up that badge and using it to prove what it's allowed to do. The Lambda function itself doesn't have any permissions on its own; it needs to assume a role to get those permissions.

The first step in this process is creating a **trust policy** that allows AWS Lambda to assume the role. Without this trust policy, Lambda wouldn't be able to assume the role and get the permissions that it needs.

Let's create a trust policy (`trust-policy.json`):

```
{
  "Version": "2012-10-17",
  "Statement": [
    {
      "Effect": "Allow",
      "Principal": {
        "Service": "lambda.amazonaws.com"
      },
      "Action": "sts:AssumeRole"
    }
  ]
}
```

This code defines a trust policy. The policy specifies that the AWS Lambda service (`lambda.amazonaws.com`) is trusted to assume this IAM role using the `sts:AssumeRole` action.

Now, create the IAM role:

```
aws iam create-role --role-name lambda-execute-role --assume-role-policy-document file://trust-policy.json
```

Attach the policy:

```
aws iam attach-role-policy --role-name lambda-execute-role --policy-arn arn:aws:iam::aws:policy/service-role/AWSLambdaBasicExecutionRole
```

The `AWSLambdaBasicExecutionRole` policy gives the Lambda function basic permissions, such as writing logs to CloudWatch. When the Lambda function runs, it will automatically assume this role and have the permissions it needs to execute properly.

Now that we've created the IAM role and attached the basic execution policy, the Lambda function has the necessary permissions to run. This completes the setup for enabling AWS Lambda to execute securely with the correct permissions in place.

Deploying the Lambda function

Once we have written the Lambda function code and set up the necessary IAM role, the next step is to deploy it to AWS so it can start responding to events.

Deployment involves uploading the packaged code and specifying how the function should be run.

Let's create the Lambda function:

```
aws lambda create-function \
  --function-name urlShortenerFunction \
  --runtime provided.al2 \
  --role arn:aws:iam::123456789012:role/lambda-execute-role \
  --handler bootstrap \
  --zip-file fileb://function.zip
```

This command uses the **AWS CLI** to create a new Lambda function named `urlShortenerFunction`. It specifies `provided.al2` as the runtime (for custom runtime on Amazon Linux 2), assigns it an IAM role (`lambda-execute-role`) for permissions, and sets `bootstrap` as the entry point handler. The function code is uploaded as a zipped file (`function.zip`).

This command registers the function with AWS Lambda, making it ready to be triggered.

Testing the Lambda function

After deploying a Lambda function, it's important to verify that it works as expected. Testing the function helps ensure that the input is processed correctly and the output meets the requirements before integrating it into a larger system.

Let's invoke the function:

```
aws lambda invoke \
  --function-name urlShortenerFunction \
  --payload '{"url": "https://example.com"}' \
  response.json
```

View the response:

```
cat response.json
```

This example shows how to invoke the deployed `urlShortenerFunction` using the AWS CLI. It sends a test payload containing a URL (`https://example.com`) and writes the function's response to a file named `response.json`.

The second command (`cat response.json`) is used to display the contents of the response, allowing us to check the output and confirm that the function behaves as intended.

Updating the function

As the application evolves, the Lambda function will likely need updates to fix bugs, improve logic, or add new features. When changes are made to the function code, the updated code must be recompiled into a new binary and repackaged into a zip file before deploying it to AWS Lambda.

Make changes to `main.go` as needed, then rebuild the Go binary and package it into a ZIP file:

```
GOOS=linux GOARCH=amd64 go build -o bootstrap main.go
zip function.zip bootstrap
```

The first command compiles the updated main.go file into a new bootstrap executable that's compatible with the Lambda Linux environment. The second command creates a fresh function. zip file containing this new binary, replacing any previous version.

Update the Lambda function code with the new package:

```
aws lambda update-function-code \
  --function-name urlShortenerFunction \
  --zip-file fileb://function.zip
```

This snippet outlines how to update an existing AWS Lambda function. After modifying `main.go`, the code is rebuilt for the Linux environment with the appropriate architecture (`GOOS=linux GOARCH=amd64`), and the output binary is named `bootstrap`.

This binary is then zipped into `function.zip`. Finally, the `aws lambda update-function-code` command uploads the new ZIP package, replacing the current function code with the updated version.

Cleaning up resources

Once we are done testing or no longer need the Lambda function and its associated resources, we clean them up. This helps avoid unnecessary AWS charges and keeps the AWS environment organized and secure.

Run the following command to delete the Lambda function:

```
aws lambda delete-function --function-name urlShortenerFunction
```

Run the following command to detach the policy and delete the IAM role:

```
aws iam detach-role-policy --role-name lambda-execute-role --policy-arn
arn:aws:iam::aws:policy/service-role/AWSLambdaBasicExecutionRole
aws iam delete-role --role-name lambda-execute-role
```

This code deletes the deployed Lambda function named `urlShortenerFunction`. It then removes the associated IAM role permissions by first detaching the AWS-managed policy and finally deleting the `lambda-execute-role` role. This ensures that all the resources created for this Lambda function are properly cleaned up.

In this section, we covered the full life cycle of building and deploying a Lambda function, from setting up the development environment and compiling the code for AWS Lambda to packaging, deploying, and testing the function. We also saw how to update the function when changes are made, and how to clean up the associated AWS resources to avoid unwanted costs.

Now that our Lambda function is up and running, the next step is to make it event-driven by configuring triggers, which define what should invoke the function and when.

Managing triggers and event sources

Managing triggers and event sources is a very important pattern when building event-driven applications. In this section, we focus on configuring AWS Lambda functions to respond to events from Amazon S3 and API Gateway, using a URL shortener as a practical example.

AWS Lambda can be invoked by various AWS services through triggers. Common event sources include Amazon S3 (for object events) and API Gateway (for HTTP requests). Configuring these triggers allows Lambda functions to respond automatically to specific events.

Setting up an S3 trigger

Sometimes we want the application to automatically respond when a file is uploaded to an S3 bucket. Setting up an S3 trigger for a Lambda function allows us to build an event-driven workflow where the function is invoked automatically as soon as new objects are added.

```
package main

import (
    "context"
    "fmt"
    "github.com/aws/aws-lambda-go/events"
    "github.com/aws/aws-lambda-go/lambda"
)

func handler(ctx context.Context, s3Event events.S3Event) error {
    for _, record := range s3Event.Records {
        s3 := record.S3
        fmt.Printf("New object uploaded: %s\n", s3.Object.Key)
    }
    return nil
}

func main() {
    lambda.Start(handler)
}
```

This Lambda function is triggered by S3 events. It receives `S3Event` data whenever a new object is uploaded. The `handler` function loops through the records in the event and prints the key (`name`) of each uploaded object. The main function starts the Lambda with the handler.

Setting up an API Gateway trigger

To make a Lambda function accessible over HTTP, we can set it up to be triggered by API Gateway. This allows users to send requests to the function through a public REST API, which is especially useful for building web and mobile backends.

```
package main

import (
    "context"
    "encoding/json"
    "github.com/aws/aws-lambda-go/events"
    "github.com/aws/aws-lambda-go/lambda"
)

type Request struct {
    URL string `json:"url"`
}

type Response struct {
    ShortURL string `json:"short_url"`
}

func handler(ctx context.Context, request events.
APIGatewayProxyRequest) (    events.APIGatewayProxyResponse, error
) {
    var req Request
    err := json.Unmarshal([]byte(request.Body), &req)
    if err != nil {
        return events.APIGatewayProxyResponse{StatusCode: 400}, err
    }

    shortURL := "https://short.ly/" + "abc123" // Placeholder logic

    res := Response{ShortURL: shortURL}
    resBody, _ := json.Marshal(res)

    return events.APIGatewayProxyResponse{
        StatusCode: 200,
        Body:       string(resBody),
    }, nil
}

func main() {
    lambda.Start(handler)
}
```

This Lambda function handles HTTP requests from API Gateway. The `handler` function receives an `APIGatewayProxyRequest`, parses the incoming JSON to extract a URL, and returns a shortened version in the response.

The response is structured with an **HTTP 200** status code and a JSON body containing the shortened URL. The main function starts the Lambda function using the `lambda.Start` method.

We explored how to configure common event sources such as Amazon S3 and API Gateway to trigger Lambda functions. These triggers allow the function to run automatically in response to file uploads, API calls, and other events.

Next, we'll take this further by integrating AWS Lambda with additional AWS services, such as **Simple Notification Service** (**SNS**), **Simple Queue Service** (**SQS**), and DynamoDB, unlocking even more powerful and scalable serverless workflows.

Integrating AWS Lambda with other AWS services

Integrating AWS Lambda with other AWS services is a very important pattern for building scalable, serverless applications. In this section, we'll explore how to connect Lambda functions with services such as API Gateway, Amazon SNS, Amazon DynamoDB, and Amazon SQS.

Integrating Lambda with API Gateway

API Gateway acts as a front door for Lambda functions, allowing us to expose them as RESTful APIs. For a URL shortener, we might have an endpoint that accepts a long URL and returns a shortened version. When a client sends a `POST` request to this endpoint, API Gateway invokes the corresponding Lambda function. The function processes the request, generates a short URL, and returns the response. This setup enables us to build a serverless API without managing any infrastructure.

The Lambda function code itself doesn't change when we add API Gateway in front of it. API Gateway simply acts as a proxy that receives HTTP requests from clients and triggers the Lambda function with that data. The function still receives the same event structure and returns the same response format that we've been using in previous examples. The main difference is that instead of manually invoking the function or triggering it from another AWS service, users can now call it through a standard HTTP endpoint such as `https://api.example.com/shorten`. This makes the Lambda function accessible to any client that can make HTTP requests, such as web browsers, mobile apps, or other services.

Integrating Lambda with Amazon SNS

Amazon SNS allows us to decouple microservices by enabling asynchronous communication. In the context of a URL shortener, you might want to notify other parts of your system whenever a new URL is shortened. To achieve this, the Lambda function can publish a message to an SNS topic after creating a short URL. Other services subscribed to this topic can then process the message accordingly.

```
package main

import (
    "context"
    "fmt"
    "github.com/aws/aws-sdk-go-v2/aws"
    "github.com/aws/aws-sdk-go-v2/config"
    "github.com/aws/aws-sdk-go-v2/service/sns"
)

func main() {
    cfg, err := config.LoadDefaultConfig(context.TODO())
    if err != nil {
        panic("configuration error: " + err.Error())
    }

    client := sns.NewFromConfig(cfg)

    input := &sns.PublishInput{
        Message:  aws.String("New URL shortened: https://short.ly/
abc123"),
        TopicArn: aws.String(
            "arn:aws:sns:us-west-2:123456789012:NewURLTopic"
        ),
    }

    result, err := client.Publish(context.TODO(), input)
    if err != nil {
        panic("publish error: " + err.Error())
    }
```

```
    fmt.Println("Message ID:", *result.MessageId)
}
```

This code publishes a message to the NewURLTopic Amazon SNS topic. We first load the default AWS configuration and create an SNS client. Then, we send a message with a shortened URL to the topic so other services subscribed to that topic can receive it. Other services subscribed to this topic can then act upon the new URL information.

Using DynamoDB with AWS Lambda

When a user submits a URL to be shortened, the Lambda function can generate a unique short code and store it in a DynamoDB table along with the original URL. Subsequent requests to the short URL can trigger another Lambda function that queries DynamoDB to retrieve the original URL and redirect the user accordingly.

```
package main

import (
    "context"
    "fmt"
    "github.com/aws/aws-lambda-go/lambda"
    "github.com/aws/aws-sdk-go-v2/aws"
    "github.com/aws/aws-sdk-go-v2/config"
    "github.com/aws/aws-sdk-go-v2/service/dynamodb"
    "github.com/aws/aws-sdk-go-v2/service/dynamodb/dynamodbiface"
    "github.com/aws/aws-sdk-go-v2/service/dynamodb/types"
)

type Request struct {
    ShortCode string `json:"short_code"`
    LongURL string `json:"long_url"`
}

func handler(ctx context.Context, req Request) (string, error) {
    cfg, err := config.LoadDefaultConfig(ctx)
    if err != nil {
        return "", fmt.Errorf("unable to load SDK config, %v", err)
    }
```

```
    svc := dynamodb.NewFromConfig(cfg)

    input := &dynamodb.PutItemInput{
        TableName: aws.String("URLMappings"),
        Item: map[string]types.AttributeValue{
            "ShortCode": &types.AttributeValueMemberS{Value: req.ShortCode
            },
            "LongURL": &types.AttributeValueMemberS{Value: req.LongURL},
        },
    }

    _, err = svc.PutItem(ctx, input)
    if err != nil {
        return "", fmt.Errorf("failed to put item, %v", err)
    }

    return fmt.Sprintf(
        "Short URL created: https://short.ly/%s", req.ShortCode
    ), nil
}

func main() {
    lambda.Start(handler)
}
```

This Lambda function stores short code and its corresponding long URL in a DynamoDB table called `URLMappings`.

When triggered, it loads the AWS configuration, initializes a DynamoDB client, and uses the `PutItem` API to insert the short code and the long URL as key-value pairs.

If the operation succeeds, it returns a success message with the generated short URL.

Leveraging DynamoDB Streams

DynamoDB Streams can be utilized to capture changes to the DynamoDB table in real time. For instance, whenever a new URL mapping is added, a stream record is generated. A Lambda function can be configured to process these stream records, enabling functionalities such as analytics, notifications, or data replication.

```
package main

import (
    "context"
    "fmt"
    "github.com/aws/aws-lambda-go/events"
    "github.com/aws/aws-lambda-go/lambda"
)

func handler(ctx context.Context, event events.DynamoDBEvent) {
    for _, record := range event.Records {
        fmt.Printf("Processing record ID: %s\n", record.EventID)
        if record.EventName == "INSERT" {
            newImage := record.Change.NewImage
            shortCode := newImage["ShortCode"].String()
            longURL := newImage["LongURL"].String()
            fmt.Printf(
                "New URL mapping added: %s -> %s\n", shortCode, longURL
            )
            // Additional processing can be done here
        }
    }
}

func main() {
    lambda.Start(handler)
}
```

This function processes each record in the DynamoDB stream, specifically handling `INSERT` events to identify new URL mappings. Such processing can be extended to trigger notifications, update caches, or perform other auxiliary tasks.

Using Amazon SQS with AWS Lambda

Integrating AWS Lambda with Amazon SQS is a powerful approach to building scalable, decoupled, and event-driven applications. In the context of a URL shortener, SQS can be used to handle tasks such as processing URL shortening requests asynchronously, managing analytics, or handling retries for failed operations. This integration allows for efficient message handling without the need to manage infrastructure.

When a user submits a URL to be shortened, the application can send a message to an SQS queue containing the URL data. A Lambda function, configured to poll this queue, retrieves the message, processes the URL shortening logic, and stores the result in a database or returns it to the user. This decouples the request handling from the processing logic, allowing for better scalability and fault tolerance.

```
package main

import (
    "context"
    "fmt"
    "github.com/aws/aws-lambda-go/events"
    "github.com/aws/aws-lambda-go/lambda"
)

func handler(ctx context.Context, sqsEvent events.SQSEvent) error {
    for _, message := range sqsEvent.Records {
        fmt.Printf(
            "Processing message ID: %s,
            Body: %s\n",
            message.MessageId,
            message.Body
        )
        // URL shortening logic
    }
    return nil
}

func main() {
    lambda.Start(handler)
}
```

In this example, the Lambda function processes each message received from the SQS queue, where each message contains data necessary for URL shortening.

Benefits of integrating SQS with Lambda

Integrating Amazon SQS with AWS Lambda allows us to queue messages for asynchronous processing, enabling the system to remain responsive under heavy load. This setup is especially useful for background tasks, batch jobs, or handling spikes in traffic without over-provisioning infrastructure. Here are the benefits:

- **Asynchronous processing**: By decoupling the message producer and consumer, the system can handle varying loads without immediate processing, improving responsiveness
- **Scalability**: Lambda functions can scale automatically in response to the number of messages in the SQS queue, ensuring efficient processing during peak times
- **Fault tolerance**: If a Lambda function fails to process a message, SQS can retain the message and retry processing, or route it to a dead-letter queue for further analysis
- **Cost efficiency**: With serverless architecture, you only pay for the compute time you consume, making it a cost-effective solution for handling background tasks

Managing secrets in Lambda functions

When building serverless applications, we often need to work with sensitive information such as database passwords, API keys, or authentication tokens. Hardcoding these secrets directly in the Lambda function code is a security risk. If someone gets access to the code, they'll have access to all secrets. Instead, AWS provides a service called **AWS Secrets Manager** that stores and manages secrets securely.

Why use AWS Secrets Manager?

AWS Secrets Manager helps to protect access to applications, services, and IT resources. Instead of embedding credentials in the code, we store them in Secrets Manager and a Lambda function retrieves them at runtime. This approach offers several benefits:

- Secrets are encrypted and stored securely
- It's possible to rotate secrets automatically without changing the code
- It's possible to control who has access to which secrets using IAM policies
- All secret access is logged for auditing purposes

Storing a secret

Before the Lambda function can use a secret, we need to store it in AWS Secrets Manager. Let's say our URL shortener needs to connect to a database. We can store the database credentials as a secret:

```
aws secretsmanager create-secret \
  --name urlshortener/db/credentials \
  --description "Database credentials for URL shortener" \
  --secret-string '{"username":"admin","password":"secure-password"}'
```

This command creates a secret named `urlshortener/db/credentials` that contains the database username and password in JSON format.

Retrieving secrets in Lambda functions

Now let's see how to retrieve and use this secret in a Lambda function:

```
type DBCredentials struct {
    Username string `json:"username"`
    Password string `json:"password"`
}

func getSecret(
    ctx context.Context, secretName string) (DBCredentials, error
) {
    cfg, err := config.LoadDefaultConfig(ctx)
    if err != nil {
        return DBCredentials{}, fmt.Errorf(
            "failed to load config: %w", err
        )
    }

    client := secretsmanager.NewFromConfig(cfg)

    result, err := client.GetSecretValue(
        ctx, &secretsmanager.GetSecretValueInput{
            SecretId: &secretName,
        }
    )
    if err != nil {
```

```
        return DBCredentials{}, fmt.Errorf(
            "failed to get secret: %w", err
        )
    }

    var credentials DBCredentials
    if err := json.Unmarshal([]byte(*result.
SecretString), &credentials);      err != nil {
        return DBCredentials{}, fmt.Errorf(
            "failed to parse secret: %w", err
        )
    }

    return credentials, nil
}
```

This code defines a `getSecret` function that retrieves a secret from AWS Secrets Manager. The function loads the AWS configuration, creates a Secrets Manager client, and calls `GetSecretValue` to fetch the secret. It then parses the JSON string into a `DBCredentials` struct.

Granting Lambda permissions to access secrets

For the Lambda function to access Secrets Manager, we need to add the appropriate permissions to its IAM role. Update the IAM role policy to include Secrets Manager permissions:

```
aws iam attach-role-policy \
  --role-name lambda-execute-role \
  --policy-arn arn:aws:iam::aws:policy/SecretsManagerReadWrite
```

Alternatively, for better security, create a custom policy that only allows reading specific secrets:

```
{
  "Version": "2012-10-17",
  "Statement": [
    {
      "Effect": "Allow",
      "Action": [
        "secretsmanager:GetSecretValue"
      ],
      "Resource":
```

```
            "arn:aws:secretsmanager:us-west-2:123456789012:
            secret:urlshortener/*"
        }
    ]
}
```

This policy only allows the Lambda function to read secrets that start with `urlshortener/`, following the principle of least privilege.

Caching secrets for better performance

Retrieving secrets from Secrets Manager on every Lambda invocation can add latency and cost. A common best practice is to cache the secret and reuse it across invocations:

```
var cachedCredentials *DBCredentials

func getSecret(ctx context.Context, secretName string) (
    DBCredentials, error
) {
    // Return cached credentials if available
    if cachedCredentials != nil {
        return *cachedCredentials, nil
    }

    cfg, err := config.LoadDefaultConfig(ctx)
    if err != nil {
        return DBCredentials{}, fmt.Errorf(
            "failed to load config: %w", err
        )
    }

    client := secretsmanager.NewFromConfig(cfg)

    result, err := client.GetSecretValue(
        ctx, &secretsmanager.GetSecretValueInput{
            SecretId: &secretName,
        }
    )
    if err != nil {
```

```
        return DBCredentials{}, fmt.Errorf(
            "failed to get secret: %w", err
        )
    }

    var credentials DBCredentials
    if err := json.Unmarshal([]byte(*result.
SecretString), &credentials);     err != nil {
        return DBCredentials{}, fmt.Errorf(
            "failed to parse secret: %w", err
        )
    }

    // Cache the credentials for future invocations
    cachedCredentials = &credentials

    return credentials, nil
}
```

By storing the credentials in a package-level variable (for example, `cachedCredentials`), the secret is only retrieved from Secrets Manager during the first invocation. Subsequent invocations within the same Lambda execution environment will use the cached value, reducing latency and API calls.

Best practices for secrets management

When working with secrets in Lambda functions, follow these best practices:

- **Never hardcode secrets**: Always use Secrets Manager or environment variables for sensitive data
- **Use specific secret names**: Organize secrets with clear naming patterns, such as `app/environment/resource`
- **Apply least privilege**: Grant Lambda functions access only to the secrets they need
- **Enable secret rotation**: Use Secrets Manager's automatic rotation feature for database credentials
- **Cache wisely**: Cache secrets to improve performance, but be aware that cached values won't update until the Lambda environment is recycled
- **Monitor access**: Enable CloudTrail logging to track who accesses which secrets and when
- **Use encryption**: Secrets Manager encrypts secrets at rest using AWS KMS keys

By following these practices, we ensure that the serverless applications handle sensitive information securely while maintaining good performance and operational efficiency.

Summary

The first section explained how AWS Lambda functions are created, deployed, and configured using the AWS Management Console and SDKs. We outlined how to package function logic, define runtime settings, and manage permissions to ensure secure and efficient execution. Practical examples, such as creating a URL shortener, illustrated how serverless code can be deployed to respond to specific tasks without provisioning infrastructure.

We then covered how to connect Lambda functions with event sources such as S3 and API Gateway. These integrations enable event-driven workflows, where functions are automatically triggered by changes such as file uploads or incoming HTTP requests. This approach supports efficient and scalable architectures by reducing the need for always-on resources while maintaining responsiveness to events.

The chapter concluded by demonstrating how AWS Lambda can interact with other AWS services, such as Amazon SNS, DynamoDB, and SQS. These services allow functions to send notifications, store structured data, and handle background tasks through queues. Together, these integrations form the foundation of powerful, modular, and serverless applications that can scale with demand and remain easy to maintain.

In the next chapter, we'll switch to serverless development on Azure using Azure Functions. You'll learn how to create lightweight, scalable functions that respond to events, and connect them with other Azure services to build powerful, event-driven solutions.

14

Serverless Computing Using Azure Functions

Serverless computing with Azure Functions offers a highly efficient and cost-effective way to build scalable cloud applications without the complexity of managing infrastructure. By abstracting away server provisioning, patching, and scaling, Azure Functions allows developers to focus purely on writing business logic. This leads to faster development cycles, lower operational overhead, and seamless scalability as workloads increase. Azure functions automatically respond to various triggers, such as HTTP requests, timers, or data changes, making them ideal for creating reactive, event-driven applications.

In enterprise and cloud-native environments, Azure Functions enables seamless integration with a wide range of Azure services, such as Azure Storage, Event Hubs, Cosmos DB, and more. This integration option simplifies the orchestration of tasks, such as file processing, data transformation, and real-time analytics. Whether used to power backend APIs, automate workflows, or process data streams, Azure Functions provides a flexible and robust base for building modern applications that scale dynamically based on demand.

In this chapter, we will cover the following topics:

- Creating and deploying Azure functions using the Azure SDK
- Setting up triggers to automatically run functions in response to events
- Using bindings to simplify data input and output in functions
- Connecting Azure Functions with Azure Storage to read and write data
- Integrating with Event Hubs to process event streams in real time

Creating and deploying Azure functions

Creating and deploying Azure Functions using the Azure SDK for Go allows developers to build serverless logic in a scalable, event-driven architecture. Azure Functions supports multiple languages, and although Go is not a built-in runtime, it can still be used effectively with custom handlers. This section explains how to configure, develop, and deploy Go-based Azure functions using the Azure SDK.

To begin, a Go application must be structured to serve HTTP requests since Azure functions will invoke the binary via HTTP when using custom handlers. For a URL shortener example, a function can accept a long URL, store it in a data store, and return a shortened URL.

```
package main

import (
    "encoding/json"
    "fmt"
    "log"
    "math/rand"
    "net/http"
    "os"
    "time"
)

type ShortenRequest struct {
    URL string `json:"url"`
}

type ShortenResponse struct {
    ShortURL string `json:"short_url"`
}

func main() {
    http.HandleFunc("/shorten", handleShorten)
    port := os.Getenv("FUNCTIONS_CUSTOMHANDLER_PORT")
    log.Fatal(http.ListenAndServe(":"+port, nil))
}
```

```
func handleShorten(w http.ResponseWriter, r *http.Request) {
    var req ShortenRequest
    json.NewDecoder(r.Body).Decode(&req)

    rand.Seed(time.Now().UnixNano())
    shortCode := fmt.Sprintf("%06d", rand.Intn(1000000))
    shortURL := fmt.Sprintf("https://short.ly/%s", shortCode)

    resp := ShortenResponse{ShortURL: shortURL}
    w.Header().Set("Content-Type", "application/json")
    json.NewEncoder(w).Encode(resp)
}
```

This code sets up a basic HTTP server that accepts a JSON payload with a URL and returns a shortened version. Azure Functions can run this binary using a custom handler defined in the `host.json` file.

```
{
  "version": "2.0",
  "extensions": {
    "http": {
      "routePrefix": "api"
    }
  },
  "customHandler": {
    "description": {
      "defaultExecutablePath": "./urlshortener"
    },
    "enableForwardingHttpRequest": true
  }
}
```

The `function.json` file defines the route and method for the function endpoint.

```
{
  "bindings": [
    {
      "authLevel": "function",
      "type": "httpTrigger",
```

```
        "direction": "in",
        "name": "req",
        "methods": ["post"]
      },
      {
        "type": "http",
        "direction": "out",
        "name": "$return"
      }
    ]
}
```

To deploy, the Go code is compiled into a binary and placed in the function's root directory. Then, using the Azure CLI, the function app is created and deployed.

Here's how to compile for Azure:

```
go build -o urlshortener main.go
```

The Azure SDK enables creating the resource group, storage account, and function app required to deploy the function.

```
import (
    "context"
    "github.com/Azure/azure-sdk-for-go/sdk/
        resourcemanager/resources/armresources"
    "github.com/Azure/azure-sdk-for-go/sdk/azidentity"
    "log"
)

func createResourceGroup(
    subscriptionID, resourceGroupName, location string
) {
    cred, err := azidentity.NewDefaultAzureCredential(nil)
    if err != nil {
        log.Fatalf("failed to obtain credential: %v", err)
    }

    ctx := context.Background()
    client, err := armresources.NewResourceGroupsClient(
```

```
            subscriptionID, cred, nil
        )
        if err != nil {
            log.Fatalf("failed to create client: %v", err)
        }

        _, err = client.CreateOrUpdate(
            ctx,
            resourceGroupName,
            armresources.ResourceGroup{
                Location: &location,
            },
            nil,
        )
        if err != nil {
            log.Fatalf("failed to create resource group: %v", err)
        }
    }
```

Deployment steps include packaging the binary and function files into a zip archive and pushing them to Azure using either the Azure CLI or SDK.

Azure functions provide automatic scaling and monitoring capabilities, and they integrate seamlessly with services such as Azure Monitor and Application Insights.

The Go custom handler approach maintains compatibility with Azure Functions' features such as deployment slots, function proxies, and identity integration, making it suitable for production-grade serverless workloads.

Logging can be implemented using `fmt.Println` or structured logging frameworks. Azure captures standard output and error streams from the handler, which are then displayed in the portal or via Log Analytics.

This model allows building efficient serverless microservices, such as the URL shortener, that operate at scale without the burden of server management.

Further enhancements could include connecting to Azure Storage or Cosmos DB to store shortened URLs, which are explored in the *Integrating Azure Blob Storage integration*, *Integrating Azure Event Hubs integration*, and *Integrating Azure Queue Storage integration* sections, focusing on service integrations.

With the Azure SDK, the entire lifecycle of Azure functions can be automated: from infrastructure setup and deployment to management and monitoring – bringing a powerful developer experience to Go-based serverless applications.

Setting up triggers and bindings

In this section, the focus is on setting up triggers and bindings for Azure Functions using Go through custom handlers. This approach enables the creation of event-driven applications, such as a URL shortener, by responding to various events and simplifying data input and output operations.

Understanding triggers and bindings

Azure Functions operate on the concept of triggers and bindings. A trigger defines how a function is invoked, such as through an HTTP request, a timer, or a message in a queue. Bindings, on the other hand, provide a declarative way to connect to other services for input and output operations. With custom handlers, these are configured in the `function.json` file, allowing the function to interact with various Azure services without hardcoding the integrations.

Implementing an HTTP trigger

For a URL shortener, an HTTP trigger can be used to accept incoming requests. The `function.json` file would specify the trigger type and methods:

```
{
  "bindings": [
    {
      "authLevel": "function",
      "type": "httpTrigger",
      "direction": "in",
      "name": "req",
      "methods": ["post"]
    },
    {
      "type": "http",
      "direction": "out",
      "name": "res"
    }
  ]
}
```

The application would handle the HTTP request, process the URL shortening logic, and return the response.

Using timer triggers

To perform periodic tasks, such as cleaning up expired URLs, a timer trigger can be set up. The `function.json` file would include the following:

```
{
  "bindings": [
    {
      "name": "timer",
      "type": "timerTrigger",
      "direction": "in",
      "schedule": "0 0 * * * *"
    }
  ]
}
```

This configuration schedules the function to run at the top of every hour, allowing for automated maintenance tasks.

Integrating with Azure Storage

To store the mapping between original and shortened URLs, Azure Table Storage can be utilized. An output binding in the `function.json` file would look like this:

```
{
  "bindings": [
    {
      "name": "outputTable",
      "type": "table",
      "direction": "out",
      "tableName": "UrlMappings",
      "connection": "AzureWebJobsStorage"
    }
  ]
}
```

In the handler, the response would include the data to be stored, formatted as expected by Azure Table Storage.

Processing queue messages

For handling tasks asynchronously, such as processing analytics data, Azure Queue Storage can be integrated. An output binding would be defined in `function.json` as follows:

```
{
  "bindings": [
    {
      "name": "outputQueue",
      "type": "queue",
      "direction": "out",
      "queueName": "analyticsqueue",
      "connection": "AzureWebJobsStorage"
    }
  ]
}
```

The function would send messages to this queue, which can then be processed by other functions or services.

After setting up triggers and bindings, we now understand how to build event-driven Azure functions that respond to HTTP requests and timers. We've also explored how input and output bindings simplify data access and interaction with external systems.

Next, we'll take this further by integrating Azure Functions with key services such as Azure Blob Storage, Event Hubs, and Queue Storage. These integrations allow functions to handle large-scale file processing, real-time event ingestion, and background task execution.

Integrating Azure Functions with Azure services

Integrating Azure Functions with various Azure services allows for the creation of scalable, event-driven applications. Using Go with custom handlers, developers can build serverless solutions that interact seamlessly with services such as Azure Storage and Event Hubs. In this chapter, we'll explore these integrations through the examples of the URL shortener application.

Integrating Azure Blob Storage

To store the mapping between original and shortened URLs, Azure Blob Storage can be utilized. An output binding in the `function.json` file can be defined as follows:

```
{
  "bindings": [
    {
      "name": "outputBlob",
      "type": "blob",
      "direction": "out",
      "path": "shorturls/{rand-guid}.json",
      "connection": "AzureWebJobsStorage"
    }
  ]
}
```

In the handler, the function writes the URL mapping to the response, which the Azure Functions host then writes to the specified blob path.

Integrating Azure Event Hubs

For processing high-throughput event data, such as tracking URL access logs, Azure Event Hubs can be integrated. An output binding in the `function.json` file can be defined as follows:

```
{
  "bindings": [
    {
      "name": "outputEventHub",
      "type": "eventHub",
      "direction": "out",
      "eventHubName": "urlaccesslogs",
      "connection": "EventHubConnectionAppSetting"
    }
  ]
}
```

The function sends messages to the event hub by writing to the response, which the Azure Functions host forwards to the specified event hub.

Integrating Azure Queue Storage

To handle background processing tasks, such as sending notifications or performing analytics, Azure Queue Storage can be used. An output binding in the `function.json` file can be defined as follows:

```
{
  "bindings": [
    {
      "name": "outputQueue",
      "type": "queue",
      "direction": "out",
      "queueName": "taskqueue",
      "connection": "AzureWebJobsStorage"
    }
  ]
}
```

The function writes messages to the response, which the Azure Functions host then places into the specified queue.

By configuring these bindings in the `function.json` file and handling the logic, Azure functions with custom handlers provide a flexible and efficient way to build serverless applications. This approach allows for seamless integration with various Azure services, enabling the development of scalable and maintainable solutions, such as a URL shortener.

Best practices for DevOps engineers

Before we wrap up this chapter, let's take a moment to discuss Go best practices that are especially important for DevOps engineers. Writing clean, maintainable code is very important when building tools and automation that your team will rely on. Let's explore some practical guidelines that will make your Go code easier to read, test, and maintain.

Keeping functions small and focused

Functions should do one thing and do it well. This makes the code easier to understand, test, and reuse.

Here's a bad practice example:

```
func processURL(url string) error {
    if url == "" {
        return fmt.Errorf("URL is empty")
    }
    if !strings.HasPrefix(url, "http") {
        return fmt.Errorf("invalid URL format")
    }

    rand.Seed(time.Now().UnixNano())
    shortCode := fmt.Sprintf("%06d", rand.Intn(1000000))

    client := getDBClient()
    data := map[string]string{"url": url, "code": shortCode}
    if err := client.Insert(data); err != nil {
        return err
    }

    emailClient := getEmailClient()
    if err := emailClient.Send("New URL created"); err != nil {
        log.Printf("failed to send email: %v", err)
    }

    return nil
}
```

Here's a good practice example:

```
func validateURL(url string) error {
    if url == "" {
        return fmt.Errorf("URL is empty")
    }
    if !strings.HasPrefix(url, "http") {
        return fmt.Errorf("invalid URL format")
    }
    return nil
}
```

```
func generateShortCode() string {
    rand.Seed(time.Now().UnixNano())
    return fmt.Sprintf("%06d", rand.Intn(1000000))
}

func storeURLMapping(url, shortCode string) error {
    client := getDBClient()
    data := map[string]string{"url": url, "code": shortCode}
    return client.Insert(data)
}

func processURL(url string) error {
    if err := validateURL(url); err != nil {
        return err
    }

    shortCode := generateShortCode()

    if err := storeURLMapping(url, shortCode); err != nil {
        return err
    }

    notifyURLCreated(url, shortCode)

    return nil
}
```

By breaking the large function into smaller pieces, each function has a single responsibility. This makes the code easier to test, debug, and understand. If the validation logic needs to change, you only need to modify the `validateURL` function.

Handling errors properly

Go's explicit error handling is one of its strengths. Never ignore errors and always provide context when returning them.

Here's a bad practice example:

```
func deployFunction(name string) {
    client, _ := azidentity.NewDefaultAzureCredential(nil)
```

```
    resourceGroup, _ := createResourceGroup("my-rg", "eastus")
    functionApp, _ := createFunctionApp(client, name)
    deploy(functionApp)
}
```

Here's a good practice example:

```
func deployFunction(name string) error {
    client, err := azidentity.NewDefaultAzureCredential(nil)
    if err != nil {
        return fmt.Errorf("failed to create Azure credential: %w", err)
    }

    resourceGroup, err := createResourceGroup("my-rg", "eastus")
    if err != nil {
        return fmt.Errorf("failed to create resource group: %w", err)
    }

    functionApp, err := createFunctionApp(client, name)
    if err != nil {
        return fmt.Errorf(
            "failed to create function app %s: %w", name, err
        )
    }

    if err := deploy(functionApp); err != nil {
        return fmt.Errorf("failed to deploy function app: %w", err)
    }

    return nil
}
```

The good example checks every error and wraps it with context using `%w`. This creates an error chain that helps to understand exactly where things went wrong. When this function fails, we'll see a clear message such as **failed to deploy function app: failed to create function app my-func: connection timeout** instead of just **connection timeout**.

Using meaningful variable names

Variable names should clearly describe what they contain. Avoid single-letter variables except for common cases such as loop counters or short-lived variables.

Here's a bad practice example:

```
func processData(d []byte) error {
    var r ShortenRequest
    if err := json.Unmarshal(d, &r); err != nil {
        return err
    }

    s := generateCode()
    u := fmt.Sprintf("https://short.ly/%s", s)

    m := map[string]string{"c": s, "u": r.URL}
    return saveMapping(m)
}
```

Here's a good practice example:

```
func processData(requestBody []byte) error {
    var request ShortenRequest
    if err := json.Unmarshal(requestBody, &request); err != nil {
        return err
    }

    shortCode := generateCode()
    shortURL := fmt.Sprintf("https://short.ly/%s", shortCode)

    mapping := map[string]string{
        "code": shortCode,
        "original_url": request.URL,
    }
    return saveMapping(mapping)
}
```

Descriptive names make the code self-documenting. Anyone reading the code immediately understands what `shortCode` and `originalURL` represent, without having to guess or look at the surrounding context.

Don't panic, return errors

In DevOps tools, unexpected crashes can break automated workflows. Use `panic` only for truly unrecoverable situations, such as programming errors. For expected failures, return errors.

Here's a bad practice example:

```
func loadConfig(path string) Config {
    data, err := os.ReadFile(path)
    if err != nil {
        panic(fmt.Sprintf("config not found: %v", err))
    }

    var config Config
    if err := json.Unmarshal(data, &config); err != nil {
        panic(fmt.Sprintf("invalid config: %v", err))
    }

    return config
}
```

Here's a good practice example:

```
func loadConfig(path string) (Config, error) {
    data, err := os.ReadFile(path)
    if err != nil {
        return Config{}, fmt.Errorf("failed to read config file: %w", err)
    }

    var config Config
    if err := json.Unmarshal(data, &config); err != nil {
        return Config{}, fmt.Errorf(
            "failed to parse config file: %w", err
        )
    }

    return config, nil
}
```

The good version returns an error instead of panicking. This allows the calling code to decide how to handle the failure – maybe retry, use default values, or log an error and exit gracefully. This is especially important in long-running services where a panic would crash the entire application.

Using context for cancellation and timeouts

When making external calls to cloud services or databases, always use `context` to set timeouts and enable cancellation. This prevents operations from hanging indefinitely.

Here's a bad practice example:

```
func uploadToStorage(data []byte) error {
    client := getStorageClient()
    _, err := client.Upload(data)
    return err
}
```

Here's a good practice example:

```
func uploadToStorage(ctx context.Context, data []byte) error {
  client := getStorageClient()
  // Create a context with timeout
  uploadCtx, cancel := context.WithTimeout(ctx, 30*time.Second)
  defer cancel()
  _, err := client.UploadWithContext(uploadCtx, data)
  if err != nil {
    return fmt.Errorf("upload failed: %w", err)
  }
  return nil
}
```

Using `context` with timeouts ensures that if Azure Storage is slow or unreachable, the function won't hang forever. After 30 seconds, it will return an error, and the application can handle it appropriately. This is critical for building reliable DevOps tools.

Structuring the code with clear packages

Organize the code into packages based on functionality, not just file types. This makes the code base easier to navigate and understand.

Here's a bad structure example:

```
app/
    handlers.go
    models.go
    utils.go
    clients.go
```

Here's a good structure example:

```
app/
    cmd/
        main.go
    internal/
        urlshortener/
            service.go
            storage.go
        azure/
            client.go
            auth.go
        config/
            config.go
```

This structure groups related code together. The `urlshortener` package contains all URL shortening logic, the `azure` package handles Azure interactions, and `config` manages configuration. This makes it easy to find code and understand what each part of the application does.

Writing testable code

Design the code so it's easy to test. Use interfaces to make dependencies replaceable with mocks during testing.

This would be hard to test:

```
func shortenURL(url string) (string, error) {
   cred, _ := azidentity.NewDefaultAzureCredential(nil)
    client, _ := azblob.NewClient(
        "https://myaccount.blob.core.windows.net/", cred, nil
    )

    shortCode := generateCode()
    data := fmt.Sprintf(`{"url": "%s", "code": "%s"}`, url, shortCode)
```

```
    _, err := client.Upload(context.Background(), []byte(data))
    if err != nil {
        return "", err
    }

    return shortCode, nil
}
```

This would be easy to test:

```
type StorageClient interface {
    Upload(ctx context.Context, data []byte) error
}

type URLShortener struct {
    storage StorageClient
}

func (u *URLShortener) ShortenURL(ctx context.Context, url string) (
    string, error
) {
    shortCode := generateCode()
    data := fmt.Sprintf(`{"url": "%s", "code": "%s"}`, url, shortCode)

    if err := u.storage.Upload(ctx, []byte(data)); err != nil {
        return "", fmt.Errorf("failed to store URL: %w", err)
    }

    return shortCode, nil
}
```

The testable version uses an interface for storage, which means we can create a mock storage client for testing that doesn't actually connect to Azure. This makes tests faster and more reliable, and doesn't require Azure credentials.

Using configuration over hardcoding

Never hardcode values such as URLs, credentials, or timeouts. Use environment variables or configuration files.

This would be bad practice:

```
func connectToAzure() (*azblob.Client, error) {
    return azblob.NewClient(
        "https://mystorageaccount.blob.core.windows.net/",
        nil,
        nil,
    )
}
```

This would be good practice:

```
type Config struct {
    StorageAccountURL string
    Timeout time.Duration
    MaxRetries int
}
func loadConfig() Config {
    return Config{
        StorageAccountURL: os.Getenv("AZURE_STORAGE_URL"),
        Timeout: 30 * time.Second,
        MaxRetries: 3,
    }
}
func connectToAzure(config Config) (*azblob.Client, error) {
    if config.StorageAccountURL == "" {
        return nil, fmt.Errorf("AZURE_STORAGE_URL not set")
    }
return azblob.NewClient(config.StorageAccountURL, nil, nil)
}
```

Using configuration makes the code work in different environments (*development*, *staging*, *production*) without code changes. We just change the environment variables.

Logging appropriately

Use structured logging and log at appropriate levels. Too much logging creates noise; too little makes debugging difficult.

Here's a bad practice example:

```
func deployFunction(name string) error {
    fmt.Println("Starting deployment")
    fmt.Println("Creating resource group")
    rg, err := createResourceGroup()
    fmt.Println("Resource group created")
    fmt.Println("Creating function app")
    app, err := createFunctionApp(name)
    fmt.Println("Function app created")
    fmt.Println("Deploying")
    deploy(app)
    fmt.Println("Done")
    return nil
}
```

Here's a good practice example:

```
func deployFunction(name string) error {
    log.Printf("Starting deployment of function: %s", name)

    rg, err := createResourceGroup()
    if err != nil {
        return fmt.Errorf("failed to create resource group: %w", err)
    }
    log.Printf("Created resource group: %s", rg.Name)

    app, err := createFunctionApp(name)
    if err != nil {
        return fmt.Errorf("failed to create function app: %w", err)
    }
    log.Printf("Created function app: %s", app.Name)

    if err := deploy(app); err != nil {
        return fmt.Errorf("deployment failed: %w", err)
    }

    log.Printf("Successfully deployed function: %s", name)
    return nil
}
```

Good logging includes context (such as the function name) and only logs important events. This makes it easier to troubleshoot issues in production without being overwhelmed by unnecessary information.

Documenting exported functions and types

Any function, type, or constant that's exported (starts with a capital letter) should have a comment explaining what it does.

Here's a bad practice example:

```
type Config struct {
    URL     string
    Timeout int
}

func NewService(cfg Config) *Service {
    return &Service{config: cfg}
}
```

Here's a good practice example:

```
// Config holds the configuration for the URL shortener service.
// It includes the storage URL and timeout settings for operations.
type Config struct {
    // URL is the Azure Storage account URL
    URL string

    // Timeout is the maximum duration in seconds for operations
    Timeout int
}

// NewService creates a new URL shortener service with the given configuration.
// It returns an initialized service ready to process requests.
func NewService(cfg Config) *Service {
    return &Service{config: cfg}
}
```

Documentation helps other developers (and your future self) understand how to use the code without reading the implementation. The go `doc` command can also extract these comments to create automatic documentation.

Key takeaways for DevOps engineers

When writing Go code for DevOps tools and automation, consider the following:

- **Prioritize reliability**: Handle all errors, use timeouts, and avoid panics
- **Make it maintainable**: Use clear names, write small functions, and document the code
- **Design for testing**: Use interfaces and dependency injection to make code testable
- **Think about operations**: Add appropriate logging and use configuration for flexibility
- **Keep it simple**: Don't over-engineer; Go's simplicity is a strength

Following these practices will help to build DevOps tools that are reliable, maintainable, and easy for the team to work with. Clean code isn't just about aesthetics; it directly impacts how quickly we can fix bugs, add features, and onboard new team members.

Summary

Serverless computing with Azure Functions offers a powerful way to build applications that scale automatically and run only when needed, reducing the burden of managing infrastructure. This chapter introduced the fundamental concepts of Azure Functions and explained how functions can be created and deployed using the Azure SDK for Go. The focus was placed on setting up the development environment, writing function logic in Go, and deploying it to Azure to run in a cloud-native, event-driven model.

The chapter continued by exploring how triggers and bindings work in Azure Functions to simplify the way data is received and sent. Triggers are used to automatically execute functions in response to events such as HTTP requests or timer schedules. Bindings connect functions to data sources such as Azure Storage, allowing inputs and outputs to be managed declaratively. These tools help reduce boilerplate code and enable smoother integration with external systems.

Finally, the chapter dived into the integration of Azure Functions with other Azure services such as Blob Storage, Event Hubs, and Queue Storage. These integrations allow Azure Functions to act as the glue between components in a larger cloud system. Real-world scenarios, including a URL shortener application, demonstrated how Azure Functions can process events, store data, and interact with distributed services efficiently. Through this, applications can be designed to respond dynamically to cloud events with minimal infrastructure complexity.

As we have reached the end of this book, we have taken a deep dive into building modern, cloud-native applications with Go, starting from crafting CLI tools and APIs, to integrating with Prometheus for observability, developing custom Terraform providers, and embracing serverless architectures on AWS and Azure.

Whether your next step is contributing to a production-grade DevOps pipeline, scaling distributed systems, or building internal tools for your team, the knowledge you've gained here will help you with practical skills and real-world patterns to tackle those challenges confidently.

Keep exploring, keep building, and continue learning as the Go ecosystem and cloud landscape evolve.

We hope you enjoyed reading this book and found it valuable in your development journey.

15

Unlock Your Exclusive Benefits

Your copy of this book includes the following exclusive benefits:

- Next-gen Packt Reader
- DRM-free PDF/ePub downloads

Follow the guide below to unlock them. The process takes only a few minutes and needs to be completed once.

Unlock this Book's Free Benefits in 3 Easy Steps

Step 1

Keep your purchase invoice ready for *Step 3*. If you have a physical copy, scan it using your phone and save it as a PDF, JPG, or PNG.

For more help on finding your invoice, visit `https://www.packtpub.com/unlock-benefits/help`.

> **Note:** If you bought this book directly from Packt, no invoice is required. After *Step 2*, you can access your exclusive content right away.

Step 2

Scan the QR code or go to `packtpub.com/unlock`.

On the page that opens (similar to *Figure 15.1* on desktop), search for this book by name and select the correct edition.

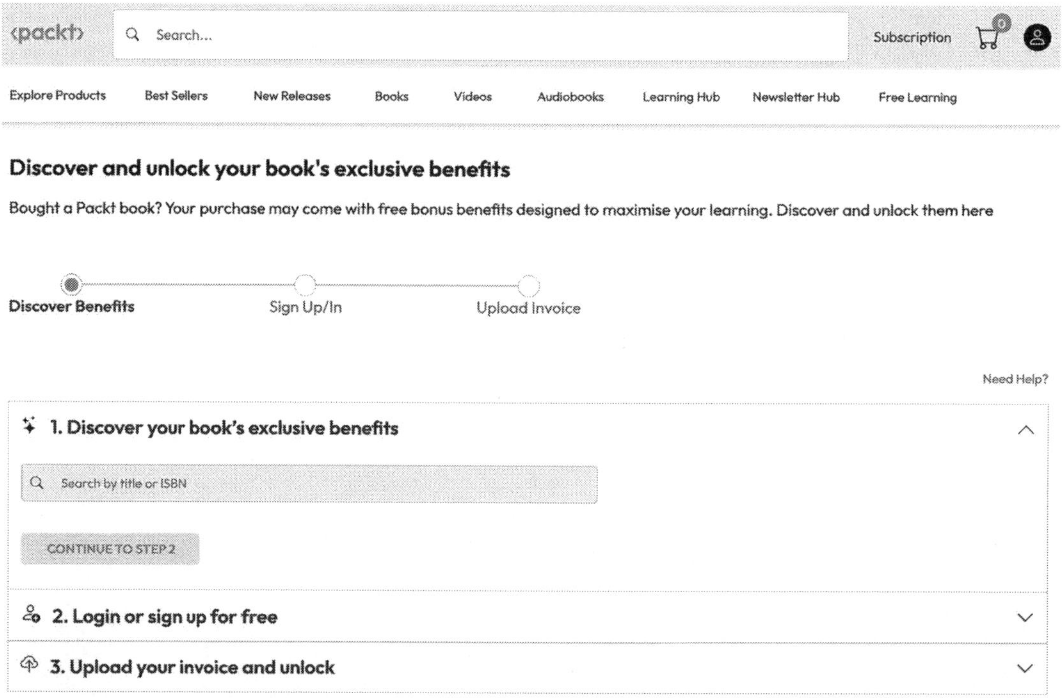

Figure 15.1: Packt unlock landing page on desktop

Step 3

After selecting your book, sign in to your Packt account or create one for free. Then upload your invoice (PDF, PNG, or JPG, up to 10 MB). Follow the on-screen instructions to finish the process.

Need help?

If you get stuck and need help, visit `https://www.packtpub.com/unlock-benefits/help` for a detailed FAQ on how to find your invoices and more. This QR code will take you to the help page.

Note: If you are still facing issues, reach out to `customercare@packt.com`.

Stay Sharp in Cloud and DevOps – Join 44,000+ Subscribers of CloudPro

CloudPro is a weekly newsletter for cloud professionals who want to stay current on the fast-evolving world of cloud computing, DevOps, and infrastructure engineering.

Every issue delivers focused, high-signal content on topics like:

- AWS, GCP & multi-cloud architecture
- Containers, Kubernetes & orchestration
- Infrastructure as Code (IaC) with Terraform, Pulumi, etc.
- Platform engineering & automation workflows
- Observability, performance tuning, and reliability best practices

Whether you're a cloud engineer, SRE, DevOps practitioner, or platform lead, CloudPro helps you stay on top of what matters, without the noise.

Scan the QR code to join for free and get weekly insights straight to your inbox:

`https://packt.link/cloudpro`

Other Books You May Enjoy

If you enjoyed this book, you may be interested in these other books by Packt:

Platform Engineering for Architects

Max Körbächer, Andreas Grabner, Hilliary Lipsig

ISBN: 978-1-83620-359-9

- Make informed decisions aligned with your organization's platform needs
- Identify missing platform capabilities and manage that technical debt effectively
- Develop critical user journeys to enhance platform functionality
- Define platform purpose, principles, and key performance indicators
- Use data-driven insights to guide product decisions
- Design and implement platform reference and target architectures

Azure for Developers, Third Edition

Kamil Mrzygłód

ISBN: 978-1-83620-351-3

- Integrate data solutions like Azure Storage and managed SQL databases into your applications
- Embed monitoring into your application using Application Insights SDK
- Develop serverless solutions with Azure Functions and Durable Functions
- Automate CI/CD workflows with GitHub Actions and Azure integration
- Build and manage containers using Azure Container Apps, Azure Container Registry (ACR), and App Service
- Design powerful workflows with both low-code and full-code approaches
- Enhance applications with AI and machine learning components

Packt is searching for authors like you

If you're interested in becoming an author for Packt, please visit authors.packt.com and apply today. We have worked with thousands of developers and tech professionals, just like you, to help them share their insight with the global tech community. You can make a general application, apply for a specific hot topic that we are recruiting an author for, or submit your own idea.

Share your thoughts

Now you've finished *Mastering Go for DevOps*, we'd love to hear your thoughts! Scan the QR code below to go straight to the Amazon review page for this book and share your feedback or leave a review on the site that you purchased it from.

https://packt.link/r/1837027331

Your review is important to us and the tech community and will help us make sure we're delivering excellent quality content.

Index

A

B

C

D

O

P

R

Made in United States
Orlando, FL
04 November 2026

90201379R00203